中华人民共和国
恢复国际海事组织合法席位50周年
THE 50TH ANNIVERSARY OF THE RESTORATION OF THE LAWFUL
SEAT OF THE PEOPLE'S REPUBLIC OF CHINA IN IMO

国际海事条约汇编
（综合文本）

A COLLECTION OF
INTERNATIONAL MARITIME TREATIES
（CONSOLIDATED EDITION）

第四卷　2006年海事劳工公约
Volume IV　Maritime Labour Convention, 2006

中华人民共和国交通运输部国际合作司
大连海事大学　编译

大连海事大学出版社
DALIAN MARITIME UNIVERSITY PRESS

ⓒ 中华人民共和国交通运输部国际合作司　大连海事大学　2023

图书在版编目（CIP）数据

国际海事条约汇编：综合文本. 第四卷，2006 年海
事劳工公约：英汉对照／中华人民共和国交通运输部国
际合作司，大连海事大学编译. —— 大连：大连海事大学
出版社，2023.9
书名原文：A COLLECTION OF INTERNATIONAL
MARITIME TREATIES（CONSOLIDATED EDITION）Volume
Ⅳ Maritime Labour Convention,2006
ISBN 978-7-5632-4454-6

Ⅰ. ①国… Ⅱ. ①中… ②大… Ⅲ. ①海洋法—国际
条约—汇编—汉、英 Ⅳ. ①D993.5

中国国家版本馆 CIP 数据核字（2023）第 156257 号

大连海事大学出版社出版

地址：大连市黄浦路523号　邮编：116026　电话：0411-84729665（营销部）　84729480（总编室）
http://press.dlmu.edu.cn　E-mail:dmupress@dlmu.edu.cn

辽宁新华印务有限公司印装　　　　　　大连海事大学出版社发行

2023 年 9 月第 1 版　　　　　　　　　　2023 年 9 月第 1 次印刷
幅面尺寸：184 mm×260 mm　　　　　　　　　　　印张：16.25
字数：374 千　　　　　　　　　　　　　　印数：1~1000 册

出版人：刘明凯

责任编辑：席香吉　　　　　　　　　　责任校对：董洪英　高　颖
封面设计：解瑶瑶　　　　　　　　　　版式设计：解瑶瑶

ISBN 978-7-5632-4454-6　　定价：73.00 元

前　言

为满足广大航运、造船、船检、海事、外贸、保险、法律等部门的工作人员及相关的教学人员了解、掌握和执行国际海事条约的需要,1992 年交通部外事司(现交通运输部国际合作司)曾在其译校和保存的有关条约的基础上,与大连海运学院(现大连海事大学)一起,以中英文对照的形式,编译出版了《国际海事条约汇编》(以下简称《汇编》)。在这 30 年间,《国际海上人命安全公约》《国际防止船舶造成污染公约》等重要的国际公约进行了多次的修改,《2006 年海事劳工公约》《国际防止船舶造成污染公约 1997 年议定书》等多部新公约和议定书通过,《汇编》始终保持更新,保持本系列书籍内容的完整性。为了便利读者阅读和使用,编者认为有必要对重要的公约进行整理,以中英文对照综合文本的形式再次出版。

我国是名副其实的航运大国、造船大国、海员大国,在国际航运业中占有举足轻重的地位。我国是国际海事组织(IMO)A 类理事国,在国际海事事务中扮演着越来越重要的角色。2021 年 12 月 15 日,国际海事组织第 32 届大会通过了《国际海事组织公约》修正案,生效后中文文本将成为其正式文本之一。今年也是我国恢复国际海事组织合法席位 50 周年,在这一时刻,重新整理四个支柱性海事公约的中英文综合文本,既是《汇编》在新时代的传承,也是向我国恢复国际海事组织合法席位 50 周年献礼,具有重要的历史意义和现实意义。

本次出版的《国际海事条约汇编》(综合文本)共四卷,分别为《国际海上人命安全公约》《国际防止船舶造成污染公约》《1978 年海员培训、发证和值班标准国际公约》《2006 年海事劳工公约》,均收录了截至 2023 年 12 月 31 日前生效的公约修正案,整理成综合文本。编者后续将根据工作需要和公约修改的频率、程度出版其他公约的综合文本和更新现有版本,尽量与国际海事组织、国际劳工组织出版的公约综合文本保持同步。希望本系列书籍能够为相关行业从业人员在研究和实施公约的过程中提供参考。

本卷前言

　　《2006 年海事劳工公约》于 2006 年 2 月 7 日至 23 日召开的第 94 届国际劳工大会上获高票通过,其目的是实现海员体面工作与生活,被称为海员的"权利法案",也是国际海事法规体系中的支柱性公约之一。中国于 2015 年 8 月 29 日经十二届全国人大常委会第十六次会议审议批准加入《2006 年海事劳工公约》,公约于 2016 年 11 月 12 日对中国正式生效。

　　《2006 年海事劳工公约》整合了国际劳工组织 37 项公约和 31 项建议书,对海员上船工作的最低要求,就业条件,起居舱室、娱乐设施、食品和膳食服务,健康保护、医疗、福利和社会保障保护,遵守与执行等做出了规定。

　　本卷所载《经修正的 2006 年海事劳工公约》为《2006 年海事劳工公约》及生效日期在 2023 年 12 月 31 日之前的修正案的综合文本。

　　在本卷编译过程中,交通运输部国际合作司王宏伟、李冠玉、陈星森、张琨琨,大连海事大学赵友涛,大连海事大学航海学院章文俊、李桢、王艳华、费珊珊、韩佳霖和大连海事大学出版社对此项工作给予了大力支持,在此表示衷心感谢。由于编译工作时间仓促,书中难免有疏漏和错误,敬请读者批评指正。

Contents

目　录

2006年海事劳工公约

Maritime Labour Convention, 2006

MARITIME LABOUR CONVENTION, 2006, as amended

Adopted by the International Labour Conference at its 94th (**Maritime**) **Session** (2006)

Amendments approved by the International Labour Conference at its 103rd **Session** (2014)

Amendments approved by the International Labour Conference at its 105th **Session** (2016)

Amendments approved by the International Labour Conference at its 107th **Session** (2018)

Preamble

The General Conference of the International Labour Organization,

Having been convened at Geneva by the Governing Body of the International Labour Office, and having met in its Ninety-fourth Session on 7 February 2006, and

Desiring to create a single, coherent instrument embodying as far as possible all up-to-date standards of existing international maritime labour Conventions and Recommendations, as well as the fundamental principles to be found in other international labour Conventions, in particular:

— the Forced Labour Convention, 1930 (No. 29);

— the Freedom of Association and Protection of the Right to Organise Convention, 1948 (No. 87);

— the Right to Organise and Collective Bargaining Convention, 1949 (No. 98);

— the Equal Remuneration Convention, 1951 (No. 100);

— the Abolition of Forced Labour Convention, 1957 (No. 105);

— the Discrimination (Employment and Occupation) Convention, 1958 (No. 111);

— the Minimum Age Convention, 1973 (No. 138);

— the Worst Forms of Child Labour Convention, 1999 (No. 182); and

经修正的 2006 年海事劳工公约

2006 年第 94 届国际(海事)劳工大会上通过

第 103 届国际劳工大会批准 2014 年修正案

第 105 届国际劳工大会批准 2016 年修正案

第 107 届国际劳工大会批准 2018 年修正案

序言

国际劳工组织大会,

经国际劳工局理事会召集,于 2006 年 2 月 7 日在日内瓦举行了其第 94 届会议,并

希望制订一项条理统一的单一文件,尽可能体现现有国际海事劳工公约和建议书中的所有最新标准以及其他国际劳工公约,特别是以下公约中的基本原则:

——《1930 年强迫劳动公约》(第 29 号);

——《1948 年自由结社和保护组织权利公约》(第 87 号);

——《1949 年组织权利和集体谈判权利公约》(第 98 号);

——《1951 年同酬公约》(第 100 号);

——《1957 年废除强迫劳动公约》(第 105 号);

——《1958 年(就业和职业)歧视公约》(第 111 号);

——《1973 年最低年龄公约》(第 138 号);

——《1999 年最恶劣形式的童工劳动公约》(第 182 号);并

Mindful of the core mandate of the Organization, which is to promote decent conditions of work, and

Recalling the ILO Declaration on Fundamental Principles and Rights at Work, 1998, and

Mindful also that seafarers are covered by the provisions of other ILO instruments and have other rights which are established as fundamental rights and freedoms applicable to all persons, and

Considering that, given the global nature of the shipping industry, seafarers need special protection, and

Mindful also of the international standards on ship safety, human security and quality ship management in the International Convention for the Safety of Life at Sea, 1974, as amended, the Convention on the International Regulations for Preventing Collisions at Sea, 1972, as amended, and the seafarer training and competency requirements in the International Convention on Standards of Training, Certification and Watchkeeping for Seafarers, 1978, as amended, and

Recalling that the United Nations Convention on the Law of the Sea, 1982, sets out a general legal framework within which all activities in the oceans and seas must be carried out and is of strategic importance as the basis for national, regional and global action and cooperation in the marine sector, and that its integrity needs to be maintained, and

Recalling that Article 94 of the United Nations Convention on the Law of the Sea, 1982, establishes the duties and obligations of a flag State with regard to, inter alia, labour conditions, crewing and social matters on ships that fly its flag, and

Recalling paragraph 8 of article 19 of the Constitution of the International Labour Organisation which provides that in no case shall the adoption of any Convention or Recommendation by the Conference or the ratification of any Convention by any Member be deemed to affect any law, award, custom or agreement which ensures more favourable conditions to the workers concerned than those provided for in the Convention or Recommendation, and

Determined that this new instrument should be designed to secure the widest possible acceptability among governments, shipowners and seafarers committed to the principles of decent work, that it should be readily updateable and that it should lend itself to effective implementation and enforcement, and

Having decided upon the adoption of certain proposals for the realization of such an instrument, which is the only item on the agenda of the session, and

Having determined that these proposals shall take the form of an international Convention;

Adopts this twenty-third day of February of the year two thousand and six the following Convention, which may be cited as the Maritime Labour Convention, 2006.

意识到本组织倡导体面劳动条件的核心使命,并

忆及 1998 年《国际劳工组织工作中的基本原则和权利宣言》,并

意识到海员也受国际劳工组织其他文件保护,且享有已确立的其他适用于所有人的基本权利和自由;并

认为由于航运业的全球性特点,海员需要特殊保护,并

意识到经修正的《1974 年国际海上人命安全公约》和经修正的《1972 年国际海上避碰规则公约》中关于船舶安全、人身保安和船舶质量管理的国际标准,以及经修正的《1978 年海员培训、发证和值班标准国际公约》中的海员培训和适任要求,并

忆及《1982 年联合国海洋法公约》规定了一个总体法律框架,海洋中的所有活动都必须在此框架下展开,它是海事部门进行国家、地区和全球性活动和合作的基础,具有战略性意义,其完整性需要得到维持,并

忆及《1982 年联合国海洋法公约》第九十四条特别确立了船旗国对悬挂其旗帜的船舶上的劳动条件、船员配备和社会事务所承担的责任和义务;并

忆及《国际劳工组织章程》第十九条第八款规定,无论在何种情况下,大会通过任何公约或建议书或者任何成员国批准任何公约都不能被视为影响到那些确保有关工人得到优于公约或建议书所规定条件的法律、裁定、惯例或协议,并

决定此新文件的制订应保证得到致力于体面劳动原则的各国政府、船东和工人尽可能最广泛的接受,且能够方便更新并保证得到有效的实施和执行,并

决定通过某些建议以完成这一文件,这是本届会议的唯一一项议程,并

决定这些建议应采取一项国际公约的形式;

于 2006 年 2 月 23 日通过以下公约,引用时可称之为《2006 年海事劳工公约》。

General obligations

Article I

1 Each Member which ratifies this Convention undertakes to give complete effect to its provisions in the manner set out in Article VI in order to secure the right of all seafarers to decent employment.

2 Members shall cooperate with each other for the purpose of ensuring the effective implementation and enforcement of this Convention.

Definitions and scope of application

Article II

1 For the purpose of this Convention and unless provided otherwise in particular provisions, the term:

   (**a**) *competent authority* means the minister, government department or other authority having power to issue and enforce regulations, orders or other instructions having the force of law in respect of the subject matter of the provision concerned;

   (**b**) *declaration of maritime labour compliance* means the declaration referred to in Regulation 5.1.3;

   (**c**) *gross tonnage* means the gross tonnage calculated in accordance with the tonnage measurement regulations contained in Annex I to the International Convention on Tonnage Measurement of Ships, 1969, or any successor Convention; for ships covered by the tonnage measurement interim scheme adopted by the International Maritime Organization, the gross tonnage is that which is included in the REMARKS column of the International Tonnage Certificate (1969);

   (**d**) *maritime labour certificate* means the certificate referred to in Regulation 5.1.3;

   (**e**) *requirements of this Convention* refers to the requirements in these Articles and in the Regulations and Part A of the Code of this Convention;

   (**f**) *seafarer* means any person who is employed or engaged or works in any capacity on board a ship to which this Convention applies;

   (**g**) *seafarers' employment agreement* includes both a contract of employment and articles of agreement;

一般义务

第一条

1　批准本公约的各成员国承诺按第六条规定的方式全面履行公约的规定,以确保海员体面就业的权利。

2　成员国应为确保有效实施和执行本公约之目的而相互合作。

定义和适用范围

第二条

1　除非具体条款另行规定,就本公约而言:

（a）　"主管当局"一词系指有权就公约规定的事项颁布和实施具有法律效力的法规、命令或其他指令的部长、政府部门或其他当局;

（b）　"海事劳工符合声明"一词系指规则 5.1.3 所述之声明;

（c）　"总吨位"一词系指根据《1969 年船舶吨位丈量国际公约》附则 I 或任何后续公约中的吨位丈量规则所计算出的总吨位;对于国际海事组织通过的临时吨位丈量表所包括的船舶,总吨位为填写在"国际吨位证书（1969）"的"备注"栏中的总吨位;

（d）　"海事劳工证书"一词系指规则 5.1.3 中所提及的证书;

（e）　"本公约的要求"一词系指本公约的正文条款和规则及守则 A 部分中的要求;

（f）　"海员"一词系指在本公约所适用的船舶上以任何职务受雇、从业或工作的任何人员;

（g）　"海员就业协议"一词包括就业合同和协议条款;

(h) *seafarer recruitment and placement service* means any person, company, institution, agency or other organization, in the public or the private sector, which is engaged in recruiting seafarers on behalf of shipowners or placing seafarers with shipowners;

(i) *ship* means a ship other than one which navigates exclusively in inland waters or waters within, or closely adjacent to, sheltered waters or areas where port regulations apply;

(j) *shipowner* means the owner of the ship or another organization or person, such as the manager, agent or bareboat charterer, who has assumed the responsibility for the operation of the ship from the owner and who, on assuming such responsibility, has agreed to take over the duties and responsibilities imposed on shipowners in accordance with this Convention, regardless of whether any other organization or persons fulfil certain of the duties or responsibilities on behalf of the shipowner.

2   Except as expressly provided otherwise, this Convention applies to all seafarers.

3   In the event of doubt as to whether any categories of persons are to be regarded as seafarers for the purpose of this Convention, the question shall be determined by the competent authority in each Member after consultation with the shipowners' and seafarers' organizations concerned with this question.

4   Except as expressly provided otherwise, this Convention applies to all ships, whether publicly or privately owned, ordinarily engaged in commercial activities, other than ships engaged in fishing or in similar pursuits and ships of traditional build such as dhows and junks. This Convention does not apply to warships or naval auxiliaries.

5   In the event of doubt as to whether this Convention applies to a ship or particular category of ships, the question shall be determined by the competent authority in each Member after consultation with the shipowners' and seafarers' organizations concerned.

6   Where the competent authority determines that it would not be reasonable or practicable at the present time to apply certain details of the Code referred to in Article VI, paragraph 1, to a ship or particular categories of ships flying the flag of the Member, the relevant provisions of the Code shall not apply to the extent that the subject matter is dealt with differently by national laws or regulations or collective bargaining agreements or other measures. Such a determination may only be made in consultation with the shipowners' and seafarers' organizations concerned and may only be made with respect to ships of less than 200 gross tonnage not engaged in international voyages.

7   Any determinations made by a Member under paragraph 3 or 5 or 6 of this Article shall be communicated to the Director-General of the International Labour Office, who shall notify the Members of the Organization.

8   Unless expressly provided otherwise, a reference to this Convention constitutes at the same time a reference to the Regulations and the Code.

（h）　"海员招募和安置服务机构"一词系指公共或私营部门中代表船东招募海员或与船东协商安排海员上船的任何个人、公司、团体、部门或其他机构；

（i）　"船舶"一词系指除专门在内河或在遮蔽水域之内或其紧邻水域或适用港口规定的区域航行的船舶以外的船舶；

（j）　"船东"一词系指船舶所有人或从船舶所有人那里承担了船舶经营责任并在承担这种责任时已同意接受船东根据本公约所承担的职责和责任的任何其他组织或个人，如管理人、代理或光船承租人，无论是否有任何其他组织或个人代表船东履行了某些职责或责任。

2　除非另有明文规定，本公约适用于所有海员。

3　如果就某类人员是否应被视为本公约所指的海员存在疑问，应由各成员国的主管当局与此问题所涉及的船东和海员组织进行协商后做出决定。

4　除非另有明文规定，本公约适用于除从事捕鱼或类似捕捞的船舶和用传统方法制造的船舶，例如独桅三角帆船和舢板以外的通常从事商业活动的所有船舶，无论其为公有还是私有。本公约不适用于军舰和军事辅助船。

5　如果就本公约是否适用于某一船舶或特定类别船舶存在疑问，该问题应由各成员国的主管当局与有关船东和海员组织进行协商后做出决定。

6　如果主管当局确定目前对悬挂该成员国旗帜的一艘船舶或特定类别船舶适用第六条第1款中所述守则的某些细节不合理或不可行，只要该事项由国家法律或法规或集体谈判协议或其他措施来处理，主管当局可以决定守则的有关规定不适用于该事项。此决定只能在与有关的船东或海员组织协商后做出，且只能针对那些不从事国际航行的 200 总吨以下船舶。

7　一成员国根据本条第 3 或 5 或 6 款所做的任何决定均应通报国际劳工局局长，局长应通知本组织成员。

8　除非另有明文规定，提及本公约同时意味着提及规则和守则。

Fundamental rights and principles

Article III

Each Member shall satisfy itself that the provisions of its law and regulations respect, in the context of this Convention, the fundamental rights to:

(**a**)   freedom of association and the effective recognition of the right to collective bargaining;

(**b**)   the elimination of all forms of forced or compulsory labour;

(**c**)   the effective abolition of child labour; and

(**d**)   the elimination of discrimination in respect of employment and occupation.

Seafarers' employment and social rights

Article IV

1   Every seafarer has the right to a safe and secure workplace that complies with safety standards.

2   Every seafarer has a right to fair terms of employment.

3   Every seafarer has a right to decent working and living conditions on board ship.

4   Every seafarer has a right to health protection, medical care, welfare measures and other forms of social protection.

5   Each Member shall ensure, within the limits of its jurisdiction, that the seafarers' employment and social rights set out in the preceding paragraphs of this Article are fully implemented in accordance with the requirements of this Convention. Unless specified otherwise in the Convention, such implementation may be achieved through national laws or regulations, through applicable collective bargaining agreements or through other measures or in practice.

基本权利和原则

第三条

就本公约所涉事项,各成员国应自行确认其法律和法规的规定尊重以下基本权利:

(**a**)　自由结社权和集体谈判权;

(**b**)　消除所有形式的强迫和强制劳动;

(**c**)　有效废除童工劳动;和

(**d**)　消除就业和职业方面的歧视。

海员的就业和社会权利

第四条

1　每一海员均有在符合安全标准的安全且受保护的工作场所工作的权利。

2　每一海员均有获得公平的就业条件的权利。

3　每一海员均有获得体面的船上工作和生活条件的权利。

4　每一海员均有享受健康保护、医疗、福利措施及其他形式的社会保障的权利。

5　各成员国在其管辖范围内应确保本条上述各款所规定的海员就业和社会权利按照本公约的要求得以充分实施。除非本公约中另有专门规定,此种实施可通过国家法律或法规、适用的集体谈判协议或其他措施或者实践来实现。

Implementation and enforcement responsibilities

Article V

1   Each Member shall implement and enforce laws or regulations or other measures that it has adopted to fulfil its commitments under this Convention with respect to ships and seafarers under its jurisdiction.

2   Each Member shall effectively exercise its jurisdiction and control over ships that fly its flag by establishing a system for ensuring compliance with the requirements of this Convention, including regular inspections, reporting, monitoring and legal proceedings under the applicable laws.

3   Each Member shall ensure that ships that fly its flag carry a maritime labour certificate and a declaration of maritime labour compliance as required by this Convention.

4   A ship to which this Convention applies may, in accordance with international law, be inspected by a Member other than the flag State, when the ship is in one of its ports, to determine whether the ship is in compliance with the requirements of this Convention.

5   Each Member shall effectively exercise its jurisdiction and control over seafarer recruitment and placement services, if these are established in its territory.

6   Each Member shall prohibit violations of the requirements of this Convention and shall, in accordance with international law, establish sanctions or require the adoption of corrective measures under its laws which are adequate to discourage such violations.

7   Each Member shall implement its responsibilities under this Convention in such a way as to ensure that the ships that fly the flag of any State that has not ratified this Convention do not receive more favourable treatment than the ships that fly the flag of any State that has ratified it.

Regulations and Parts A and B of the Code

Article VI

1   The Regulations and the provisions of Part A of the Code are mandatory. The provisions of Part B of the Code are not mandatory.

实施和执行责任

第五条

1 各成员国应对其管辖下的船舶和海员实施和执行其为履行本公约所做出之承诺而通过的法律或法规或其他措施。

2 各成员国应通过建立确保遵守本公约要求的制度,对悬挂其旗帜的船舶有效地行使管辖和控制,包括定期检查、报告、监督和执行可适用法律下的法律程序。

3 各成员国应确保悬挂其旗帜的船舶持有本公约所要求的海事劳工证书和海事劳工符合声明。

4 适用本公约的船舶,当其位于除船旗国以外的成员国的某港口时,可根据国际法受到该成员国的检查以确定其是否符合本公约的要求。

5 各成员国应对在其领土内设立的海员招募和安置服务机构有效行使其管辖和控制。

6 各成员国应对违反本公约要求的行为予以禁止,并应根据国际法,在其法律中规定制裁或要求采取改正措施,这些制裁或措施应足以阻止此种违反行为。

7 各成员国应以确保悬挂未批准本公约之任何国家旗帜的船舶得不到比悬挂已批准本公约之任何国家旗帜的船舶更优惠待遇的方式履行本公约赋予的责任。

规则以及守则之 A 部分和 B 部分

第六条

1 规则和守则 A 部分的规定具有强制性。守则 B 部分为非强制性。

2 Each Member undertakes to respect the rights and principles set out in the Regulations and to implement each Regulation in the manner set out in the corresponding provisions of Part A of the Code. In addition, the Member shall give due consideration to implementing its responsibilities in the manner provided for in Part B of the Code.

3 A Member which is not in a position to implement the rights and principles in the manner set out in Part A of the Code may, unless expressly provided otherwise in this Convention, implement Part A through provisions in its laws and regulations or other measures which are substantially equivalent to the provisions of Part A.

4 For the sole purpose of paragraph 3 of this Article, any law, regulation, collective agreement or other implementing measure shall be considered to be substantially equivalent, in the context of this Convention, if the Member satisfies itself that:

   (a) it is conducive to the full achievement of the general object and purpose of the provision or provisions of Part A of the Code concerned; and

   (b) it gives effect to the provision or provisions of Part A of the Code concerned.

Consultation with shipowners' and seafarers' organizations

Article VII

Any derogation, exemption or other flexible application of this Convention for which the Convention requires consultation with shipowners' and seafarers' organizations may, in cases where representative organizations of shipowners or of seafarers do not exist within a Member, only be decided by that Member through consultation with the Committee referred to in Article XIII.

Entry into force

Article VIII

1 The formal ratifications of this Convention shall be communicated to the Director-General of the International Labour Office for registration.

2 This Convention shall be binding only upon those Members of the International Labour Organization whose ratifications have been registered by the Director-General.

3 This Convention shall come into force 12 months after the date on which there have been registered ratifications by at least 30 Members with a total share in the world gross tonnage of ships of at least 33 per cent.

4 Thereafter, this Convention shall come into force for any Member 12 months after the date on which its ratification has been registered.

2   各成员国保证尊重规则中规定的权利和原则,并按守则 A 部分的相关内容所规定的方式实施每条规则。此外,成员国还应充分考虑到按守则 B 部分给出的方式履行其责任。

3   除非本公约另有明文规定,不能按守则 A 部分规定的方式履行权利和原则的成员国,可以通过实质上等效于 A 部分规定的法律和法规的规定或其他措施来实施 A 部分。

4   单就本条第 3 款而言,法律、法规、集体协议或其他履约措施只有在成员国自行确认以下情况时才应被视为实质上等效于本公约的规定:

  (a)   它有助于充分达到守则 A 部分有关规定的总体目标和目的;且

  (b)   它落实了守则 A 部分的有关规定。

与船东和海员组织协商

第七条

如果在一成员国内不存在船东或海员的代表组织,公约中要求与船东和海员组织进行协商的任何对本公约的偏离、免除或其他灵活适用,只能由该成员国通过与第十三条所述之委员会协商决定。

生效

第八条

1   对本公约的正式批准书应送请国际劳工局局长登记。

2   本公约只对其批准书已由国际劳工局局长登记的国际劳工组织成员国具有约束力。

3   本公约应在合计占世界船舶总吨位至少 33% 的至少 30 个成员国的批准书已经登记之日 12 个月后生效。

4   此后,对于任何成员国,本公约将于其批准书经登记之日 12 个月后对其生效。

Denunciation

Article IX

1   A Member which has ratified this Convention may denounce it after the expiration of ten years from the date on which the Convention first comes into force, by an act communicated to the Director-General of the International Labour Office for registration. Such denunciation shall not take effect until one year after the date on which it is registered.

2   Each Member which does not, within the year following the expiration of the period of ten years mentioned in paragraph 1 of this Article, exercise the right of denunciation provided for in this Article, shall be bound for another period of ten years and, thereafter, may denounce this Convention at the expiration of each new period of ten years under the terms provided for in this Article.

Effect of entry into force

Article X

This Convention revises the following Conventions:

Minimum Age (Sea) Convention, 1920 (No. 7)

Unemployment Indemnity (Shipwreck) Convention, 1920 (No. 8)

Placing of Seamen Convention, 1920 (No. 9)

Medical Examination of Young Persons (Sea) Convention, 1921 (No. 16)

Seamen's Articles of Agreement Convention, 1926 (No. 22)

Repatriation of Seamen Convention, 1926 (No. 23)

Officers' Competency Certificates Convention, 1936 (No. 53)

Holidays with Pay (Sea) Convention, 1936 (No. 54)

Shipowners' Liability (Sick and Injured Seamen) Convention, 1936 (No. 55)

Sickness Insurance (Sea) Convention, 1936 (No. 56)

Hours of Work and Manning (Sea) Convention, 1936 (No. 57)

Minimum Age (Sea) Convention (Revised), 1936 (No. 58)

退出

第九条

1 已批准本公约的成员国可自公约初次生效之日起满 10 年后向国际劳工局局长通知退出并请其登记。此项退出应自登记之日起一年后发生效力。

2 在本条第 1 款所述 10 年期满后的 1 年内未行使本条所规定之退出权利的成员国,即需再遵守 10 年,此后每当新的 10 年期满,可依本条的规定退出本公约。

生效的影响

第十条

本公约修订以下公约:

《1920 年(海上)最低年龄公约》(第 7 号)

《1920 年(海难)失业赔偿公约》(第 8 号)

《1920 年海员安置公约》(第 9 号)

《1921 年(海上)未成年人体检公约》(第 16 号)

《1926 年海员协议条款公约》(第 22 号)

《1926 年海员遣返公约》(第 23 号)

《1936 年高级船员适任证书公约》(第 53 号)

《1936 年(海上)带薪假期公约》(第 54 号)

《1936 年船东(对病、伤海员)责任公约》(第 55 号)

《1936 年(海上)疾病保险公约》(第 56 号)

《1936 年(海上)工时和配员公约》(第 57 号)

《1936 年(海上)最低年龄公约(修订)》(第 58 号)

Food and Catering (Ships' Crews) Convention, 1946 (No. 68)

Certification of Ships' Cooks Convention, 1946 (No. 69)

Social Security (Seafarers) Convention, 1946 (No. 70)

Paid Vacations (Seafarers) Convention, 1946 (No. 72)

Medical Examination (Seafarers) Convention, 1946 (No. 73)

Certification of Able Seamen Convention, 1946 (No. 74)

Accommodation of Crews Convention, 1946 (No. 75)

Wages, Hours of Work and Manning (Sea) Convention, 1946 (No. 76)

Paid Vacations (Seafarers) Convention (Revised), 1949 (No. 91)

Accommodation of Crews Convention (Revised), 1949 (No. 92)

Wages, Hours of Work and Manning (Sea) Convention (Revised), 1949 (No. 93)

Wages, Hours of Work and Manning (Sea) Convention (Revised), 1958 (No. 109)

Accommodation of Crews (Supplementary Provisions) Convention, 1970 (No. 133)

Prevention of Accidents (Seafarers) Convention, 1970 (No. 134)

Continuity of Employment (Seafarers) Convention, 1976 (No. 145)

Seafarers' Annual Leave with Pay Convention, 1976 (No. 146)

Merchant Shipping (Minimum Standards) Convention, 1976 (No. 147)

Protocol of 1996 to the Merchant Shipping (Minimum Standards) Convention, 1976 (No. 147)

Seafarers' Welfare Convention, 1987 (No. 163)

Health Protection and Medical Care (Seafarers) Convention, 1987 (No. 164)

Social Security (Seafarers) Convention (Revised), 1987 (No. 165)

Repatriation of Seafarers Convention (Revised), 1987 (No. 166)

Labour Inspection (Seafarers) Convention, 1996 (No. 178)

Recruitment and Placement of Seafarers Convention, 1996 (No. 179)

Seafarers' Hours of Work and the Manning of Ships Convention, 1996 (No. 180)

《1946 年(船上船员)食品和膳食公约》(第 68 号)

《1946 年船上厨师发证公约》(第 69 号)

《1946 年(海员)社会保障公约》(第 70 号)

《1946 年(海员)带薪休假公约》(第 72 号)

《1946 年(海员)体检公约》(第 73 号)

《1946 年一等水手证书公约》(第 74 号)

《1946 年船员起居舱室公约》(第 75 号)

《1946 年(海上)工资、工时和配员公约》(第 76 号)

《1949 年(海员)带薪休假公约(修订)》(第 91 号)

《1949 年船员起居舱室公约(修订)》(第 92 号)

《1949 年(海上)工资、工时和配员公约(修订)》(第 93 号)

《1958 年(海上)工资、工时和配员公约(修订)》(第 109 号)

《1970 年船员起居舱室(补充规定)公约》(第 133 号)

《1970 年防止事故(海员)公约》(第 134 号)

《1976 年(海员)连续就业公约》(第 145 号)

《1976 年海员带薪年休假公约》(第 146 号)

《1976 年商船(最低标准)公约》(第 147 号)

《〈1976 年商船(最低标准)公约〉(第 147 号)的 1996 年议定书》

《1987 年海员福利公约》(第 163 号)

《1987 年(海员)健康保护和医疗公约》(第 164 号)

《1987 年(海员)社会保障公约(修订)》(第 165 号)

《1987 年海员遣返公约(修订)》(第 166 号)

《1996 年(海员)劳动监察公约》(第 178 号)

《1996 年海员招募和安置公约》(第 179 号)

《1996 年海员工时和船舶配员公约》(第 180 号)

Depositary functions

Article XI

1 The Director-General of the International Labour Office shall notify all Members of the International Labour Organization of the registration of all ratifications, acceptances and denunciations under this Convention.

2 When the conditions provided for in paragraph 3 of Article VIII have been fulfilled, the Director-General shall draw the attention of the Members of the Organization to the date upon which the Convention will come into force.

Article XII

The Director-General of the International Labour Office shall communicate to the Secretary-General of the United Nations for registration in accordance with Article 102 of the Charter of the United Nations full particulars of all ratifications, acceptances and denunciations registered under this Convention.

Special Tripartite Committee

Article XIII

1 The Governing Body of the International Labour Office shall keep the working of this Convention under continuous review through a committee established by it with special competence in the area of maritime labour standards.

2 For matters dealt with in accordance with this Convention, the Committee shall consist of two representatives nominated by the Government of each Member which has ratified this Convention, and the representatives of Shipowners and Seafarers appointed by the Governing Body after consultation with the Joint Maritime Commission.

3 The Government representatives of Members which have not yet ratified this Convention may participate in the Committee but shall have no right to vote on any matter dealt with in accordance with this Convention. The Governing Body may invite other organizations or entities to be represented on the Committee by observers.

4 The votes of each Shipowner and Seafarer representative in the Committee shall be weighted so as to ensure that the Shipowners' group and the Seafarers' group each have half the voting power of the total number of governments which are represented at the meeting concerned and entitled to vote.

保存人职责

第十一条

1 国际劳工局局长应将各成员国就本公约所交存的所有批准书、接受书和退出书的登记情况通报国际劳工组织的全体成员国。

2 在第八条第 3 款规定的条件得到满足后,局长应提请本组织各成员国注意本公约开始生效的日期。

第十二条

国际劳工局局长应按照《联合国宪章》第一百零二条的规定,将根据本公约登记的所有批准、接受和退出的详细情况送请联合国秘书长进行登记。

三方专门委员会

第十三条

1 国际劳工局理事会应通过其所设立的一个在海事劳工标准领域有专长的委员会保持对公约发挥作用的情况进行审议。

2 就根据本公约处理的事项而言,委员会应由已批准本公约的各成员国政府指派的两名代表和理事会经与联合海事委员会协商后指定的船东和海员代表组成。

3 尚未批准本公约的成员国的政府代表可以参加委员会,但对根据本公约处理的任何事项无表决权。理事会可以邀请其他组织或机构以观察员的身份出席委员会。

4 应对委员会中每个船东和海员代表的票数予以加权,以保证船东组和海员组各自拥有出席有关会议并有表决权的政府投票权总数的一半。

Amendment of this Convention

Article XIV

1   Amendments to any of the provisions of this Convention may be adopted by the General Conference of the International Labour Organization in the framework of article 19 of the Constitution of the International Labour Organisation and the rules and procedures of the Organization for the adoption of Conventions. Amendments to the Code may also be adopted following the procedures in Article XV.

2   In the case of Members whose ratifications of this Convention were registered before the adoption of the amendment, the text of the amendment shall be communicated to them for ratification.

3   In the case of other Members of the Organization, the text of the Convention as amended shall be communicated to them for ratification in accordance with article 19 of the Constitution.

4   An amendment shall be deemed to have been accepted on the date when there have been registered ratifications, of the amendment or of the Convention as amended, as the case may be, by at least 30 Members with a total share in the world gross tonnage of ships of at least 33 per cent.

5   An amendment adopted in the framework of article 19 of the Constitution shall be binding only upon those Members of the Organization whose ratifications have been registered by the Director-General of the International Labour Office.

6   For any Member referred to in paragraph 2 of this Article, an amendment shall come into force 12 months after the date of acceptance referred to in paragraph 4 of this Article or 12 months after the date on which its ratification of the amendment has been registered, whichever date is later.

7   Subject to paragraph 9 of this Article, for Members referred to in paragraph 3 of this Article, the Convention as amended shall come into force 12 months after the date of acceptance referred to in paragraph 4 of this Article or 12 months after the date on which their ratifications of the Convention have been registered, whichever date is later.

8   For those Members whose ratification of this Convention was registered before the adoption of an amendment but which have not ratified the amendment, this Convention shall remain in force without the amendment concerned.

本公约的修正案

第十四条

1 对本公约任何规定的修正案均可由国际劳工组织大会在《国际劳工组织章程》第十九条和本组织通过公约的议事规则的框架下予以通过。对守则的修正案还可按第十五条的程序通过。

2 对于在修正案通过前登记了其对本公约的批准书的成员国,应将修正案的文本送交它们以供批准。

3 对于本组织的其他成员国,应根据《国际劳工组织章程》第十九条将经修正的公约文本送交它们以供批准。

4 修正案应在合计占世界船舶吨位至少 33% 的至少 30 个成员国对修正案或经修正公约(视实际情况)的批准书已经登记后视为已被接受。

5 在章程第十九条框架下通过的修正案应只对那些批准书已交国际劳工局局长登记的本组织成员国具有约束力。

6 对于本条第 2 款所述的任何成员国,修正案应于本条第 4 款中所述的接受之日起 12 个月后生效,或于其对修正案的批准书登记之日起 12 个月后生效,以较晚者为准。

7 取决于本条第 9 款的规定,对于本条第 3 款所述的成员国,经修正的公约应于本条第 4 款中所述的接受之日起 12 个月后生效,或于其对公约的批准书登记之日起 12 个月后生效,以较晚者为准。

8 对于其批准本公约的批准书在有关修正案通过之前登记但并没有批准修正案的成员国,未做相关修正的公约应继续对其有效。

9 Any Member whose ratification of this Convention is registered after the adoption of the amendment but before the date referred to in paragraph 4 of this Article may, in a declaration accompanying the instrument of ratification, specify that its ratification relates to the Convention without the amendment concerned. In the case of a ratification with such a declaration, the Convention shall come into force for the Member concerned 12 months after the date on which the ratification was registered. Where an instrument of ratification is not accompanied by such a declaration, or where the ratification is registered on or after the date referred to in paragraph 4, the Convention shall come into force for the Member concerned 12 months after the date on which the ratification was registered and, upon its entry into force in accordance with paragraph 7 of this Article, the amendment shall be binding on the Member concerned unless the amendment provides otherwise.

Amendments to the Code

Article XV

1 The Code may be amended either by the procedure set out in Article XIV or, unless expressly provided otherwise, in accordance with the procedure set out in the present Article.

2 An amendment to the Code may be proposed to the Director-General of the International Labour Office by the government of any Member of the Organization or by the group of Shipowner representatives or the group of Seafarer representatives who have been appointed to the Committee referred to in Article XIII. An amendment proposed by a government must have been proposed by, or be supported by, at least five governments of Members that have ratified the Convention or by the group of Shipowner or Seafarer representatives referred to in this paragraph.

3 Having verified that the proposal for amendment meets the requirements of paragraph 2 of this Article, the Director-General shall promptly communicate the proposal, accompanied by any comments or suggestions deemed appropriate, to all Members of the Organization, with an invitation to them to transmit their observations or suggestions concerning the proposal within a period of six months or such other period (which shall not be less than three months nor more than nine months) prescribed by the Governing Body.

4 At the end of the period referred to in paragraph 3 of this Article, the proposal, accompanied by a summary of any observations or suggestions made under that paragraph, shall be transmitted to the Committee for consideration at a meeting. An amendment shall be considered adopted by the Committee if:

(**a**) at least half the governments of Members that have ratified this Convention are represented in the meeting at which the proposal is considered; and

(**b**) a majority of at least two-thirds of the Committee members vote in favour of the amendment; and

9 在修正案通过以后但在本条第 4 款所述日期之前登记了对本公约的批准书的任何成员国,可在批准书后附上一份声明,明确其批准书涉及的是未经相关修正的公约。在批准书附有这样一份声明的情况下,本公约将在批准书登记之日 12 个月后对该有关成员国生效。如果批准书未附有这样一份声明,或者批准书于第 4 款所述日期或之后登记,本公约将在批准书登记之日 12 个月以后对该有关成员国生效,并且,在修正案根据本条第 7 款生效后,该修正案对该有关成员国有约束力,除非修正案另有规定。

对守则的修正案

第十五条

1 守则既可以按第十四条规定的程序修订,或者,除非另有明文规定,也可以根据本条规定的程序修订。

2 本组织的任何成员国政府或被指定参加第十三条所述委员会的船东代表组或海员代表组可向国际劳工局局长提出对守则的修正案。由一国政府提出的修正案必须得到至少 5 个已批准本公约的成员国政府的共同提议或支持,或者得到本款所述船东代表组或海员代表组的共同提议或支持。

3 经核实关于修正案的提议满足本条第 2 款的要求后,局长应立即将此提议连同任何适当的评论或建议通知给本组织的所有成员国,并请成员国在 6 个月内或理事会规定的其他时间期限(不应少于 3 个月,也不应超过 9 个月)内提出其对该提议的意见或建议。

4 在本条第 3 款所述的期限届满后,应将该提议连同成员国根据该款所提出的意见或建议的要点提交给委员会召开会议审议。在下述情况下应视为修正案已获得了委员会的通过,如果:

（**a**） 至少有半数以上已批准本公约的成员国政府出席审议该提议之会议;并

（**b**） 委员会成员中至少有三分之二的多数投票支持修正案;并

(c) this majority comprises the votes in favour of at least half the government voting power, half the Shipowner voting power and half the Seafarer voting power of the Committee members registered at the meeting when the proposal is put to the vote.

5 Amendments adopted in accordance with paragraph 4 of this Article shall be submitted to the next session of the Conference for approval. Such approval shall require a majority of two-thirds of the votes cast by the delegates present. If such majority is not obtained, the proposed amendment shall be referred back to the Committee for reconsideration should the Committee so wish.

6 Amendments approved by the Conference shall be notified by the Director-General to each of the Members whose ratifications of this Convention were registered before the date of such approval by the Conference. These Members are referred to below as "the ratifying Members". The notification shall contain a reference to the present Article and shall prescribe the period for the communication of any formal disagreement. This period shall be two years from the date of the notification unless, at the time of approval, the Conference has set a different period, which shall be a period of at least one year. A copy of the notification shall be communicated to the other Members of the Organization for their information.

7 An amendment approved by the Conference shall be deemed to have been accepted unless, by the end of the prescribed period, formal expressions of disagreement have been received by the Director-General from more than 40 per cent of the Members which have ratified the Convention and which represent not less than 40 per cent of the gross tonnage of the ships of the Members which have ratified the Convention.

8 An amendment deemed to have been accepted shall come into force six months after the end of the prescribed period for all the ratifying Members except those which had formally expressed their disagreement in accordance with paragraph 7 of this Article and have not withdrawn such disagreement in accordance with paragraph 11. However:

(a) before the end of the prescribed period, any ratifying Member may give notice to the Director-General that it shall be bound by the amendment only after a subsequent express notification of its acceptance; and

(b) before the date of entry into force of the amendment, any ratifying Member may give notice to the Director-General that it will not give effect to that amendment for a specified period.

9 An amendment which is the subject of a notice referred to in paragraph 8(a) of this Article shall enter into force for the Member giving such notice six months after the Member has notified the Director-General of its acceptance of the amendment or on the date on which the amendment first comes into force, whichever date is later.

10 The period referred to in paragraph 8(b) of this Article shall not go beyond one year from the date of entry into force of the amendment or beyond any longer period determined by the Conference at the time of approval of the amendment.

（c）　此多数票中至少包含了对提议进行表决时在会议注册的委员会成员中政府表决权的半数支持票、船东表决权的半数支持票和海员表决权的半数支持票。

5　根据本条第 4 款通过的修正案应提交下一届大会批准。这种批准要求出席大会代表三分之二多数投票支持。如果没有获得这种多数,若委员会愿意的话,应将建议修正案送回委员会重新审议。

6　局长应将经大会批准的修正案通知给其对本公约的批准书在大会批准修正案前业经登记的每一成员国。下文称此种成员国为“批约成员国”。该通知应援引本条,并应规定提出任何正式异议的期限。除非大会在批准时确定了不同期限(应至少为一年),此期限应为自通知之日起两年。通知的副本应送本组织的其他成员国供其知晓。

7　除非局长在规定的期限内收到超过 40% 的已批准本公约成员国的正式不同意见,并且它们代表着不少于已批准公约成员国船舶总吨位的 40%,大会通过的修正案应视为已被接受。

8　视为已被接受的修正案应于规定期限结束之日 6 个月后对所有批约成员国生效,根据本条第 7 款正式表示了不同意见且没有根据第 11 款撤销该不同意见的批约成员国除外。但是:

（a）　任何批约成员国可在规定的期限结束前通知局长,只有其将来明确通知其接受后,才受修正案的约束;以及

（b）　任何批约成员国可在修正案生效之日前通知局长,在一段确定的期间内自己将不执行该修正案。

9　本条第 8(a)款所述通知中所指的修正案对于做出该通知的成员国来说,应于该成员国通知国际劳工局局长其接受修正案之日起 6 个月后对其生效,或于修正案初次生效之日对其生效,以较晚者为准。

10　本条第 8(b)款所述期间自修正案生效之日起不应超过 1 年或超过大会批准修正案时确定的任何更长时间。

11 A Member that has formally expressed disagreement with an amendment may withdraw its disagreement at any time. If notice of such withdrawal is received by the Director-General after the amendment has entered into force, the amendment shall enter into force for the Member six months after the date on which the notice was registered.

12 After entry into force of an amendment, the Convention may only be ratified in its amended form.

13 To the extent that a maritime labour certificate relates to matters covered by an amendment to the Convention which has entered into force:

(**a**) a Member that has accepted that amendment shall not be obliged to extend the benefit of the Convention in respect of the maritime labour certificates issued to ships flying the flag of another Member which:

(**i**) pursuant to paragraph 7 of this Article, has formally expressed disagreement to the amendment and has not withdrawn such disagreement; or

(**ii**) pursuant to paragraph 8 (a) of this Article, has given notice that its acceptance is subject to its subsequent express notification and has not accepted the amendment; and

(**b**) a Member that has accepted the amendment shall extend the benefit of the Convention in respect of the maritime labour certificates issued to ships flying the flag of another Member that has given notice, pursuant to paragraph 8(b) of this Article, that it will not give effect to that amendment for the period specified in accordance with paragraph 10 of this Article.

Authoritative languages

Article XVI

The English and French versions of the text of this Convention are equally authoritative.

11 对一修正案正式表示过不同意见的成员国可以随时撤销其不同意见。如果国际劳工局局长在修正案生效以后收到此种撤销通知,修正案应于该通知登记之日 6 个月后对该成员国生效。

12 一修正案生效后,只能批准经修正的公约。

13 只要海事劳工证书与已生效的公约修正案所涉及的事项有关:

（**a**） 接受了一项修正案的成员国没有义务在签发的海事劳工证书方面将公约的益处扩展到悬挂下述另一成员国旗帜的船舶:

（**i**） 根据本条第 7 款,正式表示了对修正案的不同意见且未撤销该不同意见者;或

（**ii**） 根据本条第 8(a)款,通知了其对修正案的接受取决于后来的明确通知且尚未接受该修正案者;以及

（**b**） 如果某成员国根据本条第 8(b) 款做出了在本条第 10 款规定的期间内其将不执行修正案的通知,接受了该修正案的成员国在签发的海事劳工证书方面应将公约的益处扩展到悬挂上述成员国旗帜的船舶。

作准语言

第十六条

本公约的英文本和法文本同等作准。

Explanatory note to the Regulations and Code of the Maritime Labour Convention

1   This explanatory note, which does not form part of the Maritime Labour Convention, is intended as a general guide to the Convention.

2   The Convention comprises three different but related parts: the Articles, the Regulations and the Code.

3   The Articles and Regulations set out the core rights and principles and the basic obligations of Members ratifying the Convention. The Articles and Regulations can only be changed by the Conference in the framework of article 19 of the Constitution of the International Labour Organisation (see Article XIV of the Convention).

4   The Code contains the details for the implementation of the Regulations. It comprises Part A (mandatory Standards) and Part B (non-mandatory Guidelines). The Code can be amended through the simplified procedure set out in Article XV of the Convention. Since the Code relates to detailed implementation, amendments to it must remain within the general scope of the Articles and Regulations.

5   The Regulations and the Code are organized into general areas under five Titles:

Title 1: Minimum requirements for seafarers to work on a ship

Title 2: Conditions of employment

Title 3: Accommodation, recreational facilities, food and catering

Title 4: Health protection, medical care, welfare and social security protection

Title 5: Compliance and enforcement

6   Each Title contains groups of provisions relating to a particular right or principle (or enforcement measure in Title 5), with connected numbering. The first group in Title 1, for example, consists of Regulation 1.1, Standard A1.1 and Guideline B1.1, relating to minimum age.

7   The Convention has three underlying purposes:

(a)   to lay down, in its Articles and Regulations, a firm set of rights and principles;

(b)   to allow, through the Code, a considerable degree of flexibility in the way Members implement those rights and principles; and

(c)   to ensure, through Title 5, that the rights and principles are properly complied with and enforced.

海事劳工公约的规则和守则的解注

1 本解注旨在作为对海事劳工公约的一般性指导,不构成公约的组成部分。

2 本公约由三个不同但相关的部分构成:条款、规则和守则。

3 条款和规则规定了核心权利和原则以及批准本公约的成员国的基本义务。条款和规则只能由大会在《国际劳工组织章程》第十九条的框架下修改(见公约第十四条)。

4 守则包含了规则的实施细节。它由 A 部分(强制性标准)和 B 部分(非强制性导则)组成。守则可以通过公约第十五条规定的简化程序来修订。由于守则涉及具体实施,对守则的修正必须仍放在条款和规则的总体范畴内。

5 规则和守则按以下标题被划归为五个领域:

标题一:海员上船工作的最低要求

标题二:就业条件

标题三:起居舱室、娱乐设施、食品和膳食服务

标题四:健康保护、医疗、福利和社会保障

标题五:遵守与执行

6 每一标题包含了关于具体权利和原则(或标题五中的执行措施)的几组规定,这几组规定的编号相关联。例如,标题一的第一组包括关于最低年龄的规则 1.1、标准 A1.1 和导则 B1.1。

7 本公约有三个根本目标:

(**a**)   在正文和规则中规定一套确定的权利和原则;

(**b**)   通过守则允许成员国在履行这些权利和原则的方式上有相当程度的灵活性;和

(**c**)   通过标题五确保这些权利和原则得以妥善遵守和执行。

8   There are two main areas for flexibility in implementation: one is the possibility for a Member, where necessary (see Article VI, paragraph 3), to give effect to the detailed requirements of Part A of the Code through substantial equivalence (as defined in Article VI, paragraph 4).

9   The second area of flexibility in implementation is provided by formulating the mandatory requirements of many provisions in Part A in a more general way, thus leaving a wider scope for discretion as to the precise action to be provided for at the national level. In such cases, guidance on implementation is given in the non-mandatory Part B of the Code. In this way, Members which have ratified this Convention can ascertain the kind of action that might be expected of them under the corresponding general obligation in Part A, as well as action that would not necessarily be required. For example, Standard A4.1 requires all ships to provide prompt access to the necessary medicines for medical care on board ship [paragraph 1(b)] and to "carry a medicine chest" [paragraph 4(a)]. The fulfilment in good faith of this latter obligation clearly means something more than simply having a medicine chest on board each ship. A more precise indication of what is involved is provided in the corresponding Guideline B4.1.1 (paragraph 4) so as to ensure that the contents of the chest are properly stored, used and maintained.

10 Members which have ratified this Convention are not bound by the guidance concerned and, as indicated in the provisions in Title 5 on port State control, inspections would deal only with the relevant requirements of this Convention (Articles, Regulations and the Standards in Part A). However, Members are required under paragraph 2 of Article VI to give due consideration to implementing their responsibilities under Part A of the Code in the manner provided for in Part B. If, having duly considered the relevant Guidelines, a Member decides to provide for different arrangements which ensure the proper storage, use and maintenance of the contents of the medicine chest, to take the example given above, as required by the Standard in Part A, then that is acceptable. On the other hand, by following the guidance provided in Part B, the Member concerned, as well as the ILO bodies responsible for reviewing implementation of international labour Conventions, can be sure without further consideration that the arrangements the Member has provided for are adequate to implement the responsibilities under Part A to which the Guideline relates.

8　在实施中有两个方面的灵活性:其一是成员国在必要时(见第六条第 3 款)通过实质上等效(按第六条第 4 款所定义)来执行守则 A 部分的具体要求的可能性。

9　实施中灵活性的第二个方面是通过将 A 部分许多规定的强制性要求表述得更加宽泛来实现的,这样就为在国家的层面上采取确切的行动留出了更广泛的自主权。在这种情况下,守则中非强制性的 B 部分给出了实施指导。这样,已批准本公约的成员国可以确定在 A 部分相应的一般性义务下它们应当采取什么样的行动,以及可能未必要求的行动。例如,标准 A4.1 要求在所有船舶上能够迅速取得用于船上医疗所必需的药品[第 1 (b)款]并"配备一个医药箱"[第 4(a)款]。忠实履行后者的义务明显意味着不仅仅是简单地在每艘船上配备一个医药箱。在相应的导则 B4.1.1 中(第 4 款)对于所涉及的问题给出了更为准确的指示,以便确保妥善地存放、使用和维护医药箱内的物品。

10　已批准本公约的成员国不受相关导则的约束,而且,正如关于港口国监督的标题五中的规定所指出,检查只针对本公约的有关要求(条款、规则和 A 部分的标准)。但是,根据第六条第 2 款,要求成员国在履行其在 A 部分下的责任时对 B 部分所提供的方式给以充分考虑。用上文所举的例子,如果在充分考虑相关导则后,成员国决定做出不同的安排来确保按 A 部分标准的要求对医药箱中的物品进行妥善存放、使用和维护,则是可以接受的。另一方面,通过遵循 B 部分给出的指南,有关成员国以及国际劳工组织负责审议国际劳工公约实施的机构能够确定成员国做出的安排充分履行了导则所涉及的 A 部分中的责任,而无须做进一步考虑。

THE REGULATIONS AND THE CODE

Title 1
Minimum requirements for seafarers to work on a ship

Regulation 1.1
Minimum age

Purpose: To ensure that no under-age persons work on a ship

1   No person below the minimum age shall be employed or engaged or work on a ship.

2   The minimum age at the time of the initial entry into force of this Convention is 16 years.

3   A higher minimum age shall be required in the circumstances set out in the Code.

Standard A1.1   Minimum age

1   The employment, engagement or work on board a ship of any person under the age of 16 shall be prohibited.

2   Night work of seafarers under the age of 18 shall be prohibited. For the purposes of this Standard, "night" shall be defined in accordance with national law and practice. It shall cover a period of at least nine hours starting no later than midnight and ending no earlier than 5 a.m.

3   An exception to strict compliance with the night work restriction may be made by the competent authority when:

   (**a**)   the effective training of the seafarers concerned, in accordance with established programmes and schedules, would be impaired; or

   (**b**)   the specific nature of the duty or a recognized training programme requires that the seafarers covered by the exception perform duties at night and the authority determines, after consultation with the shipowners' and seafarers' organizations concerned, that the work will not be detrimental to their health or well-being.

规则和守则

标题一
海员上船工作的最低要求

规则 1.1
最低年龄

目的:确保未成年人不得上船工作

1　低于最低年龄的人不得在船上受雇、受聘或工作。

2　在本公约生效伊始,最低年龄为 16 岁。

3　在守则规定的情形中应要求更高的最低年龄。

标准 A1.1　最低年龄

1　应禁止任何 16 岁以下的人员受雇、受聘或到船上工作。

2　应禁止 18 岁以下的海员在夜间工作。就本标准而言,"夜间"应根据国家法律或实践来定义。它应该包括从不晚于午夜开始至不早于上午 5 点钟结束的一段至少 9 个小时的时段。

3　在下列情况下主管当局可以对严格遵守关于夜间工作的限制做出例外:

（a）　根据已经确定的项目和日程安排,有关海员的有效培训将被扰乱;或

（b）　职责的具体性质或认可的培训项目要求所涉及的海员例外履行夜间职责,且主管当局在与有关船东和海员组织协商后确定该工作不会对他们的健康或福利产生有害影响。

4 The employment, engagement or work of seafarers under the age of 18 shall be prohibited where the work is likely to jeopardize their health or safety. The types of such work shall be determined by national laws or regulations or by the competent authority, after consultation with the shipowners' and seafarers' organizations concerned, in accordance with relevant international standards.

Guideline B1. 1   Minimum age

1 When regulating working and living conditions, Members should give special attention to the needs of young persons under the age of 18.

Regulation 1. 2
Medical certificate

Purpose: To ensure that all seafarers are medically fit to perform their duties at sea

1 Seafarers shall not work on a ship unless they are certified as medically fit to perform their duties.

2 Exceptions can only be permitted as prescribed in the Code.

Standard A1. 2   Medical certificate

1 The competent authority shall require that, prior to beginning work on a ship, seafarers hold a valid medical certificate attesting that they are medically fit to perform the duties they are to carry out at sea.

2 In order to ensure that medical certificates genuinely reflect seafarers' state of health, in light of the duties they are to perform, the competent authority shall, after consultation with the shipowners' and seafarers' organizations concerned, and giving due consideration to applicable international guidelines referred to in Part B of this Code, prescribe the nature of the medical examination and certificate.

3 This Standard is without prejudice to the International Convention on Standards of Training, Certification and Watchkeeping for Seafarers, 1978, as amended ("STCW"). A medical certificate issued in accordance with the requirements of STCW shall be accepted by the competent authority, for the purpose of Regulation 1. 2. A medical certificate meeting the substance of those requirements, in the case of seafarers not covered by STCW, shall similarly be accepted.

4 The medical certificate shall be issued by a duly qualified medical practitioner or, in the case of a certificate solely concerning eyesight, by a person recognized by the competent authority as qualified to issue such a certificate. Practitioners must enjoy full professional independence in exercising their medical judgement in undertaking medical examination procedures.

4 应禁止雇用或聘用 18 岁以下的海员从事可能损害其健康或安全的工作。这些工作的类型应由国家法律或法规确定,或由主管当局根据相关国际标准与有关船东和海员组织协商后确定。

导则 B1.1　最低年龄

1 在对工作和生活条件进行规范时,成员国应特别注意 18 岁以下未成年人的需要。

规则 1.2
体检证书

目的:确保所有海员的健康状况适合履行其海上职责

1 除非海员的健康状况经证明适合履行其职责,否则不得上船工作。

2 只有在本守则规定的情况下才允许例外。

标准 A1.2　体检证书

1 主管当局应要求,海员在上船工作之前持有有效的体检证书,证明其健康状况适合其将在海上履行的职责。

2 为了确保体检证书真实地反映海员的健康状况,主管当局应根据其将要履行的职责,并充分考虑到本守则 B 部分给出的适用国际性导则,与船东和海员组织协商后规定体格检查和证书的性质。

3 本标准并不损害经修正的《1978 年海员培训、发证和值班标准国际公约》("1978 年 STCW 公约")。就规则 1.2 而言,主管当局应接受根据 STCW 公约的要求签发的体检证书。对于 STCW 公约未包括的海员,满足那些要求的实质性内容的体检证书应同样予以接受。

4 体检证书应由有正规资格的医师签发,或者,对于只涉及视力的证书而言,由经主管当局认可的具备签发证书资格的人员签发。医师在履行体检程序时必须享有充分的职业独立性来进行其医学判断。

5   Seafarers that have been refused a certificate or have had a limitation imposed on their ability to work, in particular with respect to time, field of work or trading area, shall be given the opportunity to have a further examination by another independent medical practitioner or by an independent medical referee.

6   Each medical certificate shall state in particular that:

   (a)   the hearing and sight of the seafarer concerned, and the colour vision in the case of a seafarer to be employed in capacities where fitness for the work to be performed is liable to be affected by defective colour vision, are all satisfactory; and

   (b)   the seafarer concerned is not suffering from any medical condition likely to be aggravated by service at sea or to render the seafarer unfit for such service or to endanger the health of other persons on board.

7   Unless a shorter period is required by reason of the specific duties to be performed by the seafarer concerned or is required under STCW:

   (a)   a medical certificate shall be valid for a maximum period of two years unless the seafarer is under the age of 18, in which case the maximum period of validity shall be one year;

   (b)   a certification of colour vision shall be valid for a maximum period of six years.

8   In urgent cases the competent authority may permit a seafarer to work without a valid medical certificate until the next port of call where the seafarer can obtain a medical certificate from a qualified medical practitioner, provided that:

   (a)   the period of such permission does not exceed three months; and

   (b)   the seafarer concerned is in possession of an expired medical certificate of recent date.

9   If the period of validity of a certificate expires in the course of a voyage, the certificate shall continue in force until the next port of call where the seafarer can obtain a medical certificate from a qualified medical practitioner, provided that the period shall not exceed three months.

10   The medical certificates for seafarers working on ships ordinarily engaged on international voyages must as a minimum be provided in English.

Guideline B1. 2   Medical certificate

Guideline B1. 2. 1   International guidelines

1   The competent authority, medical practitioners, examiners, shipowners, seafarers' representatives and all other persons concerned with the conduct of medical fitness examinations of seafarer candidates and serving seafarers should follow the ILO/WHO Guidelines for Conducting Pre-sea and Periodic Medical Fitness Examinations for Seafarers, including any subsequent versions, and any other applicable international guidelines published by the International Labour Organization, the International Maritime Organization or the World Health Organization.

5　对于被拒绝发证的海员，或在其工作能力方面，特别是关于时间、工作内容或航行区域方面被施加了限制的海员，应给予他们由另一位独立的医师或独立的鉴定人做进一步检查的机会。

6　每份体检证书应特别载明：

（a）　有关海员的听力和视力以及那些受雇职务所从事的工作将会受到不良色觉视力影响的人员的色觉视力全部符合要求；以及

（b）　该海员未患有任何由于在海上工作而可能会而加重，或使其变得不适合从事此种工作，或威胁船上其他人员健康的疾患。

7　除非由于有关海员将履行的特殊职责或根据 STCW 公约的规定要求更短的期间：

（a）　体检证书的最长有效期为两年，除非海员低于 18 岁，在这种情况下体检证书的最长有效期应为一年；

（b）　色觉视力证书的最长有效期应为六年。

8　在紧急情况下，主管当局可以允许没有有效体检证书的海员工作直至该海员可以从合格的医师那里取得一份体检证书的下一停靠港，条件是：

（a）　所允许的期间不超过 3 个月；并且

（b）　该海员持有最近过期的体检证书。

9　如果在某航行途中证书到期，该证书应继续有效至该海员能够从合格医师那里取得体检证书的下一停靠港，条件是这段时间不超过 3 个月。

10　在通常从事国际航行的船舶上工作的海员的体检证书至少必须用英文写成。

导则 B1.2　体检证书

导则 B1.2.1　国际导则

1　主管当局、医师、体检人员、船东、海员的代表和所有其他对求职海员和在职海员实施体格健康检查的有关人员应遵循《ILO/WHO 海员上船工作前和定期体格健康检查实施指南》，包括其任何修订版本以及国际劳工组织、国际海事组织或世界卫生组织出版的任何其他适用的国际导则。

Regulation 1. 3
Training and qualifications

Purpose: To ensure that seafarers are trained or qualified to carry out their duties on board ship

1   Seafarers shall not work on a ship unless they are trained or certified as competent or otherwise qualified to perform their duties.

2   Seafarers shall not be permitted to work on a ship unless they have successfully completed training for personal safety on board ship.

3   Training and certification in accordance with the mandatory instruments adopted by the International Maritime Organization shall be considered as meeting the requirements of paragraphs 1 and 2 of this Regulation.

4   Any Member which, at the time of its ratification of this Convention, was bound by the Certification of Able Seamen Convention, 1946 (No. 74), shall continue to carry out the obligations under that Convention unless and until mandatory provisions covering its subject matter have been adopted by the International Maritime Organization and entered into force, or until five years have elapsed since the entry into force of this Convention in accordance with paragraph 3 of Article Ⅷ, whichever date is earlier.

Regulation 1. 4
Recruitment and placement

Purpose: To ensure that seafarers have access to an efficient and well-regulated seafarer recruitment and placement system

1   All seafarers shall have access to an efficient, adequate and accountable system for finding employment on board ship without charge to the seafarer.

2   Seafarer recruitment and placement services operating in a Member's territory shall conform to the standards set out in the Code.

3   Each Member shall require, in respect of seafarers who work on ships that fly its flag, that shipowners who use seafarer recruitment and placement services that are based in countries or territories in which this Convention does not apply, ensure that those services conform to the requirements set out in the Code.

Standard A1. 4   Recruitment and placement

1   Each Member that operates a public seafarer recruitment and placement service shall ensure that the service is operated in an orderly manner that protects and promotes seafarers' employment rights as provided in this Convention.

规则 1.3
培训和资格

目的:确保海员经过培训并具备履行其船上职责的资格

1 除非海员经过培训或经证明适任或者具备履行其职责的资格,否则不得在船上工作。

2 除非海员成功地完成了船上个人安全培训,否则不得允许其在船上工作。

3 按国际海事组织通过的强制性文件进行的培训和发证应被视为满足本规则第 1 和 2 款的要求。

4 任何在批准本公约时受《1946 年一等水手公约》(第 74 号)约束的成员国,应继续履行该公约的义务,除非并且直到国际海事组织通过了覆盖该公约事项的强制性规定并已生效,或者直到本公约根据第八条第 3 款生效后已经过去了 5 年,以较早的日期为准。

规则 1.4
招募和安置

目的:确保海员有机会利用高效和规范的海员招募和安置系统

1 所有海员应能够利用高效、充分和可靠,并且不向海员收费的系统寻找船上就业的机会。

2 在成员国领土内开办的海员招募和安置服务机构应符合本守则所规定的标准。

3 关于在悬挂其旗帜的船舶上工作的海员,各成员国应要求,如果船东利用那些在本公约不适用的国家或领土内设立的招募和安置服务机构,应保证这些服务机构符合本规则的要求。

标准 A1.4 招募和安置

1 开办公共海员招募和安置服务机构的各成员国应确保该服务机构以保护和促进本公约所规定的海员就业权利的方式有序运作。

2   Where a Member has private seafarer recruitment and placement services operating in its territory whose primary purpose is the recruitment and placement of seafarers or which recruit and place a significant number of seafarers, they shall be operated only in conformity with a standardized system of licensing or certification or other form of regulation. This system shall be established, modified or changed only after consultation with the shipowners' and seafarers' organizations concerned. In the event of doubt as to whether this Convention applies to a private recruitment and placement service, the question shall be determined by the competent authority in each Member after consultation with the shipowners' and seafarers' organizations concerned. Undue proliferation of private seafarer recruitment and placement services shall not be encouraged.

3   The provisions of paragraph 2 of this Standard shall also apply to the extent that they are determined by the competent authority, in consultation with the shipowners' and seafarers' organizations concerned, to be appropriate in the context of recruitment and placement services operated by a seafarers' organization in the territory of the Member for the supply of seafarers who are nationals of that Member to ships which fly its flag. The services covered by this paragraph are those fulfilling the following conditions:

(a)   the recruitment and placement service is operated pursuant to a collective bargaining agreement between that organization and a shipowner;

(b)   both the seafarers' organization and the shipowner are based in the territory of the Member;

(c)   the Member has national laws or regulations or a procedure to authorize or register the collective bargaining agreement permitting the operation of the recruitment and placement service; and

(d)   the recruitment and placement service is operated in an orderly manner and measures are in place to protect and promote seafarers' employment rights comparable to those provided in paragraph 5 of this Standard.

4   Nothing in this Standard or Regulation 1.4 shall be deemed to:

(a)   prevent a Member from maintaining a free public seafarer recruitment and placement service for seafarers in the framework of a policy to meet the needs of seafarers and shipowners, whether the service forms part of or is coordinated with a public employment service for all workers and employers; or

(b)   impose on a Member the obligation to establish a system for the operation of private seafarer recruitment or placement services in its territory.

5   A Member adopting a system referred to in paragraph 2 of this Standard shall, in its laws and regulations or other measures, at a minimum:

(a)   prohibit seafarer recruitment and placement services from using means, mechanisms or lists intended to prevent or deter seafarers from gaining employment for which they are qualified;

2 如果某成员国有以招募和安置海员为主要目的或招募和安置相当数量海员的私营海员招募和安置服务机构在其领土内运营,这些服务机构必须依照一种标准化的发放许可证或发证或其他形式的规范制度运营。这种制度必须在与有关的船东和海员组织协商后才能建立、修改或改变。在对本公约是否适用于某一私营招募和安置服务机构存有疑问时,该问题应由各成员国的主管当局与有关船东和海员组织协商决定。不应鼓励私营海员招募和安置服务机构过度扩散。

3 本标准第 2 款的规定还应适用于——适用程度由主管当局与有关船东和海员组织协商确定认为合适——在成员国领土内由海员组织运营的招募和安置服务机构向悬挂该成员国旗帜的船舶提供本国海员的情况。本款所包括的服务机构为满足以下条件者:

(**a**) 该招募和安置服务机构根据该海员组织与船东之间的集体谈判协议运营;

(**b**) 海员组织和船东均设立于成员国的领土之内;

(**c**) 该成员国有国家法律或法规或程序对允许运营招募和安置服务机构的集体谈判协议进行授权或登记;和

(**d**) 招募和安置服务机构以有序的方式运营,并具备与本标准第 5 款所规定者相当的保护和促进海员就业权利的措施。

4 本标准或规则 1.4 中的任何规定都不应被视为:

(**a**) 阻止一成员国在满足海员和船东需要的政策框架内为海员维持一个免费的海员招募和安置服务机构,无论该服务机构是作为面向所有工人和雇主的公共就业服务机构的一部分还是与之相协调;或

(**b**) 向成员国施加在其领土内建立一个供私营海员招募和安置服务机构运作的制度的义务。

5 采用了本标准第 2 段所述之制度的成员国,应至少在其法律和法规或其他措施中:

(**a**) 禁止海员招募和安置服务机构利用各种方式、机制或清单来阻止或者阻挠海员获得其所称职的工作;

(**b**)   require that no fees or other charges for seafarer recruitment or placement or for providing employment to seafarers are borne directly or indirectly, in whole or in part, by the seafarer, other than the cost of the seafarer obtaining a national statutory medical certificate, the national seafarer's book and a passport or other similar personal travel documents, not including, however, the cost of visas, which shall be borne by the shipowner; and

(**c**)   ensure that seafarer recruitment and placement services operating in its territory:

     (**i**)   maintain an up-to-date register of all seafarers recruited or placed through them, to be available for inspection by the competent authority;

     (**ii**)   make sure that seafarers are informed of their rights and duties under their employment agreements prior to or in the process of engagement and that proper arrangements are made for seafarers to examine their employment agreements before and after they are signed and for them to receive a copy of the agreements;

     (**iii**)   verify that seafarers recruited or placed by them are qualified and hold the documents necessary for the job concerned, and that the seafarers' employment agreements are in accordance with applicable laws and regulations and any collective bargaining agreement that forms part of the employment agreement;

     (**iv**)   make sure, as far as practicable, that the shipowner has the means to protect seafarers from being stranded in a foreign port;

     (**v**)   examine and respond to any complaint concerning their activities and advise the competent authority of any unresolved complaint;

     (**vi**)   establish a system of protection, by way of insurance or an equivalent appropriate measure, to compensate seafarers for monetary loss that they may incur as a result of the failure of a recruitment and placement service or the relevant shipowner under the seafarers' employment agreement to meet its obligations to them.

6   The competent authority shall closely supervise and control all seafarer recruitment and placement services operating in the territory of the Member concerned. Any licences or certificates or similar authorizations for the operation of private services in the territory are granted or renewed only after verification that the seafarer recruitment and placement service concerned meets the requirements of national laws and regulations.

7   The competent authority shall ensure that adequate machinery and procedures exist for the investigation, if necessary, of complaints concerning the activities of seafarer recruitment and placement services, involving, as appropriate, representatives of shipowners and seafarers.

（**b**） 要求海员招募或安置或者为海员提供就业的费用或其他收费不得直接或间接、全部或部分地由该海员承担,海员取得国家法定体检证书、国家海员服务簿、护照或其他类似个人旅行证件的费用除外,但除外的费用不包括签证费,签证费应由船东负担;以及

（**c**） 确保其领土内的海员招募和安置服务机构:

　（**i**）　维持一份其所招募或安置的所有海员的最新登记册,以备主管当局检查;

　（**ii**）　保证海员在受聘前或受聘过程中被告知其在就业协议上的权利和职责,并为海员在签署就业协议之前和之后对之进行核阅以及确保他们收到一份该协议的副本做出适当安排;

　（**iii**）　核实被其招募和安置的海员是合格的并持有从事相关工作所必需的证书,并核实海员就业协议符合所适用的法律和法规和构成就业协议一部分的任何集体谈判协议;

　（**iv**）　尽实际可能确保船东有保护海员免于流落外国港口的手段;

　（**v**）　对有关其活动的任何投诉进行核查并做出反应,并将任何未解决的投诉报告主管当局;

　（**vi**）　建立一个保护机制,通过保险或适当的等效措施,赔偿由于招募和安置服务机构或有关船东未能按就业协议履行对海员的义务而可能给海员造成的资金损失。

6　主管当局应密切监督和控制在有关成员国领土内运营的所有海员招募和安置服务机构。只有经过核验表明有关海员招募和安置服务符合其国家法律和法规的要求后才为其核发或换新在该领土内的经营许可或证书或类似授权。

7　主管当局应确保存在适当的机制和程序,在必要时对关于海员招募和安置服务机构活动的投诉开展调查,并视情况请船东和海员的代表参与。

8 Each Member which has ratified this Convention shall, in so far as practicable, advise its nationals on the possible problems of signing on a ship that flies the flag of a State which has not ratified the Convention, until it is satisfied that standards equivalent to those fixed by this Convention are being applied. Measures taken to this effect by the Member that has ratified this Convention shall not be in contradiction with the principle of free movement of workers stipulated by the treaties to which the two States concerned may be parties.

9 Each Member which has ratified this Convention shall require that shipowners of ships that fly its flag, who use seafarer recruitment and placement services based in countries or territories in which this Convention does not apply, ensure, as far as practicable, that those services meet the requirements of this Standard.

10 Nothing in this Standard shall be understood as diminishing the obligations and responsibilities of shipowners or of a Member with respect to ships that fly its flag.

Guideline B1. 4   Recruitment and placement

Guideline B1. 4. 1   Organizational and operational guidelines

1 When fulfilling its obligations under Standard A1. 4, paragraph 1, the competent authority should consider:

(**a**)   taking the necessary measures to promote effective cooperation among seafarer recruitment and placement services, whether public or private;

(**b**)   the needs of the maritime industry at both the national and international levels, when developing training programmes for seafarers that form the part of the ship's crew that is responsible for the ship's safe navigation and pollution prevention operations, with the participation of shipowners, seafarers and the relevant training institutions;

(**c**)   making suitable arrangements for the cooperation of representative shipowners' and seafarers' organizations in the organization and operation of the public seafarer recruitment and placement services, where they exist;

(**d**)   determining, with due regard to the right to privacy and the need to protect confidentiality, the conditions under which seafarers' personal data may be processed by seafarer recruitment and placement services, including the collection, storage, combination and communication of such data to third parties;

(**e**)   maintaining an arrangement for the collection and analysis of all relevant information on the maritime labour market, including the current and prospective supply of seafarers that work as crew classified by age, sex, rank and qualifications, and the industry's requirements, the collection of data on age or sex being admissible only for statistical purposes or if used in the framework of a programme to prevent discrimination based on age or sex;

8 批准了本公约的各成员国应尽实际可能,将与一艘悬挂未批准本公约国家的旗帜的船舶签定上船协议可能引起的问题告知其本国国民,直至其认为与本公约所确定的标准等效的标准在该船得以实施。已批准本公约的成员国为此而采取的措施不应与相关的两个国家可能都已加入的条约所规定的工人自由流动原则相矛盾。

9 已批准本公约的各成员国应要求悬挂其旗帜船舶的船东,如果使用了在本公约不适用的国家或领土内设立的海员招募和安置服务机构,尽实际可能确保这些服务机构符合本标准的要求。

10 本标准的任何要求都不得被理解为减少了船东或成员国对悬挂本国旗帜的船舶的义务和责任。

导则 B1.4　招募和安置

导则 B1.4.1　组织和操作导则

1 在履行其在标准 A1.4 第 1 款下的义务时,主管当局应考虑:

（**a**）采取必要的措施促进海员招募和安置服务机构间的有效合作,无论其为公共或私营;

（**b**）在船东、海员和相关培训机构的参与下,为那些参与负责船舶安全航行和防污染操作的海员制订培训计划时,考虑到国家和国际海运业的需要;

（**c**）如果存在公共招募和安置服务机构,为有代表性的船东和海员组织在公共招募和安置服务机构的组织和运作方面的合作做出适当的安排;

（**d**）充分考虑到隐私权和保密需要,确定在何种条件下海员的个人资料可由海员招募和安置服务机构来处理,包括这些资料的收集、存储、合并以及向第三方传送;

（**e**）对收集和分析海事劳动力市场的所有相关信息做出安排,其中包括根据年龄、性别、等级和资质以及航运业的要求分类的海员目前和预期供应情况,有关年龄或性别数据的收集只能用于统计目的,或者只能用于防止年龄或性别歧视的项目框架中;

(**f**) ensuring that the staff responsible for the supervision of public and private seafarer recruitment and placement services for ship's crew with responsibility for the ship's safe navigation and pollution prevention operations have had adequate training, including approved sea-service experience, and have relevant knowledge of the maritime industry, including the relevant maritime international instruments on training, certification and labour standards;

(**g**) prescribing operational standards and adopting codes of conduct and ethical practices for seafarer recruitment and placement services; and

(**h**) exercising supervision of the licensing or certification system on the basis of a system of quality standards.

2 In establishing the system referred to in Standard A1.4, paragraph 2, each Member should consider requiring seafarer recruitment and placement services, established in its territory, to develop and maintain verifiable operational practices. These operational practices for private seafarer recruitment and placement services and, to the extent that they are applicable, for public seafarer recruitment and placement services should address the following matters:

(**a**) medical examinations, seafarers' identity documents and such other items as may be required for the seafarer to gain employment;

(**b**) maintaining, with due regard to the right to privacy and the need to protect confidentiality, full and complete records of the seafarers covered by their recruitment and placement system, which should include but not be limited to:

(**i**) the seafarers' qualifications;

(**ii**) record of employment;

(**iii**) personal data relevant to employment; and

(**iv**) medical data relevant to employment;

(**c**) maintaining up-to-date lists of the ships for which the seafarer recruitment and placement services provide seafarers and ensuring that there is a means by which the services can be contacted in an emergency at all hours;

(**d**) procedures to ensure that seafarers are not subject to exploitation by the seafarer recruitment and placement services or their personnel with regard to the offer of engagement on particular ships or by particular companies;

(**e**) procedures to prevent the opportunities for exploitation of seafarers arising from the issue of joining advances or any other financial transaction between the shipowner and the seafarers which are handled by the seafarer recruitment and placement services;

(**f**) clearly publicizing costs, if any, which the seafarer will be expected to bear in the recruitment process;

(**g**) ensuring that seafarers are advised of any particular conditions applicable to the job for which they are to be engaged and of the particular shipowner's policies relating to their employment;

（**f**）　确保负责监督那些为承担船舶安全航行和防污染操作职责的船员服务的公共和私营海员招募和安置服务机构的人员受到过适当培训,包括具备认可的海上服务资历和关于海运业的相关知识,其中包括关于培训、发证和劳工标准的相关国际海事文件;

（**g**）　为海员招募和安置服务机构规定经营标准并通过行为准则和道德规范;以及

（**h**）　基于质量标准体系对许可或证书制度实施监督。

2　在建立标准 A1.4 第 2 款所述的制度时,成员国应考虑要求在其领土内设立的海员招募和安置服务机构制定并维持可以核验的经营规范。私营海员招募和安置服务机构以及在适用的限度内公共海员招募和安置机构的这些经营规范应涉及以下事项:

（**a**）　体格检查、海员身份证书以及海员为获得就业可能被要求的其他类似项目;

（**b**）　充分考虑到隐私权和保密的需要,保持其招募和安置系统涉及的关于海员的全面和完整的记录。此类记录应包括但不限于下列内容:

　　（**i**）　海员的资格;

　　（**ii**）　就业记录;

　　（**iii**）　与就业有关的个人资料;和

　　（**iv**）　与就业有关的健康资料;

（**c**）　保持由该海员招募和安置服务机构提供海员的船舶的最新名单,并确保存在一种可用来随时与该服务机构进行紧急联络的手段;

（**d**）　有程序确保海员在被聘用到某些特定船舶或被某些特定公司聘用,不受海员招募和安置服务机构或其工作人员的盘剥;

（**e**）　有程序防止出现通过预付上船或由海员招募和安置服务机构操纵的船东与海员之间的任何其他财务转账而产生的盘剥海员的机会;

（**f**）　清楚地公布在招募过程中需要由海员承担的费用,如果有的话;

（**g**）　确保海员被告知关于其即将从事的工作的任何特定条件以及与他们的就业相关的特定船东的政策;

(h) procedures which are in accordance with the principles of natural justice for dealing with cases of incompetence or indiscipline consistent with national laws and practice and, where applicable, with collective agreements;

(i) procedures to ensure, as far as practicable, that all mandatory certificates and documents submitted for employment are up to date and have not been fraudulently obtained and that employment references are verified;

(j) procedures to ensure that requests for information or advice by families of seafarers while the seafarers are at sea are dealt with promptly and sympathetically and at no cost; and

(k) verifying that labour conditions on ships where seafarers are placed are in conformity with applicable collective bargaining agreements concluded between a shipowner and a representative seafarers' organization and, as a matter of policy, supplying seafarers only to shipowners that offer terms and conditions of employment to seafarers which comply with applicable laws or regulations or collective agreements.

3 Consideration should be given to encouraging international cooperation between Members and relevant organizations, such as:

(a) the systematic exchange of information on the maritime industry and labour market on a bilateral, regional and multilateral basis;

(b) the exchange of information on maritime labour legislation;

(c) the harmonization of policies, working methods and legislation governing recruitment and placement of seafarers;

(d) the improvement of procedures and conditions for the international recruitment and placement of seafarers; and

(e) workforce planning, taking account of the supply of and demand for seafarers and the requirements of the maritime industry.

（h） 有根据自然公正的原则处理不称职或不守纪律情况的程序,此类程序符合国家法律和惯例,如适用集体协议应符合集体协议的规定;

（i） 有程序尽实际可能确保申请就业所提交的所有强制性证书和文件都是最新的,不是通过欺骗获得的,而且其就业情况经过核实;

（j） 有程序确保海员在海上期间其家属关于获得信息或建议的要求能够得到迅速和富有同情心的处理,且不收取费用;以及

（k） 核实海员所被安置的船舶上的劳动条件符合船东与海员代表组织所签定的适用集体谈判协议,并作为一项政策,只向那些为海员提供的就业条款和条件符合适用的法律或法规或集体协议的船东提供海员。

3 应考虑鼓励成员国和相关组织之间的国际合作,例如:

（a） 在双边、区域和多边的基础上系统地交换关于海运业和海事劳动力市场的信息;

（b） 交换关于海事劳动立法的信息;

（c） 协调涉及海员招募和安置的政策、工作方法与立法;

（d） 改善海员国际招募和安置的程序与条件;和

（e） 根据海员的供求情况和海运业的要求制订劳动力规划。

Title 2
Conditions of employment

Regulation 2. 1
Seafarers' employment agreements

Purpose: To ensure that seafarers have a fair employment agreement

1   The terms and conditions for employment of a seafarer shall be set out or referred to in a clear written legally enforceable agreement and shall be consistent with the standards set out in the Code.

2   Seafarers' employment agreements shall be agreed to by the seafarer under conditions which ensure that the seafarer has an opportunity to review and seek advice on the terms and conditions in the agreement and freely accepts them before signing.

3   To the extent compatible with the Member's national law and practice, seafarers' employment agreements shall be understood to incorporate any applicable collective bargaining agreements.

Standard A2. 1   Seafarers' employment agreements

1   Each Member shall adopt laws or regulations requiring that ships that fly its flag comply with the following requirements:

   (a)   seafarers working on ships that fly its flag shall have a seafarers' employment agreement signed by both the seafarer and the shipowner or a representative of the shipowner (or, where they are not employees, evidence of contractual or similar arrangements) providing them with decent working and living conditions on board the ship as required by this Convention;

   (b)   seafarers signing a seafarers' employment agreement shall be given an opportunity to examine and seek advice on the agreement before signing, as well as such other facilities as are necessary to ensure that they have freely entered into an agreement with a sufficient understanding of their rights and responsibilities;

   (c)   the shipowner and seafarer concerned shall each have a signed original of the seafarers' employment agreement;

   (d)   measures shall be taken to ensure that clear information as to the conditions of their employment can be easily obtained on board by seafarers, including the ship's master, and that such information, including a copy of the seafarers' employment agreement, is also accessible for review by officers of a competent authority, including those in ports to be visited; and

   (e)   seafarers shall be given a document containing a record of their employment on board the ship.

标题二
就业条件

规则 2.1
海员就业协议

目的：确保海员取得公平的就业协议

1　海员的就业条款和条件应在一项明确的法律上可执行的书面协议中加以规定或提及并应与守则中规定的标准一致。

2　海员的就业协议应在确保海员有机会对协议中的条款和条件进行审阅和征求意见并在签字前自由接受的前提下，取得海员的同意。

3　在与成员国国家法律和惯例相符合的范围内，海员的就业协议应被理解为包括了任何适用的集体谈判协议。

标准 A2.1　海员就业协议

1　各成员国应通过法律或法规要求悬挂其旗帜的船舶符合下述要求：

（**a**）　在悬挂其旗帜的船舶上工作的海员应持有一份由海员和船东或船东的代表双方签署的海员就业协议（或者，如果他们不是雇员，则为契约性或类似协议的证明）为其提供本公约所要求的体面的船上工作和生活条件；

（**b**）　签署海员就业协议的海员在签字前应有机会对协议进行审查和征询他人意见，还要为海员提供其他必要的便利，确保其在充分理解其权利和义务后自由达成协议；

（**c**）　有关船东和海员应各持有一份经签字的海员就业协议原件；

（**d**）　应采取措施确保包括船长在内的海员在船上可以容易地获得关于其就业条件的明确信息，并且这些信息，包括一份海员就业协议的副本，还应能够供主管当局的官员，包括船舶所挂靠港口的官员查验；以及

（**e**）　应发给海员一份载有其船上就业记录的文件。

2   Where a collective bargaining agreement forms all or part of a seafarers' employment agreement, a copy of that agreement shall be available on board. Where the language of the seafarers' employment agreement and any applicable collective bargaining agreement is not in English, the following shall also be available in English (except for ships engaged only in domestic voyages):

(**a**)   a copy of a standard form of the agreement; and

(**b**)   the portions of the collective bargaining agreement that are subject to a port State inspection under Regulation 5.2.

3   The document referred to in paragraph 1(e) of this Standard shall not contain any statement as to the quality of the seafarers' work or as to their wages. The form of the document, the particulars to be recorded and the manner in which such particulars are to be entered, shall be determined by national law.

4   Each Member shall adopt laws and regulations specifying the matters that are to be included in all seafarers' employment agreements governed by its national law. Seafarers' employment agreements shall in all cases contain the following particulars:

(**a**)   the seafarer's full name, date of birth or age, and birthplace;

(**b**)   the shipowner's name and address;

(**c**)   the place where and date when the seafarers' employment agreement is entered into;

(**d**)   the capacity in which the seafarer is to be employed;

(**e**)   the amount of the seafarer's wages or, where applicable, the formula used for calculating them;

(**f**)   the amount of paid annual leave or, where applicable, the formula used for calculating it;

(**g**)   the termination of the agreement and the conditions thereof, including:

  (**i**)   if the agreement has been made for an indefinite period, the conditions entitling either party to terminate it, as well as the required notice period, which shall not be less for the shipowner than for the seafarer;

  (**ii**)   if the agreement has been made for a definite period, the date fixed for its expiry; and

  (**iii**)   if the agreement has been made for a voyage, the port of destination and the time which has to expire after arrival before the seafarer should be discharged;

(**h**)   the health and social security protection benefits to be provided to the seafarer by the shipowner;

(**i**)   the seafarer's entitlement to repatriation;

(**j**)   reference to the collective bargaining agreement, if applicable; and

2 如果集体谈判协议构成海员就业协议的全部或一部分,该协议的一份副本应保留在船上。如果海员就业协议和任何适用的集体谈判协议的语言不是英语,则以下内容还应用英语提供(仅从事国内航行的船舶除外):

（**a**） 一份协议的标准格式;和

（**b**） 根据规则 5.2,集体谈判协议中要接受港口国检查的部分。

3 本标准第 1(e)款中所述的文件不得包括关于海员工作的质量和其工资的陈述。该文件的格式、将要记录的细节和这些细节将被记录的方式应由国家法律确定。

4 成员国应通过法律和法规,具体规定受其国家法律约束的所有海员就业协议需要包括的事项。在所有情况下,海员就业协议均应包括以下细节:

（**a**） 海员的全名、出生日期或年龄及出生地;

（**b**） 船东的名称和地址;

（**c**） 订立海员就业协议的地点及日期;

（**d**） 海员将担任的职务;

（**e**） 海员的工资数额,或者如果适用,用于计算工资的公式;

（**f**） 带薪年假的天数,或者如果适用,用于计算天数的公式;

（**g**） 协议的终止及其终止条件,包括:

（**i**） 如果协议没有确定期限,各方有权终止协议的条件,以及所要求的预先通知期,船东的预先通知期不得短于海员的预先通知期;

（**ii**） 如果协议有确定期限,其确定的期满日期;和

（**iii**） 如果协议是为一次航程而订,其航行之目的港,以及到达目的港后海员应被解雇前所须经历的时间;

（**h**） 将由船东提供给海员的健康和社会保障福利;

（**i**） 海员获得遣返的权利;

（**j**） 提及集体谈判协议,如适用;以及

(**k**)   any other particulars which national law may require.

5   Each Member shall adopt laws or regulations establishing minimum notice periods to be given by the seafarers and shipowners for the early termination of a seafarers' employment agreement. The duration of these minimum periods shall be determined after consultation with the shipowners' and seafarers' organizations concerned, but shall not be shorter than seven days.

6   A notice period shorter than the minimum may be given in circumstances which are recognized under national law or regulations or applicable collective bargaining agreements as justifying termination of the employment agreement at shorter notice or without notice. In determining those circumstances, each Member shall ensure that the need of the seafarer to terminate, without penalty, the employment agreement on shorter notice or without notice for compassionate or other urgent reasons is taken into account.

7   Each Member shall require that a seafarer's employment agreement shall continue to have effect while a seafarer is held captive on or off the ship as a result of acts of piracy or armed robbery against ships, regardless of whether the date fixed for its expiry has passed or either party has given notice to suspend or terminate it. For the purpose of this paragraph, the term:

(**a**)   piracy shall have the same meaning as in the United Nations Convention on the Law of the Sea, 1982;

(**b**)   armed robbery against ships means any illegal act of violence or detention or any act of depredation, or threat thereof, other than an act of piracy, committed for private ends and directed against a ship or against persons or property on board such a ship, within a State's internal waters, archipelagic waters and territorial sea, or any act of inciting or of intentionally facilitating an act described above.

Guideline B2.1   Seafarers' employment agreements

Guideline B2.1.1   Record of employment

1   In determining the particulars to be recorded in the record of employment referred to in Standard A2.1, paragraph 1(e), each Member should ensure that this document contains sufficient information, with a translation in English, to facilitate the acquisition of further work or to satisfy the sea-service requirements for upgrading or promotion. A seafarers' discharge book may satisfy the requirements of paragraph 1(e) of that Standard.

（k） 国家法律所要求的其他细节。

5 各成员国应通过法律或法规确定海员和船东提前终止海员就业协议时发出预先通知的最短期限。最短期限的长度应在与有关船东和海员组织协商后确定,但不得短于七天。

6 在国家法律或法规或者适用的集体谈判协议承认为合理的更短时间预先通知或不经通知结束就业协议的情形下,预先通知期可以比最短期限更短。在确定这些情形时,各成员国应保证考虑到海员出于值得同情的原因或其他紧急原因提前较短时间通知或不通知就终止就业协议且不因此而受处罚的需要。

7 每个成员国均应要求在海员由于海盗或者武装劫持行为被扣押在船上或被劫持离船期间,海员就业协议持续有效,无论是否已过该海员就业协议规定的到期日或者任何一方已通知中止或者终止协议。就本段而言:

（a） "海盗"一词的含义与《1982 年联合国海洋法公约》中所界定的含义相同;

（b） "武装劫持船舶"是指发生在一国内水、群岛水域和领海内,为了私人目的针对船舶或船上人员或船上财产实施或者威胁实施的任何非法暴力行为或扣押或任何掠夺行为,或者任何教唆或故意便利上述行为的行为,海盗行为除外。

导则 B2.1 海员就业协议

导则 B2.1.1 就业记录

1 在确定标准 A2.1 第 1(e) 款所述的就业记录簿将记录的细节时,各成员国应确保该文件包含足够的信息并有英文译文,以便于将来找到工作或满足升级或升迁所需的海上资历要求。海员的派遣书可满足该标准第 1(e) 款的要求。

Regulation 2. 2

Wages

Purpose: To ensure that seafarers are paid for their services

1 All seafarers shall be paid for their work regularly and in full in accordance with their employment agreements.

Standard A2. 2   Wages

1 Each Member shall require that payments due to seafarers working on ships that fly its flag are made at no greater than monthly intervals and in accordance with any applicable collective agreement.

2 Seafarers shall be given a monthly account of the payments due and the amounts paid, including wages, additional payments and the rate of exchange used where payment has been made in a currency or at a rate different from the one agreed to.

3 Each Member shall require that shipowners take measures, such as those set out in paragraph 4 of this Standard, to provide seafarers with a means to transmit all or part of their earnings to their families or dependants or legal beneficiaries.

4 Measures to ensure that seafarers are able to transmit their earnings to their families include:

(a) a system for enabling seafarers, at the time of their entering employment or during it, to allot, if they so desire, a proportion of their wages for remittance at regular intervals to their families by bank transfers or similar means; and

(b) a requirement that allotments should be remitted in due time and directly to the person or persons nominated by the seafarers.

5 Any charge for the service under paragraphs 3 and 4 of this Standard shall be reasonable in amount, and the rate of currency exchange, unless otherwise provided, shall, in accordance with national laws or regulations, be at the prevailing market rate or the official published rate and not unfavourable to the seafarer.

6 Member that adopts national laws or regulations governing seafarers' wages shall give due consideration to the guidance provided in Part B of the Code.

7 Where a seafarer is held captive on or off the ship as a result of acts of piracy or armed robbery against ships, wages and other entitlements under the seafarers' employment agreement, relevant collective bargaining agreement or applicable national laws, including the remittance of any allotments as provided in paragraph 4 of this Standard, shall continue to be paid during the entire period of captivity and until the seafarer is released and duly repatriated in accordance with Standard A2. 5. 1 or, where the seafarer dies while in captivity, until the date of death as determined in accordance with applicable national laws or regulations. The terms piracy and armed robbery against ships shall have the same meaning as in Standard A2. 1, paragraph 7.

规则 2.2

工资

目的:确保海员得到工作报酬

1 所有海员均应根据其就业协议定期获得全额工作报酬。

标准 A2.2 工资

1 各成员国应要求按不超过一个月的间隔并根据任何适用的集体协议向在悬挂其旗帜的船舶上工作的海员支付其应得的报酬。

2 应给海员一个应得报酬和实付数额的月薪账目,包括工资、额外报酬, 以及在其报酬采用的货币或兑换率不同于曾经达成一致的货币或兑换率时所用的兑换率。

3 各成员国应要求船东采取措施,例如本标准第 4 款中规定的措施,为海员提供一种将其收入的全部或部分转给其家人或受赡养人或法定受益人的方式。

4 确保海员能够将其收入转给其家人的措施包括:

(**a**) 如果其本人愿意,在海员订立协议时或在协议期间使其能够通过银行转账或类似方式拨出其工资的一定比例定期汇给其家庭的一种机制;和

(**b**) 要求在适当时间将分付数额直接汇给海员指定的人员。

5 本标准第 3 和 4 款下之服务的收费应在数额上合理,且除非另行规定,货币兑换率应根据国家法律或法规采用主要市场汇率或官方公布的汇率,而不得对海员不利。

6 各成员国在通过管理海员工资的国家法律或法规时,应充分考虑到守则 B 部分提供的指导。

7 一旦海员因为海盗或者武装劫持等行为导致被扣押在船上或被劫持离船,其海员就业协议及相关集体协议或适用的国家法律所规定的工资和其他权利,包括依据本标准第 4 段所述的任何养家费汇款,在海员整个被劫持期间应该持续地得到支付,直到海员被释放或按照标准 A2.5.1 中的规定被适当地遣返,或者,一旦海员在被扣押期间身故,直到根据适用的国内法律或法规所确定的海员身故之日为止。"针对船舶的海盗和武装劫持"一词的含义与标准 A2.1 条第 7 款中的含义一致。

Guideline B2. 2   Wages

Guideline B2. 2. 1   Specific definitions

1   For the purpose of this Guideline, the term:

(**a**)   *able seafarer* means any seafarer who is deemed competent to perform any duty which may be required of a rating serving in the deck department, other than the duties of a supervisory or specialist rating, or who is defined as such by national laws, regulations or practice, or by collective agreement;

(**b**)   *basic pay or wages* means the pay, however composed, for normal hours of work; it does not include payments for overtime worked, bonuses, allowances, paid leave or any other additional remuneration;

(**c**)   *consolidated wage* means a wage or salary which includes the basic pay and other pay-related benefits; a consolidated wage may include compensation for all overtime hours which are worked and all other pay-related benefits, or it may include only certain benefits in a partial consolidation;

(**d**)   *hours of work* means time during which seafarers are required to do work on account of the ship;

(**e**)   overtime means time worked in excess of the normal hours of work.

Guideline B2. 2. 2   Calculation and payment

1   For seafarers whose remuneration includes separate compensation for overtime worked:

(**a**)   for the purpose of calculating wages, the normal hours of work at sea and in port should not exceed eight hours per day;

(**b**)   for the purpose of calculating overtime, the number of normal hours per week covered by the basic pay or wages should be prescribed by national laws or regulations, if not determined by collective agreements, but should not exceed 48 hours per week; collective agreements may provide for a different but not less favourable treatment;

(**c**)   the rate or rates of compensation for overtime, which should be not less than one and one-quarter times the basic pay or wages per hour, should be prescribed by national laws or regulations or by collective agreements, if applicable; and

(**d**)   records of all overtime worked should be maintained by the master, or a person assigned by the master, and endorsed by the seafarer at no greater than monthly intervals.

2   For seafarers whose wages are fully or partially consolidated:

(**a**)   the seafarers' employment agreement should specify clearly, where appropriate, the number of hours of work expected of the seafarer in return for this remuneration, and any additional allowances which might be due in addition to the consolidated wage, and in which circumstances;

导则 B2.2　工资

导则 B2.2.1　具体定义

1　就本导则而言：

（**a**）　"一等水手"一词系指任何被认为能够胜任除管理或专业级别的职责以外的可能要求在甲板部工作的一名普通船员从事的任何职责的海员，或者根据国家法律、法规或惯例或集体协议被定义为一等水手的任何海员；

（**b**）　"基本报酬或工资"一词系指正常工作时间的报酬，无论这一报酬如何构成；它不包括加班报酬、奖金、津贴、带薪休假或任何其他额外酬劳；

（**c**）　"合并工资"一词系指包括基本工资和与工资有关的其他津贴在内的工资或薪资；合并工资可包括对所有加班工作给予的补偿和所有其他与工资相连的津贴，或者，它也可以包括部分合并工资内的某些津贴；

（**d**）　"工作时间"一词系指要求海员为船舶工作的时间；

（**e**）　"加班"一词系指超出正常工作时间之外工作的时间；

导则 B2.12.12　计算和支付

1　对于其报酬包括了另计的加班工作补偿的海员：

（**a**）　出于计算工资之目的，在海上和港口的正常工作时间每天不应超过 8 小时；

（**b**）　出于计算加班之目的，对于由基本报酬或工资所涵盖的每周正常工作时间，如果集体协议未予确定，应由国家法律或法规确定，但每周不得超过 48 小时；集体协议可以规定不同但不能较之更加不利的待遇；

（**c**）　加班补偿率不应低于每小时基本报酬或工资的 1.25 倍，该补偿率应由国家法律或法规或由适用的集体协议予以规定；以及

（**d**）　所有加班时间均应由船长或船长指定的人员进行记录，并至少按每月的间隔由海员签字。

2　对于其工资系全部或部分合并的海员：

（**a**）　凡适当时，海员就业协议应明确说明海员为这一报酬而需工作的时间，并说明除了合并工资外可能应支付的任何额外津贴以及在何种情况下支付；

(**b**) where hourly overtime is payable for hours worked in excess of those covered by the consolidated wage, the hourly rate should be not less than one and one-quarter times the basic rate corresponding to the normal hours of work as defined in paragraph 1 of this Guideline; the same principle should be applied to the overtime hours included in the consolidated wage;

(**c**) remuneration for that portion of the fully or partially consolidated wage representing the normal hours of work as defined in paragraph 1(a) of this Guideline should be no less than the applicable minimum wage; and

(**d**) for seafarers whose wages are partially consolidated, records of all overtime worked should be maintained and endorsed as provided for in paragraph 1 (d) of this Guideline.

3 National laws or regulations or collective agreements may provide for compensation for overtime or for work performed on the weekly day of rest and on public holidays by at least equivalent time off duty and off the ship or additional leave in lieu of remuneration or any other compensation so provided.

4 National laws and regulations adopted after consulting the representative shipowners' and seafarers' organizations or, as appropriate, collective agreements should take into account the following principles:

(**a**) equal remuneration for work of equal value should apply to all seafarers employed on the same ship without discrimination based upon race, colour, sex, religion, political opinion, national extraction or social origin;

(**b**) the seafarers' employment agreement specifying the applicable wages or wage rates should be carried on board the ship; information on the amount of wages or wage rates should be made available to each seafarer, either by providing at least one signed copy of the relevant information to the seafarer in a language which the seafarer understands, or by posting a copy of the agreement in a place accessible to seafarers or by some other appropriate means;

(**c**) wages should be paid in legal tender; where appropriate, they may be paid by bank transfer, bank cheque, postal cheque or money order;

(**d**) on termination of engagement all remuneration due should be paid without undue delay;

(**e**) adequate penalties or other appropriate remedies should be imposed by the competent authority where shipowners unduly delay, or fail to make, payment of all remuneration due;

(**f**) wages should be paid directly to seafarers' designated bank accounts unless they request otherwise in writing;

(**g**) subject to subparagraph (h) of this paragraph, the shipowner should impose no limit on seafarers' freedom to dispose of their remuneration;

（**b**）　凡对超出合并工资所涵盖的工作时间按每小时加班支付的,该小时报酬率不应低于本导则第 1 款所界定的与正常工作时间对应的基本工资率的 1. 25 倍;同样的原则也适用于包括在合并工资内的加班时间;

（**c**）　全部和部分合并工资中属于本导则第 1（a）款所界定的正常工作时间的那一部分报酬不应低于适用的最低工资;以及

（**d**）　对于其工资为部分合并的海员,应保持其所有加班的记录,并应按本导则第 1（d）款中的规定在记录上签字认可。

3　国家法律或法规或集体协议可以规定,对加班或在每周休息日和公共节假日工作的补偿,至少应以相等的休息时间和离船时间,或是以追加休假的方式,来代替报酬或为此规定的任何其他补偿。

4　在与船东和海员的代表组织协商后通过的国家法律和法规或者适当时的集体协议应考虑到以下原则:

（**a**）　同工同酬应适用于受雇于同一船舶的所有海员,不得依据种族、肤色、性别、宗教信仰、政治观点、民族血统或社会出身加以歧视;

（**b**）　具体说明适用的工资或工资率的海员就业协议应随船携带;应通过用海员懂得的语言向其提供至少一份业已签字的有关信息的副本,或通过在全体海员能够进入的地点张贴一份协议副本,或通过其他一些适宜的手段使每个海员都能获得有关工资额或工资率的信息;

（**c**）　工资应以法定方式支付;凡适宜时,可以通过银行转账、银行支票、邮政支票或汇款支付工资;

（**d**）　在终止雇用时,所有应付报酬的支付不得出现不应有的延误;

（**e**）　如果船东无理拖延支付,或未能支付所有应付报酬,主管当局应对其给以适当惩罚或强制其采取其他适当补救措施;

（**f**）　工资应直接支付给海员指定的银行账户,除非他们以书面形式提出另外的要求;

（**g**）　除依照本款（h）项规定者,船东不应对海员支配其报酬的自由施加限制;

(h) deduction from remuneration should be permitted only if:

  (i) there is an express provision in national laws or regulations or in an applicable collective agreement and the seafarer has been informed, in the manner deemed most appropriate by the competent authority, of the conditions for such deductions; and

  (ii) the deductions do not in total exceed the limit that may have been established by national laws or regulations or collective agreements or court decisions for making such deductions;

(i) no deductions should be made from a seafarer's remuneration in respect of obtaining or retaining employment;

(j) monetary fines against seafarers other than those authorized by national laws or regulations, collective agreements or other measures should be prohibited;

(k) the competent authority should have the power to inspect stores and services provided on board ship to ensure that fair and reasonable prices are applied for the benefit of the seafarers concerned; and

(l) to the extent that seafarers' claims for wages and other sums due in respect of their employment are not secured in accordance with the provisions of the International Convention on Maritime Liens and Mortgages, 1993, such claims should be protected in accordance with the Protection of Workers' Claims (Employer's Insolvency) Convention, 1992 (No. 173).

5 Each Member should, after consulting with representative shipowners' and seafarers' organizations, have procedures to investigate complaints relating to any matter contained in this Guideline.

Guideline B2.2.3 Minimum wages

1 Without prejudice to the principle of free collective bargaining, each Member should, after consulting representative shipowners' and seafarers' organizations, establish procedures for determining minimum wages for seafarers. Representative shipowners' and seafarers' organizations should participate in the operation of such procedures.

2 When establishing such procedures and in fixing minimum wages, due regard should be given to international labour standards concerning minimum wage fixing, as well as the following principles:

(a) the level of minimum wages should take into account the nature of maritime employment, crewing levels of ships, and seafarers' normal hours of work; and

(b) the level of minimum wages should be adjusted to take into account changes in the cost of living and in the needs of seafarers.

（**h**） 只有在下列情况下,才允许在报酬中做出扣减;

   （**i**） 国家法律或法规或适用的集体协议有明确规定且已通过主管当局认为最合适的方式向海员通知了此种扣减的条件;以及

   （**ii**） 扣减总额不超过国家法律或法规或集体协议或法院裁决可能已为此种扣减规定的限额;

（**i**） 不应为获得或保持就业而在海员的报酬中予以扣减;

（**j**） 除国家法律或法规、集体协议或其他措施授权者外,应禁止对海员罚款;

（**k**） 主管当局出于对有关海员利益的考虑,应有权检查船上配备的小卖部和提供的服务,以保证其价格公平合理;

（**l**） 在根据《1993 年海事优先权和抵押权国际公约》的规定无法对海员的工资和其他与就业有关的应付款项之请求给以保证的情况下,此类请求应根据《1992 年(雇主破产)保护工人债权公约》(第 173 号)予以保护。

5 各成员国应在与船东和海员组织协商后,建立对与本导则中包括的任何事项有关的投诉的调查程序。

导则 B2.2.3 最低工资

1 在不损害自由集体谈判原则的前提下,各成员国应在与船东和海员的代表组织协商后,建立确定海员最低工资的程序。船东和海员的代表组织应参与此类程序的运作。

2 在建立此类程序和确定最低工资时,应充分考虑有关确定最低工资的国际劳工标准以及以下原则:

（**a**） 最低工资的水平应考虑到海上就业的性质、船舶的配员水平和海员的正常工作时间;和

（**b**） 最低工资的水平应考虑海员生活费用和需求的变化而予以调整。

3   The competent authority should ensure:

(a)   by means of a system of supervision and sanctions, that wages are paid at not less than the rate or rates fixed; and

(b)   that any seafarers who have been paid at a rate lower than the minimum wage are enabled to recover, by an inexpensive and expeditious judicial or other procedure, the amount by which they have been underpaid.

Guideline B2.2.4   Minimum monthly basic pay or wage figure for able seafarers

1   The basic pay or wages for a calendar month of service for an able seafarer should be no less than the amount periodically set by the Joint Maritime Commission or another body authorized by the Governing Body of the International Labour Office. Upon a decision of the Governing Body, the Director-General shall notify any revised amount to the Members of the Organization.

2   Nothing in this Guideline should be deemed to prejudice arrangements agreed between shipowners or their organizations and seafarers' organizations with regard to the regulation of standard minimum terms and conditions of employment, provided such terms and conditions are recognized by the competent authority.

Regulation 2.3
Hours of work and hours of rest

Purpose: To ensure that seafarers have regulated hours of work or hours of rest

1   Each Member shall ensure that the hours of work or hours of rest for seafarers are regulated.

2   Each Member shall establish maximum hours of work or minimum hours of rest over given periods that are consistent with the provisions in the Code.

Standard A2.3   Hours of work and hours of rest

1   For the purpose of this Standard, the term:

(a)   *hours of work* means time during which seafarers are required to do work on account of the ship;

(b)   *hours of rest* means time outside hours of work; this term does not include short breaks.

2   Each Member shall within the limits set out in paragraphs 5 to 8 of this Standard either a maximum number of hours of work which shall not be exceeded in a given period of time, or a minimum number of hours of rest which shall be provided in a given period of time.

3　主管当局应保证:

（**a**）　通过监督和制裁制度,使所支付的工资不低于所确定的工资率;以及

（**b**）　已按低于最低工资的工资率领取了工资的任何海员,能通过一种花费不多且迅速的司法或其他程序,追偿对其少付的数额。

导则 B2.2.4　一等水手的月最低基本报酬或工资数额

1　一等水手一个日历月工作的基本报酬或工资不应低于联合海事委员会或者国际劳工局理事会授予权利的另一机构所定期确定的数额。理事会一旦做出决定,局长应向本组织的成员国通知任何更新的数额。

2　本导则的任何条款都不应被视为有损船东或其组织和海员组织之间就标准的最低就业条款和条件的规范所达成的协议,条件是此种条款和条件得到主管当局的承认。

规则 2.3
工作或休息时间

目的:确保海员享有规范的工作时间或休息时间

1　各成员国应确保对海员的工作时间或休息时间加以规范。

2　各成员国应确立符合守则规定的特定时间内的最长工作时间或最短休息时间。

标准 A2.3　工作时间和休息时间

1　就本标准而言:

（**a**）　"工作时间"一词系指要求海员为船舶工作的时间;

（**b**）　"休息时间"一词系指工作时间以外的时间,这一词不包括短暂的休息。

2　各成员国须在本标准第 5 至 8 款规定的范围内,确定在一段特定的时间内不得超过的最长工作小时数,或是在一段特定时间内应提供的最短休息小时数。

3   Each Member acknowledges that the normal working hours' standard for seafarers, like that for other workers, shall be based on an eight-hour day with one day of rest per week and rest on public holidays. However, this shall not prevent the Member from having procedures to authorize or register a collective agreement which determines seafarers' normal working hours on a basis no less favourable than this Standard.

4   In determining the national standards, each Member shall take account of the danger posed by the fatigue of seafarers, especially those whose duties involve navigational safety and the safe and secure operation of the ship.

5   The limits on hours of work or rest shall be as follows:

(a)   maximum hours of work shall not exceed:

(i)   14 hours in any 24-hour period; and

(ii)   72 hours in any seven-day period; or

(b)   minimum hours of rest shall not be less than:

(i)   10 hours in any 24-hour period; and

(ii)   77 hours in any seven-day period.

6   Hours of rest may be divided into no more than two periods, one of which shall be at least 6 hours in length, and the interval between consecutive periods of rest shall not exceed 14 hours.

7   Musters, fire-fighting and lifeboat drills, and drills prescribed by national laws and regulations and by international instruments, shall be conducted in a manner that minimizes the disturbance of rest periods and does not induce fatigue.

8   When a seafarer is on call, such as when a machinery space is unattended, the seafarer shall have an adequate compensatory rest period if the normal period of rest is disturbed by call-outs to work.

9   If no collective agreement or arbitration award exists or if the competent authority determines that the provisions in the agreement or award in respect of paragraph 7 or 8 of this Standard are inadequate, the competent authority shall determine such provisions to ensure the seafarers concerned have sufficient rest.

10   Each Member shall require the posting, in an easily accessible place, of a table with the shipboard working arrangements, which shall contain for every position at least:

(a)   the schedule of service at sea and service in port; and

(b)   the maximum hours of work or the minimum hours of rest required by national laws or regulations or applicable collective agreements.

11   The table referred to in paragraph 10 of this Standard shall be established in a standardized format in the working language or languages of the ship and in English.

3 各成员国承认,同其他工人一样,海员的正常工时标准应以每天 8 小时,每周休息 1 天和公共节假日休息为依据。然而,这并不妨碍成员国利用有关程序批准或登记在不低于这一标准的基础上确定海员正常工时的集体协议。

4 在确定国家标准时,各成员国应考虑到海员疲劳带来的危险,特别是那些职责涉及航行安全以及船舶的安全和保安操作的海员。

5 工作或休息时间应做如下限制:

（**a**） 最长工作时间:

（**i**） 在任何 24 小时时段内不得超过 14 小时;和

（**ii**） 在任何 7 天时间内不得超过 72 小时;或

（**b**） 最短休息时间:

（**i**） 在任何 24 小时时段内不得少于 10 小时;和

（**ii**） 在任何 7 天时间内不得少于 77 小时。

6 休息时间最多可分为两段,其中一段至少要有 6 小时,且相连的两段休息时间的间隔不得超过 14 小时。

7 集合、消防和救生艇训练,以及国家法律、法规和国际文件规定的训练应以对休息时间的影响最小和不会造成疲劳的方式进行。

8 在某一海员处于随时待命的情况下,例如机舱处于无人看管时,如果海员因被招去工作而打扰了正常的休息时间,则应给予充分的补休。

9 如果没有集体协议或仲裁裁决,或如果主管当局确定协议或裁决的条款关于本标准第 7 或第 8 款的规定不充分,则主管当局应确定此类条款以确保有关海员得到充分的休息。

10 各成员国应要求在容易进入的地点张贴一份船上工作安排表,该表格应至少包括每一岗位的下列内容:

（**a**） 在海上和在港口的工作时间表;和

（**b**） 国家法律或法规或适用的集体协议所要求的最长工作时间和最短休息时间。

11 本标准第 10 款所述的表格应按标准化的格式以船上的一种或多种工作语言和英文制定。

12 Each Member shall require that records of seafarers' daily hours of work or of their daily hours of rest be maintained to allow monitoring of compliance with paragraphs 5 to 11 inclusive of this Standard. The records shall be in a standardized format established by the competent authority taking into account any available guidelines of the International Labour Organization or shall be in any standard format prepared by the Organization. They shall be in the languages required by paragraph 11 of this Standard. The seafarers shall receive a copy of the records pertaining to them which shall be endorsed by the master, or a person authorized by the master, and by the seafarers.

13 Nothing in paragraphs 5 and 6 of this Standard shall prevent a Member from having national laws or regulations or a procedure for the competent authority to authorize or register collective agreements permitting exceptions to the limits set out. Such exceptions shall, as far as possible, follow the provisions of this Standard but may take account of more frequent or longer leave periods or the granting of compensatory leave for watchkeeping seafarers or seafarers working on board ships on short voyages.

14 Nothing in this Standard shall be deemed to impair the right of the master of a ship to require a seafarer to perform any hours of work necessary for the immediate safety of the ship, persons on board or cargo, or for the purpose of giving assistance to other ships or persons in distress at sea. Accordingly, the master may suspend the schedule of hours of work or hours of rest and require a seafarer to perform any hours of work necessary until the normal situation has been restored. As soon as practicable after the normal situation has been restored, the master shall ensure that any seafarers who have performed work in a scheduled rest period are provided with an adequate period of rest.

Guideline B2.3   Hours of work and hours of rest

Guideline B2.3.1   Young seafarers

1 At sea and in port the following provisions should apply to all young seafarers under the age of 18:

   (a)   working hours should not exceed eight hours per day and 40 hours per week and overtime should be worked only where unavoidable for safety reasons;

   (b)   sufficient time should be allowed for all meals, and a break of at least one hour for the main meal of the day should be assured; and

   (c)   a 15-minute rest period as soon as possible following each two hours of continuous work should be allowed.

2 Exceptionally, the provisions of paragraph 1 of this Guideline need not be applied if:

   (a)   they are impracticable for young seafarers in the deck, engine room and catering departments assigned to watchkeeping duties or working on a rostered shift-work system; or

   (b)   the effective training of young seafarers in accordance with established programmes and schedules would be impaired.

12 成员国应要求保持对海员的日工作时间或其日休息时间进行记录,以便监督是否符合本标准第 5 至 11 款的规定。记录应采用主管当局考虑到国际劳工组织的所有指导原则而确定的标准格式,或者应采用本组织制定的任何标准格式。它们应使用本标准第 11 款所要求的语言。海员应得到一份由船长或船长授权人员以及海员本人签字认可的有关其本人记录的副本。

13 本标准第 5 和 6 款的规定不得妨碍成员国制定国家法律或法规或者主管当局批准或注册允许超出规定限制的例外情况的集体协议的程序。此类例外应尽可能遵循本标准的规定,但可考虑给予值班海员或在短途航行船舶上工作的海员更经常或更长时间的休假或准予补休。

14 本标准的任何规定不得妨碍船长出于船舶、船上人员或货物的紧急安全需要,或出于帮助海上遇险的其他船舶或人员的目的而要求一名海员从事任何时间工作的权利。为此,船长可中止工作时间或休息时间安排,要求一名海员从事任何时间的必要工作,直至情况恢复正常。一旦情况恢复正常,船长应尽快地确保所有在计划安排的休息时间内从事工作的海员获得充足的休息时间。

导则 B2.3 工作时间和休息时间

导则 B2.3.1 未成年海员

1 在海上和港口,下述规定应适用于所有 18 岁以下的未成年海员:

(**a**) 工作时间不能超过每日 8 小时、每周 40 小时,只有在出于安全原因无法避免的情况下才加班工作;

(**b**) 各餐都要留有充分的时间,并应保证在日间正餐有至少 1 个小时的休息时间;以及

(**c**) 应允许每连续工作 2 小时后有 15 分钟的休息时间。

2 作为例外,在以下情况不必适用本导则第 1 款的规定:

(**a**) 如果对于被分配在甲板部、轮机部和膳食部担任值班职责或按班组倒班制工作的未成年海员,这样做不可行;或者

(**b**) 如果未成年海员根据既定计划和安排的培训将会受影响。

3   Such exceptional situations should be recorded, with reasons, and signed by the master.

4   Paragraph 1 of this Guideline does not exempt young seafarers from the general obligation on all seafarers to work during any emergency as provided for in Standard A2.3, paragraph 14.

Regulation 2.4
Entitlement to leave

Purpose: To ensure that seafarers have adequate leave

1   Each Member shall require that seafarers employed on ships that fly its flag are given paid annual leave under appropriate conditions, in accordance with the provisions in the Code.

2   Seafarers shall be granted shore leave to benefit their health and well-being and consistent with the operational requirements of their positions.

Standard A2.4   Entitlement to leave

1   Each Member shall adopt laws and regulations determining the minimum standards for annual leave for seafarers serving on ships that fly its flag, taking proper account of the special needs of seafarers with respect to such leave.

2   Subject to any collective agreement or laws or regulations providing for an appropriate method of calculation that takes account of the special needs of seafarers in this respect, the annual leave with pay entitlement shall be calculated on the basis of a minimum of 2.5 calendar days per month of employment. The manner in which the length of service is calculated shall be determined by the competent authority or through the appropriate machinery in each country. Justified absences from work shall not be considered as annual leave.

3   Any agreement to forgo the minimum annual leave with pay prescribed in this Standard, except in cases provided for by the competent authority, shall be prohibited.

Guideline B2.4   Entitlement to leave

Guideline B2.4.1   Calculation of entitlement

1   Under conditions as determined by the competent authority or through the appropriate machinery in each country, service off-articles should be counted as part of the period of service.

2   Under conditions as determined by the competent authority or in an applicable collective agreement, absence from work to attend an approved maritime vocational training course or for such reasons as illness or injury or for maternity should be counted as part of the period of service.

3   上述例外应予记录,说明原因,且有船长签字。

4   本导则第 1 款对未成年海员不免除标准 A2.3 第 14 款规定的关于所有海员在任何紧急情况时工作的一般义务。

规则 2.4

休假的权利

目的:确保海员有充分的休假

1   各成员国应要求悬挂其旗帜的船舶所雇用的海员在适当的条件下根据守则的规定享受带薪年休假。

2   应准许海员上岸休息以利海员的健康和福利及其职务的运作要求。

标准 A2.4   休假的权利

1   各成员国应通过法律和法规,确定在悬挂其旗帜的船舶上工作的海员的最低年休假标准,并充分考虑到海员对这种休假的特殊需要。

2   取决于对在这方面考虑到海员的特殊需要的适当计算方法作出规定的任何集体协议或法律或法规,带薪年休假的权利应以每服务一个月最低 2.5 日历天为基础加以计算。计算服务期长度的方法应由各国主管当局或通过适当的机制来确定。合理的缺勤不应被视作年假。

3   除非属于主管当局规定的情况,否则禁止达成放弃享受本标准规定的最低带薪年休假的任何协议。

导则 B2.4   休假的权利

导则 B2.4.1   假期权利的计算

1   根据各国由主管当局或通过适当机制确定的条件,合同外服务的时间应被算作服务期的一部分。

2   根据由主管当局或适用的集体协议确定的条件,因参加认可的海事职业培训班或者出于患病或受伤或因生育等原因造成的缺勤,应算作服务期的一部分。

3 The level of pay during annual leave should be at the seafarer's normal level of remuneration provided for by national laws or regulations or in the applicable seafarers' employment agreement. For seafarers employed for periods shorter than one year or in the event of termination of the employment relationship, entitlement to leave should be calculated on a pro-rata basis.

4 The following should not be counted as part of annual leave with pay:

(**a**) public and customary holidays recognized as such in the flag State, whether or not they fall during the annual leave with pay;

(**b**) periods of incapacity for work resulting from illness or injury or from maternity, under conditions as determined by the competent authority or through the appropriate machinery in each country;

(**c**) temporary shore leave granted to a seafarer while under an employment agreement; and

(**d**) compensatory leave of any kind, under conditions as determined by the competent authority or through the appropriate machinery in each country.

Guideline B2.4.2   Taking of annual leave

1 The time at which annual leave is to be taken should, unless it is fixed by regulation, collective agreement, arbitration award or other means consistent with national practice, be determined by the shipowner after consultation and, as far as possible, in agreement with the seafarers concerned or their representatives.

2 Seafarers should in principle have the right to take annual leave in the place with which they have a substantial connection, which would normally be the same as the place to which they are entitled to be repatriated. Seafarers should not be required without their consent to take annual leave due to them in another place except under the provisions of a seafarers' employment agreement or of national laws or regulations.

3 If seafarers are required to take their annual leave from a place other than that permitted by paragraph 2 of this Guideline, they should be entitled to free transportation to the place where they were engaged or recruited, whichever is nearer their home; subsistence and other costs directly involved should be for the account of the shipowner; the travel time involved should not be deducted from the annual leave with pay due to the seafarer.

4 A seafarer taking annual leave should be recalled only in cases of extreme emergency and with the seafarer's consent.

Guideline B2.4.3   Division and accumulation

1 The division of the annual leave with pay into parts, or the accumulation of such annual leave due in respect of one year together with a subsequent period of leave, may be authorized by the competent authority or through the appropriate machinery in each country.

3 在年休假期间的报酬水平应为国家法律、法规或适用的海员就业协议中规定的海员正常报酬水平。对于受雇期短于 1 年的海员,或在雇佣关系终止的情况下,休假的权利应按比例计算。

4 下述情况不应算作带薪年休假的一部分:

（**a**） 船旗国认可的公共和传统假日,不论其是否发生在带薪年休假假期内;

（**b**） 在由各国主管当局或通过适当的机制确定的条件下,因患病、受伤或因生育而不能工作期间;

（**c**） 在履行就业协议期间准许海员的短期上岸休息;以及

（**d**） 在由主管当局或通过各国适当的机制确定的条件下,任何类型的补休。

导则 B2.4.2 年休假的使用

1 除非由法规、集体协议、仲裁决定或其他符合国家惯例的方式确定,年休假的休假时间应由船东在与有关海员或其代表协商并尽可能达成一致后确定。

2 原则上海员应有权在其具有实质性联系的地点休假,该地点通常与其有权获得遣返去往之地点相同。除非在海员就业协议或国家法律或法规规定的情况下,未经海员同意,不应要求海员在另一地点休其应享的年休假。

3 如果要求海员从本导则第 2 款所允许的地点以外开始休其年休假,他们应有权免费旅行到其受雇或被招募的地点,以离其家较近者为准;补助以及其他直接相关的费用应由船东承担;旅行所花费的时间不应从海员应享的带薪年休假中扣减。

4 只有在极端紧急的情况下并取得海员的同意后才能将休年假的海员召回。

导则 B2.4.3 分段和累积休假

1 各国主管当局或通过适当的机制可批准将年休假分成几个部分,或将一年应享的此种年休假与后来的一段休假累积在一起。

2   Subject to paragraph 1 of this Guideline and unless otherwise provided in an agreement applicable to the shipowner and the seafarer concerned, the annual leave with pay recommended in this Guideline should consist of an uninterrupted period.

Guideline B2. 4. 4   Young seafarers

1   Special measures should be considered with respect to young seafarers under the age of 18 who have served six months or any other shorter period of time under a collective agreement or seafarers' employment agreement without leave on a foreign-going ship which has not returned to their country of residence in that time, and will not return in the subsequent three months of the voyage. Such measures could consist of their repatriation at no expense to themselves to the place of original engagement in their country of residence for the purpose of taking any leave earned during the voyage.

Regulation 2. 5
Repatriation

Purpose: To ensure that seafarers are able to return home

1   Seafarers have a right to be repatriated at no cost to themselves in the circumstances and under the conditions specified in the Code.

2   Each Member shall require ships that fly its flag to provide financial security to ensure that seafarers are duly repatriated in accordance with the Code.

Standard A2. 5. 1   Repatriation

1   Each Member shall ensure that seafarers on ships that fly its flag are entitled to repatriation in the following circumstances:

 (a)   if the seafarers' employment agreement expires while they are abroad;

 (b)   when the seafarers' employment agreement is terminated:

   (i)   by the shipowner; or

   (ii)   by the seafarer for justified reasons; and also

 (c)   when the seafarers are no longer able to carry out their duties under their employment agreement or cannot be expected to carry them out in the specific circumstances.

2   Each Member shall ensure that there are appropriate provisions in its laws and regulations or other measures or in collective bargaining agreements, prescribing:

 (a)   the circumstances in which seafarers are entitled to repatriation in accordance with paragraph 1(b) and (c) of this Standard;

 (b)   the maximum duration of service periods on board following which a seafarer is entitled to repatriation—such periods to be less than 12 months; and

2 除了本导则第 1 款的情形外,除非适用于有关船东和海员的协议另有规定,本导则所建议的带薪年休假应为一段连续的期间。

导则 B2.4.4　未成年海员

1 对于根据集体协议或海员就业协议在一艘前往国外的船上服务六个月或任何更短的时间,并在该段时间内没有回到过其居住国,且在该航行之后的三个月内也不会回去的 18 岁以下的未成年海员,应考虑特别的措施。此种措施可以包括将其免费送回到其居住国原来的受聘地,按其在航行期间获得的任何假期休假。

规则 2.5
遣返

目的:确保海员能够回家

1 在守则所规定的情形和条件下,海员有权利得到遣返而不向他们收取费用。

2 各成员国应要求悬挂其旗帜的船舶提供财务担保以确保海员根据守则得以合理遣返。

标准 A2.5.1　遣返

1 各成员国应确保悬挂其旗帜船舶上的海员在以下情形有权得到遣返:

　（**a**）　如果当海员在国外时海员就业协议到期;

　（**b**）　如果其海员就业协议:

　　　（**i**）　被船东终止;或

　　　（**ii**）　被海员出于合理的理由终止;以及

　（**c**）　如果海员不再具备履行其就业协议中职责的能力或在具体情形下不能指望其履行这些职责。

2 各成员国应确保在其法律和法规或其他措施中或在集体谈判协议中有适当的条款,规定:

　（**a**）　海员有权根据本标准第 1（b）和（c）款得到遣返的情形;

　（**b**）　海员在有权得到遣返前在船上服务的最长期间——这段时间应少于 12 个月;以及

(c) the precise entitlements to be accorded by shipowners for repatriation, including those relating to the destinations of repatriation, the mode of transport, the items of expense to be covered and other arrangements to be made by shipowners.

3 Each Member shall prohibit shipowners from requiring that seafarers make an advance payment towards the cost of repatriation at the beginning of their employment, and also from recovering the cost of repatriation from the seafarers' wages or other entitlements except where the seafarer has been found, in accordance with national laws or regulations or other measures or applicable collective bargaining agreements, to be in serious default of the seafarer's employment obligations.

4 National laws and regulations shall not prejudice any right of the shipowner to recover the cost of repatriation under third-party contractual arrangements.

5 If a shipowner fails to make arrangements for or to meet the cost of repatriation of seafarers who are entitled to be repatriated:

(a) the competent authority of the Member whose flag the ship flies shall arrange for repatriation of the seafarers concerned; if it fails to do so, the State from which the seafarers are to be repatriated or the State of which they are a national may arrange for their repatriation and recover the cost from the Member whose flag the ship flies;

(b) costs incurred in repatriating seafarers shall be recoverable from the shipowner by the Member whose flag the ship flies;

(c) the expenses of repatriation shall in no case be a charge upon the seafarers, except as provided for in paragraph 3 of this Standard.

6 Taking into account applicable international instruments, including the International Convention on Arrest of Ships, 1999, a Member which has paid the cost of repatriation pursuant to this Code may detain, or request the detention of, the ships of the shipowner concerned until the reimbursement has been made in accordance with paragraph 5 of this Standard.

7 Each Member shall facilitate the repatriation of seafarers serving on ships which call at its ports or pass through its territorial or internal waters, as well as their replacement on board.

8 In particular, a Member shall not refuse the right of repatriation to any seafarer because of the financial circumstances of a shipowner or because of the shipowner's inability or unwillingness to replace a seafarer.

9 Each Member shall require that ships that fly its flag carry and make available to seafarers a copy of the applicable national provisions regarding repatriation written in an appropriate language.

Standard A2.5.2 Financial security

1 In implementation of Regulation 2.5, paragraph 2, this Standard establishes requirements to ensure the provision of an expeditious and effective financial security system to assist seafarers in the event of their abandonment.

（**c**）　船东应同意给予的具体遣返权利,包括关于遣返的目的地、旅行方式、船东将负担的费用项目和将做出的其他安排方面的内容。

3　成员国应禁止船东要求海员在开始受雇时预付遣返费用,禁止船东从海员的工资或其他收益中扣回遣返费用,除非根据国家法律或法规或者其他措施或适用的集体谈判协议,海员出现严重失职而被遣返。

4　国家法律和法规不得妨碍船东根据第三方契约性安排收回遣返费用的任何权利。

5　如船东未能为有权得到遣返的海员安排遣返或负担其遣返费用:

（**a**）　船舶有权悬挂其旗帜的成员国的主管当局应安排有关海员的遣返;如果它未能这样做,海员将被遣返起程的国家或海员为其国民的国家可安排该海员的遣返,并向船舶所悬旗帜的成员国收回费用;

（**b**）　船舶所悬旗帜的成员国应能够向船东索回遣返海员发生的费用;

（**c**）　不论何种情况,均不得向海员收取遣返费用,本标准第 3 款规定的情况除外。

6　考虑到包括《1999 年国际扣船公约》在内的适用国际文件,根据本守则付出遣返费用的成员国,可滞留或要求滞留有关船东的船舶,直至船东按本标准第 5 款做出偿付。

7　各成员国应为停靠在其港口或者通过其领水或内水的船舶上工作的海员的遣返提供便利。

8　特别是,成员国不得因为船东的财政状况或因船东不能或不愿意替换海员而拒绝任何海员得到遣返的权利。

9　各成员国应要求悬挂其旗帜的船舶携带并向海员提供一份用适当的语言写成的有关遣返的适用国家规定。

标准 A2.5.2　财务担保

1　为执行规则 2.5 第 2 款,本标准做出了规定,要求确保提供迅速、有效的财务担保制度,以便在海员被遗弃时向其提供援助。

2 For the purposes of this Standard, a seafarer shall be deemed to have been abandoned where, in violation of the requirements of this Convention or the terms of the seafarers' employment agreement, the shipowner:

(**a**)   fails to cover the cost of the seafarer's repatriation; or

(**b**)   has left the seafarer without the necessary maintenance and support; or

(**c**)   has otherwise unilaterally severed their ties with the seafarer including failure to pay contractual wages for a period of at least two months.

3 Each Member shall ensure that a financial security system meeting the requirements of this Standard is in place for ships flying its flag. The financial security system may be in the form of a social security scheme or insurance or a national fund or other similar arrangements. Its form shall be determined by the Member after consultation with the shipowners' and seafarers' organizations concerned.

4 The financial security system shall provide direct access, sufficient coverage and expedited financial assistance, in accordance with this Standard, to any abandoned seafarer on a ship flying the flag of the Member.

5 For the purposes of paragraph 2(b) of this Standard, necessary maintenance and support of seafarers shall include: adequate food, accommodation, drinking water supplies, essential fuel for survival on board the ship and necessary medical care.

6 Each Member shall require that ships that fly its flag, and to which paragraph 1 or 2 of Regulation 5.1.3 applies, carry on board a certificate or other documentary evidence of financial security issued by the financial security provider. A copy shall be posted in a conspicuous place on board where it is available to the seafarers. Where more than one financial security provider provides cover, the document provided by each provider shall be carried on board.

7 The certificate or other documentary evidence of financial security shall contain the information required in Appendix A2-I. It shall be in English or accompanied by an English translation.

8 Assistance provided by the financial security system shall be granted promptly upon request made by the seafarer or the seafarer's nominated representative and supported by the necessary justification of entitlement in accordance with paragraph 2 above.

9 Having regard to Regulations 2.2 and 2.5, assistance provided by the financial security system shall be sufficient to cover the following:

(**a**)   outstanding wages and other entitlements due from the shipowner to the seafarer under their employment agreement, the relevant collective bargaining agreement or the national law of the flag State, limited to four months of any such outstanding wages and four months of any such outstanding entitlements;

(**b**)   all expenses reasonably incurred by the seafarer, including the cost of repatriation referred to in paragraph 10; and

2 就本标准而言,若船东违反本公约规定或海员就业协议条款,有以下情形的,海员应视为被遗弃:

（**a**）　未能支付海员遣返费用;或

（**b**）　造成海员得不到必要的给养和补给;或

（**c**）　以其他方式单方面断绝与海员的关系,包括至少为期两个月未能支付合同工资。

3 各成员国应确保悬挂其旗帜的船舶具有符合本标准规定的财务担保制度。财务担保制度可采取社会保障计划或保险或国家基金或其他类似形式的安排。其形式应由成员国经与相关船东组织和海员组织协商后决定。

4 财务担保制度应根据本标准向悬挂成员国旗帜的船舶上任何被遗弃的海员提供直接获取途径、充分覆盖范围和快速财政援助。

5 就本标准第 2(b)款而言,海员的必要给养和补给应包括:充足的食品、住宿、饮用水供应、在船舶上生存所必需的燃料和必要的医疗。

6 各成员国应要求悬挂其旗帜且适用规则 5.1.3 第 1 或第 2 款的船舶在船上携带一份由财务担保提供方签发的财务担保证书或其他财务担保证明文件。应在船上醒目位置张贴一份副本,供海员知悉。若有不止一个财务担保提供方提供了保障,应在船上携带每个提供方所提供的文件。

7 财务担保证书或其他财务担保证明文件应包含附件 A2-I 所要求的信息。它应为英文版或附英文译文。

8 经海员或海员指定的代表提出要求,并附上按照上文第 2 款应享权利所必要的依据,应迅速给予其由财务担保制度所提供的援助。

9 考虑到规则 2.2 和 2.5,财务担保制度所提供的援助应足以负担:

（**a**）　根据海员就业协议、相关集体谈判协议或船旗国的法律,船东应向海员支付但尚未支付的工资和其他津贴,以四个月的任何此类未付工资和四个月的任何此类未付津贴为限;

（**b**）　海员产生的所有合理费用,包括第 10 款提及的遣返费用;和

(**c**)   the essential needs of the seafarer including such items as: adequate food, clothing where necessary, accommodation, drinking water supplies, essential fuel for survival on board the ship, necessary medical care and any other reasonable costs or charges from the act or omission constituting the abandonment until the seafarer's arrival at home.

10   The cost of repatriation shall cover travel by appropriate and expeditious means, normally by air, and include provision for food and accommodation of the seafarer from the time of leaving the ship until arrival at the seafarer's home, necessary medical care, passage and transport of personal effects and any other reasonable costs or charges arising from the abandonment.

11   The financial security shall not cease before the end of the period of validity of the financial security unless the financial security provider has given prior notification of at least 30 days to the competent authority of the flag State.

12   If the provider of insurance or other financial security has made any payment to any seafarer in accordance with this Standard, such provider shall, up to the amount it has paid and in accordance with the applicable law, acquire by subrogation, assignment or otherwise, the rights which the seafarer would have enjoyed.

13   Nothing in this Standard shall prejudice any right of recourse of the insurer or provider of financial security against third parties.

14   The provisions in this Standard are not intended to be exclusive or to prejudice any other rights, claims or remedies that may also be available to compensate seafarers who are abandoned. National laws and regulations may provide that any amounts payable under this Standard can be offset against amounts received from other sources arising from any rights, claims or remedies that may be the subject of compensation under the present Standard.

Guideline B2.5   Repatriation

Guideline B2.5.1   Entitlement

1   Seafarers should be entitled to repatriation:

(**a**)   in the case covered by Standard A2.5, paragraph 1(a), upon the expiry of the period of notice given in accordance with the provisions of the seafarers' employment agreement;

(**b**)   in the cases covered by Standard A2.5, paragraph 1(b) and (c):

(**i**)   in the event of illness or injury or other medical condition which requires their repatriation when found medically fit to travel;

(**ii**)   in the event of shipwreck;

(**iii**)   in the event of the shipowner not being able to continue to fulfil their legal or contractual obligations as an employer of the seafarers by reason of insolvency, sale of ship, change of ship's registration or any other similar reason;

(c) 海员的基本需求,包括诸如此类的项目:充足的食品、必要的衣物、住宿、饮用水供应、在船上生存所必需的燃料、必要的医疗和因构成遗弃的行为或疏忽而导致的任何其他合理费用和收费,直至海员到家为止。

10 遣返费用应负担以适当和快捷的方式旅行(一般为乘飞机)的费用,并包括向海员提供自离开船舶至到家期间的食宿、必要的医疗、个人物品通行和运输以及因遗弃而产生的任何其他合理费用或收费。

11 财务担保在其有效期结束之前不得停止,除非财务担保提供方已提前至少 30 天通知船旗国主管当局。

12 若保险提供方或其他财务担保提供方已根据本标准向海员支付了任何款项,此类提供方应根据适用的法律,通过权利代位、权利转让或其他方式获得海员本应享有的权利,以不超过其所付数额为限。

13 本标准的任何规定不应影响承保人或财务担保提供方对第三方的任何追索权。

14 本标准的规定并非意在具有排他性或妨碍为赔偿被遗弃海员而提供的其他任何权利、索赔或补偿。国家法律和法规可规定任何根据本标准应支付的数额可与因本标准规定可予赔偿的任何权利、索赔或补偿而从其他来源获得的数额相抵消。

导则 B2.5　遣返

导则 B2.5.1　应享权利

1 在以下情况下海员应享有得到遣返的权利:

(**a**) 在标准 A2.5 第 1(a)款所覆盖的情况下,当根据海员就业协议的规定做出的通知期结束时;

(**b**) 在标准 A2.5 第 1(b)和(c)款所覆盖的情况下:

(**i**) 因患病或受伤或其他健康问题需要其遣返且身体状况适于旅行时;

(**ii**) 在船舶失事时;

(**iii**) 在由于破产、变卖船舶、改变船舶登记或任何其他类似原因,船东不能继续履行其作为海员雇佣者的法律或契约义务时;

(**iv**) in the event of a ship being bound for a war zone, as defined by national laws or regulations or seafarers' employment agreements, to which the seafarer does not consent to go; and

(**v**) in the event of termination or interruption of employment in accordance with an industrial award or collective agreement, or termination of employment for any other similar reason.

2 In determining the maximum duration of service periods on board following which a seafarer is entitled to repatriation, in accordance with this Code, account should be taken of factors affecting the seafarers' working environment. Each Member should seek, wherever possible, to reduce these periods in the light of technological changes and developments and might be guided by any recommendations made on the matter by the Joint Maritime Commission.

3 The costs to be borne by the shipowner for repatriation under Standard A2.5 should include at least the following:

(**a**) passage to the destination selected for repatriation in accordance with paragraph 6 of this Guideline;

(**b**) accommodation and food from the moment the seafarers leave the ship until they reach the repatriation destination;

(**c**) pay and allowances from the moment the seafarers leave the ship until they reach the repatriation destination, if provided for by national laws or regulations or collective agreements;

(**d**) transportation of 30 kg of the seafarers' personal luggage to the repatriation destination; and

(**e**) medical treatment when necessary until the seafarers are medically fit to travel to the repatriation destination.

4 Time spent awaiting repatriation and repatriation travel time should not be deducted from paid leave accrued to the seafarers.

5 Shipowners should be required to continue to cover the costs of repatriation until the seafarers concerned are landed at a destination prescribed pursuant to this Code or are provided with suitable employment on board a ship proceeding to one of those destinations.

6 Each Member should require that shipowners take responsibility for repatriation arrangements by appropriate and expeditious means. The normal mode of transport should be by air. The Member should prescribe the destinations to which seafarers may be repatriated. The destinations should include the countries with which seafarers may be deemed to have a substantial connection including:

(**a**) the place at which the seafarer agreed to enter into the engagement;

(**b**) the place stipulated by collective agreement;

(**c**) the seafarer's country of residence; or

    （ⅳ）   在船舶驶往国家法律、法规或海员就业协议所界定的战乱区域而海员不同意前往的情况下；以及

    （ⅴ）   根据仲裁裁定或集体协议而终止或中断雇佣关系，或由于其他类似原因终止雇佣关系。

2   在根据本守则确定海员在有权得到遣返前在船上服务的最长期间时，应考虑到影响海员工作环境的多种因素。凡可行时，各成员国应视技术的变化和发展而缩短这一期间，并可参考联合海事委员会就此事项所提出的建议。

3   根据标准 A2.5，在遣返方面将由船东承担的费用应至少包括以下项目：

（a）   到达根据本导则第 6 款选定的遣返目的地的旅费；

（b）   从海员离船时起至抵达遣返目的地时止的食宿费；

（c）   如果本国法律、法规或集体协议有规定，从海员离船时起至抵达遣返目的地时止的工资和津贴；

（d）   将海员个人行李 30 千克运至遣返目的地的运输费；以及

（e）   必要时，提供医治使海员身体状况适合前往遣返目的地的旅行。

4   等待遣返所用的时间和遣返旅行时间不应从海员积累的带薪年假中扣减。

5   应要求船东继续承担遣返的费用，直到有关海员到达本守则所规定的目的地，或在前往这些目的地之一的船舶上为其提供了合适的就业。

6   成员国应要求船东负责通过适当和迅速的方式对遣返做出安排。通常的旅行方式应为乘坐飞机。成员国应规定海员可被遣返的目的地。目的地应包括可视为海员与之存在实质性联系的国家，包括：

（a）   海员同意接受雇用的地点；

（b）   集体协议规定的地点；

（c）   海员的居住国；或

(**d**)　such other place as may be mutually agreed at the time of engagement.

7　Seafarers should have the right to choose from among the prescribed destinations the place to which they are to be repatriated.

8　The entitlement to repatriation may lapse if the seafarers concerned do not claim it within a reasonable period of time to be defined by national laws or regulations or collective agreements, except where they are held captive on or off the ship as a result of acts of piracy or armed robbery against ships. The terms piracy and armed robbery against ships shall have the same meaning as in Standard A2.1, paragraph 7.

Guideline B2.5.2　Implementation by Members

1　Every possible practical assistance should be given to a seafarer stranded in a foreign port pending repatriation and in the event of delay in the repatriation of the seafarer, the competent authority in the foreign port should ensure that the consular or local representative of the flag State and the seafarer's State of nationality or State of residence, as appropriate, is informed immediately.

2　Each Member should have regard to whether proper provision is made:

(**a**)　for the return of seafarers employed on a ship that flies the flag of a foreign country who are put ashore in a foreign port for reasons for which they are not responsible:

(**i**)　to the port at which the seafarer concerned was engaged; or

(**ii**)　to a port in the seafarer's State of nationality or State of residence, as appropriate; or

(**iii**)　to another port agreed upon between the seafarer and the master or shipowner, with the approval of the competent authority or under other appropriate safeguards;

(**b**)　for medical care and maintenance of seafarers employed on a ship that flies the flag of a foreign country who are put ashore in a foreign port in consequence of sickness or injury incurred in the service of the ship and not due to their own wilful misconduct.

3　If, after young seafarers under the age of 18 have served on a ship for at least four months during their first foreign-going voyage, it becomes apparent that they are unsuited to life at sea, they should be given the opportunity of being repatriated at no expense to themselves from the first suitable port of call in which there are consular services of the flag State, or the State of nationality or residence of the young seafarer. Notification of any such repatriation, with the reasons therefor, should be given to the authority which issued the papers enabling the young seafarers concerned to take up seagoing employment.

Guideline B2.5.3　Financial security

1　In implementation of paragraph 8 of Standard A2.5.2, if time is needed to check the validity of certain aspects of the request of the seafarer or the seafarer's nominated representative, this should not prevent the seafarer from immediately receiving such part of the assistance requested as is recognized as justified.

（**d**）　可能在聘用时双方同意的其他地点。

7　海员应有权从规定的目的地中选择其将被遣返的地点。

8　如果有关海员在国家法律或法规或集体协议规定的合理时间内未提出遣返要求,其应享有的遣返权利可能失效,除非其因针对船只的海盗或武装抢劫行为而被扣押在船或被劫持离船。"针对船只的海盗或武装抢劫行为"应与标准 A2.1 第 7 款中的该词含义一致。

导则 B2.5.2　成员国实施

1　对被困于外国港口等候遣返的海员应给予各种可能的实际援助。对于海员遣返受到延误的情况,外国港口的主管当局应确保立即视情况通知船旗国和海员国籍国或居住国的领事或者当地代表。

2　各成员国应关注是否做出了妥善安排:

（**a**）　将那些由于非其自身责任的原因在外国港口被置于岸上的就业于悬挂外国旗帜的船舶的海员送回到:

（**i**）　有关海员受雇的港口;或

（**ii**）　海员的国籍国或居住国(视情而定)的一个港口;或

（**iii**）　经主管当局批准或在其他适当保障的前提下,有关海员和船长或船东协商同意的另一港口;

（**b**）　医治和照料由于在船上服务期间非因其自身故意行为不当而患病、受伤,导致其在外国港口被置于岸上的受雇于悬挂外国旗帜船舶的海员。

3　首次出航国外的 18 岁以下未成年海员在船上服务至少四个月后,若显示出不适应海上生活,应给予该未成年海员从设有船旗国或者其国籍国或居住国领事馆的第一个合适的挂靠港口被免费遣返回国的机会。应向为该未成年海员签发准许其上船就业的有关当局报告任何此种遣返情况及其原因。

导则 B2.5.3　财务担保

1　为执行标准 A2.5.2 第 8 款,如果需要时间来核对海员或海员指定的代表所提要求的某些方面的有效性,这不应妨碍海员立即收到所要求的被认定为有依据的那部分援助。

Regulation 2.6

Seafarer compensation for the ship's loss or foundering

Purpose: To ensure that seafarers are compensated when a ship is lost or has foundered

1   Seafarers are entitled to adequate compensation in the case of injury, loss or unemployment arising from the ship's loss or foundering.

Standard A2.6   Seafarer compensation for the ship's loss or foundering

1   Each Member shall make rules ensuring that, in every case of loss or foundering of any ship, the shipowner shall pay to each seafarer on board an indemnity against unemployment resulting from such loss or foundering.

2   The rules referred to in paragraph 1 of this Standard shall be without prejudice to any other rights a seafarer may have under the national law of the Member concerned for losses or injuries arising from a ship's loss or foundering.

Guideline B2.6   Seafarer compensation for the ship's loss or foundering

Guideline B2.6.1   Calculation of indemnity against unemployment

1   The indemnity against unemployment resulting from a ship's foundering or loss should be paid for the days during which the seafarer remains in fact unemployed at the same rate as the wages payable under the employment agreement, but the total indemnity payable to any one seafarer may be limited to two months' wages.

2   Each Member should ensure that seafarers have the same legal remedies for recovering such indemnities as they have for recovering arrears of wages earned during the service.

Regulation 2.7

Manning levels

Purpose: To ensure that seafarers work on board ships with sufficient personnel for the safe, efficient and secure operation of the ship

1   Each Member shall require that all ships that fly its flag have a sufficient number of seafarers employed on board to ensure that ships are operated safely, efficiently and with due regard to security under all conditions, taking into account concerns about seafarer fatigue and the particular nature and conditions of the voyage.

规则 2.6
船舶灭失或沉没时对海员的赔偿

目的:确保在船舶灭失或沉没时对海员进行赔偿

1 海员有权就由于船舶灭失或沉没所造成的伤害、损失或失业得到充分的赔偿。

标准 A2.6　船舶灭失或沉没时对海员的赔偿

1 各成员国应制订规章,确保在任何船舶灭失或沉没的各种情况下,船东应就这种灭失或沉没导致的海员失业向船上每个海员支付赔偿。

2 本标准第 1 款所述的规章应不妨碍海员根据有关成员国关于船舶灭失或沉没而造成损失或伤害国家法律可能享有的其他权利。

导则 B2.6　船舶灭失或沉没时对海员的赔偿

导则 B2.6.1　失业赔偿的计算

1 对因船舶灭失或沉没而造成的失业所给予的赔偿,在海员实属失业期间,应相等于就业协议中可支付工资的比率,但向任何一个海员支付的赔偿总额可仅限于两个月的工资。

2 成员国应确保海员享有索取此种赔偿的法律救济,与其索取其服务期间的拖欠工资所享受的法律救济相同。

规则 2.7
配员水平

目的:为了船舶运营的安全、高效和保安,确保海员在人员充足的船上工作

1 各成员国应要求悬挂其旗帜的所有船舶考虑到海员的疲劳以及航行的性质和条件,在船上配有充足数目的海员以确保船舶的安全、高效操作,并充分注意到在各种条件下的保安。

Standard A2.7   Manning levels

1   Each Member shall require that all ships that fly its flag have a sufficient number of seafarers on board to ensure that ships are operated safely, efficiently and with due regard to security. Every ship shall be manned by a crew that is adequate, in terms of size and qualifications, to ensure the safety and security of the ship and its personnel, under all operating conditions, in accordance with the minimum safe manning document or an equivalent issued by the competent authority, and to comply with the standards of this Convention.

2   When determining, approving or revising manning levels, the competent authority shall take into account the need to avoid or minimize excessive hours of work to ensure sufficient rest and to limit fatigue, as well as the principles in applicable international instruments, especially those of the International Maritime Organization, on manning levels.

3   When determining manning levels, the competent authority shall take into account all the requirements within Regulation 3.2 and Standard A3.2 concerning food and catering.

Guideline B2.7   Manning levels

Guideline B2.7.1   Dispute settlement

1   Each Member should maintain, or satisfy itself that there is maintained, efficient machinery for the investigation and settlement of complaints or disputes concerning the manning levels on a ship.

2   Representatives of shipowners' and seafarers' organizations should participate, with or without other persons or authorities, in the operation of such machinery.

Regulation 2.8

Career and skill development and opportunities for seafarers' employment

Purpose: To promote career and skill development and employment opportunities for seafarers

1   Each Member shall have national policies to promote employment in the maritime sector and to encourage career and skill development and greater employment opportunities for seafarers domiciled in its territory.

Standard A2.8   Career and skill development and employment opportunities for seafarers

1   Each Member shall have national policies that encourage career and skill development and employment opportunities for seafarers, in order to provide the maritime sector with a stable and competent workforce.

2   The aim of the policies referred to in paragraph 1 of this Standard shall be to help seafarers strengthen their competencies, qualifications and employment opportunities.

3   Each Member shall, after consulting the shipowners' and seafarers' organizations concerned, establish clear objectives for the vocational guidance, education and training of seafarers whose duties on board ship primarily relate to the safe operation and navigation of the ship, including ongoing training.

标准 A2.7　配员水平

1　各成员国应要求悬挂其旗帜的所有船舶在船上配有充足的海员数目,确保船舶的安全和高效操作,并充分注意到保安。各船舶均应根据主管当局签发的最低安全配员证书或等效文件,并满足本公约的标准,从数量和资格角度配备充足的海员,确保在各种操作情况下船舶及其人员的安全和保安。

2　在确定、批准或修改配员水平时,主管当局应考虑到避免或最大限度减少过度超时工作从而确保充分休息和限制疲劳的需要,以及适用的国际文件,特别是国际海事组织的文件中关于配员的原则。

3　在确定配员水平时,主管当局应考虑到规则 3.2 和标准 A3.2 关于食品和膳食服务的所有要求。

导则 B2.7　配员水平

导则 B2.7.1　争议解决

1　各成员国应维持一种调查和解决任何关于船上配员水平的申诉或争议的高效机制,或确认其得以维持。

2　无论有无其他人员或当局的参与,船东和海员组织的代表应参与此种机制的运作。

规则 2.8
海员职业发展和技能开发及就业机会

目的:促进海员职业发展和技能开发及就业机会

1　各成员国应有促进海事部门的就业并鼓励在其领土内居住的海员的职业发展和技能开发以及更多就业机会的国家政策。

标准 A2.8　海员职业和技能开发及就业机会

1　为了向海运业提供稳定和胜任的劳动力,各成员国应制定鼓励海员职业发展和技能开发及海员就业机会的国家政策。

2　本标准第 1 款所述政策的目标应为帮助海员增强其适任性、资格和就业机会。

3　各成员国应在与有关的船东和海员组织协商后,为那些其船上职责主要涉及船舶的安全操作和航行的海员确定关于职业指导、教育和培训的明确目标,包括继续培训。

Guideline B2.8   Career and skill development and employment opportunities for seafarers

Guideline B2.8.1   Measures to promote career and skill development and employment opportunities for seafarers

1   Measures to achieve the objectives set out in Standard A2.8 might include:

(**a**)   agreements providing for career development and skills training with a shipowner or an organization of shipowners; or

(**b**)   arrangements for promoting employment through the establishment and maintenance of registers or lists, by categories, of qualified seafarers; or

(**c**)   promotion of opportunities, both on board and ashore, for further training and education of seafarers to provide for skill development and portable competencies in order to secure and retain decent work, to improve individual employment prospects and to meet the changing technology and labour market conditions of the maritime industry.

Guideline B2.8.2   Register of seafarers

1   Where registers or lists govern the employment of seafarers, these registers or lists should include all occupational categories of seafarers in a manner determined by national law or practice or by collective agreement.

2   Seafarers on such a register or list should have priority of engagement for seafaring.

3   Seafarers on such a register or list should be required to be available for work in a manner to be determined by national law or practice or by collective agreement.

4   To the extent that national laws or regulations permit, the number of seafarers on such registers or lists should be periodically reviewed so as to achieve levels adapted to the needs of the maritime industry.

5   When a reduction in the number of seafarers on such a register or list becomes necessary, all appropriate measures should be taken to prevent or minimize detrimental effects on seafarers, account being taken of the economic and social situation of the country concerned.

导则 B2.8　海员职业发展和技能开发及就业机会

导则 B2.8.1　促进海员职业发展和技能开发及就业机会的措施

1　实现标准 A2.8 所列目标的措施可以包括：

（**a**）　与船东或船东组织达成提供职业发展和技能培训的协议；或

（**b**）　通过建立和维护合格海员的分类登记册或名单的方式做出促进就业的安排；或

（**c**）　促进海员在船上和岸上接受进一步培训和教育的机会，以提供职业技能开发和发展海员自身能力，从而获得并保持体面工作，改善个人就业前景并适应海运业技术和劳动市场状况的变化。

导则 B2.8.2　海员登记册

1　如果采用登记册或名单来管理海员就业，则这些登记册和名单应按国家法律或惯例或通过集体协议所确定的方式，包括海员的所有职业类别。

2　此种登记册或名单上的海员应优先受雇出海工作。

3　应要求此种登记册或名单上的海员随时准备按国家法律或惯例或通过集体协议确定的方式工作。

4　在国家法律或法规许可的范围内，应定期审查海员登记册或名单上的海员人数，使之达到符合航运业需要的水平。

5　在此登记册或名单的总人数需要减少时，应考虑到有关国家的经济和社会状况，采取一切适当的措施，防止或最大限度地减小对海员的不利影响。

Title 3
Accommodation, recreational facilities, food and catering

Regulation 3. 1
Accommodation and recreational facilities

Purpose: To ensure that seafarers have decent accommodation and recreational facilities on board

1   Each Member shall ensure that ships that fly its flag provide and maintain decent accommodations and recreational facilities for seafarers working or living on board, or both, consistent with promoting the seafarers' health and well-being.

2   The requirements in the Code implementing this Regulation which relate to ship construction and equipment apply only to ships constructed on or after the date when this Convention comes into force for the Member concerned. For ships constructed before that date, the requirements relating to ship construction and equipment that are set out in the Accommodation of Crews Convention (Revised), 1949 (No. 92), and the Accommodation of Crews (Supplementary Provisions) Convention, 1970 (No. 133), shall continue to apply to the extent that they were applicable, prior to that date, under the law or practice of the Member concerned. A ship shall be deemed to have been constructed on the date when its keel is laid or when it is at a similar stage of construction.

3   Unless expressly provided otherwise, any requirement under an amendment to the Code relating to the provision of seafarer accommodation and recreational facilities shall apply only to ships constructed on or after the amendment takes effect for the Member concerned.

Standard A3. 1   Accommodation and recreational facilities

1   Each Member shall adopt laws and regulations requiring that ships that fly its flag:

(a)   meet minimum standards to ensure that any accommodation for seafarers, working or living on board, or both, is safe, decent and in accordance with the relevant provisions of this Standard; and

(b)   are inspected to ensure initial and ongoing compliance with those standards.

2   In developing and applying the laws and regulations to implement this Standard, the competent authority, after consulting the shipowners' and seafarers' organizations concerned, shall:

(a)   take into account Regulation 4. 3 and the associated Code provisions on health and safety protection and accident prevention, in light of the specific needs of seafarers that both live and work on board ship; and

(b)   give due consideration to the guidance contained in Part B of this Code.

标题三
起居舱室、娱乐设施、食品和膳食服务

规则 3.1
起居舱室和娱乐设施

目的:确保海员在船上有体面的起居舱室和娱乐设施

1　各成员国应确保悬挂其旗帜的船舶向工作和(或)生活在船上的海员提供并保持与促进海员的健康和福利一致的体面起居舱室和娱乐设施。

2　实施本规则的守则中与船舶建造和设备有关的要求仅适用于本公约对有关成员国生效之日或以后建造的船舶。对于该日之前建造的船舶,《1949 年船员起居舱室公约(修订)》(第 92 号)和《1970 年船员起居舱室(补充规定)公约》(第 133 号)中规定的关于船舶建造和设备的要求在该日之前应根据有关成员国的法律或实践继续在其适用的范围内适用。一艘船舶在其龙骨铺设之日或当其处于类似建造阶段应被视为已建造。

3　除非另有明文规定,守则修正案中与海员居住舱室和娱乐设施有关的任何要求应仅适用于修正案对有关成员国生效之日或以后建造的船舶。

标准 A3.1　起居舱室和娱乐设施

1　各成员国应通过法律和法规要求悬挂其旗帜的船舶:

(a)　满足最低标准,以确保在船上工作和(或)生活的海员的任何居住舱室安全、体面并符合本标准的相关规定;以及

(b)　经过检查并确保起初并持续符合这些标准。

2　在制定并适用法律和法规来实施本标准时,主管当局在与有关船东和海员组织协商后,应:

(a)　根据在船上生活并工作的海员的具体需要,考虑到规则 4.3 及相关守则中关于保护健康和安全及防止事故的规定;以及

(b)　充分考虑到本守则 B 部分所载的指导。

3 The inspections required under Regulation 5.1.4 shall be carried out when:

(**a**) a ship is registered or re-registered; or

(**b**) the seafarer accommodation on a ship has been substantially altered.

4 The competent authority shall pay particular attention to ensuring implementation of the requirements of this Convention relating to:

(**a**) the size of rooms and other accommodation spaces;

(**b**) heating and ventilation;

(**c**) noise and vibration and other ambient factors;

(**d**) sanitary facilities;

(**e**) lighting; and

(**f**) hospital accommodation.

5 The competent authority of each Member shall require that ships that fly its flag meet the minimum standards for on-board accommodation and recreational facilities that are set out in paragraphs 6 to 17 of this Standard.

6 With respect to general requirements for accommodation:

(**a**) there shall be adequate headroom in all seafarer accommodation; the minimum permitted headroom in all seafarer accommodation where full and free movement is necessary shall be not less than 203 centimetres; the competent authority may permit some limited reduction in headroom in any space, or part of any space, in such accommodation where it is satisfied that such reduction:

(**i**) is reasonable; and

(**ii**) will not result in discomfort to the seafarers;

(**b**) the accommodation shall be adequately insulated;

(**c**) in ships other than passenger ships, as defined in Regulation 2(e) and (f) of the International Convention for the Safety of Life at Sea, 1974, as amended (the "SOLAS Convention"), sleeping rooms shall be situated above the load line amidships or aft, except that in exceptional cases, where the size, type or intended service of the ship renders any other location impracticable, sleeping rooms may be located in the fore part of the ship, but in no case forward of the collision bulkhead;

(**d**) in passenger ships, and in special ships constructed in compliance with the IMO Code of Safety for Special Purpose Ships, 1983, and subsequent versions (hereinafter called "special purpose ships"), the competent authority may, on condition that satisfactory arrangements are made for lighting and ventilation, permit the location of sleeping rooms below the load line, but in no case shall they be located immediately beneath working alleyways;

3 在出现以下情形时应进行规则 5.1.4 所要求的检查：

（**a**） 在登记一艘船舶或重新登记一艘船舶时；或

（**b**） 对船上的海员起居舱室做了实质性改动时。

4 主管当局应特别注意确保实施本公约关于以下方面的要求：

（**a**） 房间和其他起居舱室空间的尺寸；

（**b**） 取暖和通风；

（**c**） 噪声和振动及其他环境因素；

（**d**） 卫生设施；

（**e**） 照明；和

（**f**） 医务室。

5 各成员国的主管当局应要求悬挂其旗帜的船舶满足本标准第 6 至 17 款中规定的船上起居舱室和娱乐设施最低标准。

6 关于居住舱室的一般要求：

（**a**） 海员所有起居舱室具有充足的净高；所有需要海员充分和自由移动的起居舱室的最低允许净高不得低于 203 厘米；主管当局可准许在任何起居舱室或舱室的一部分酌量有限降低上述高度，如果主管当局认为该降低：

（**i**） 是合理的；且

（**ii**） 不会给海员带来不适；

（**b**） 起居舱室应予充分隔热；

（**c**） 在经修订的《1974 年国际海上人命安全公约》（"SOLAS 公约"）第 2（e） 和（f） 条所定义的客船以外的船舶上，卧室应位于船舶的中部或尾部的载重线以上，但在特殊情况下，因船舶的大小、类型或其预期的用途使卧室放在其他位置不可行，卧室可放在船艏部，但无论如何不得放在防撞舱壁之前；

（**d**） 在客船上以及在根据国际海事组织《1983 年特殊用途船舶安全规则》及其后续版本而建造的特殊船舶（以下称为"特殊用途船舶"）上，如果对照明和通风状况做出了满意的安排，主管当局可准许将海员卧室放在载重线以下，但无论如何不得置于紧贴工作通道之下；

(**e**)   there shall be no direct openings into sleeping rooms from cargo and machinery spaces or from galleys, storerooms, drying rooms or communal sanitary areas; that part of a bulkhead separating such places from sleeping rooms and external bulkheads shall be efficiently constructed of steel or other approved substance and be watertight and gastight;

(**f**)   the materials used to construct internal bulkheads, panelling and sheeting, floors and joinings shall be suitable for the purpose and conducive to ensuring a healthy environment;

(**g**)   proper lighting and sufficient drainage shall be provided; and

(**h**)   accommodation and recreational and catering facilities shall meet the requirements in Regulation 4.3, and the related provisions in the Code, on health and safety protection and accident prevention, with respect to preventing the risk of exposure to hazardous levels of noise and vibration and other ambient factors and chemicals on board ships, and to provide an acceptable occupational and onboard living environment for seafarers.

7   With respect to requirements for ventilation and heating:

(**a**)   sleeping rooms and mess rooms shall be adequately ventilated;

(**b**)   ships, except those regularly engaged in trade where temperate climatic conditions do not require this, shall be equipped with air conditioning for seafarer accommodation, for any separate radio room and for any centralized machinery control room;

(**c**)   all sanitary spaces shall have ventilation to the open air, independently of any other part of the accommodation; and

(**d**)   adequate heat through an appropriate heating system shall be provided, except in ships exclusively on voyages in tropical climates.

8   With respect to requirements for lighting, subject to such special arrangements as may be permitted in passenger ships, sleeping rooms and mess rooms shall be lit by natural light and provided with adequate artificial light.

9   When sleeping accommodation on board ships is required, the following requirements for sleeping rooms apply:

(**a**)   in ships other than passenger ships, an individual sleeping room shall be provided for each seafarer; in the case of ships of less than 3,000 gross tonnage or special purpose ships, exemptions from this requirement may be granted by the competent authority after consultation with the shipowners' and seafarers' organizations concerned;

(**b**)   separate sleeping rooms shall be provided for men and for women;

(**c**)   sleeping rooms shall be of adequate size and properly equipped so as to ensure reasonable comfort and to facilitate tidiness;

（e）　卧室不得与货物和机器处所、厨房、仓库、烘干房或公共卫生区域直接相通；将上述处所与卧室分开的舱壁部分和外部舱壁应使用钢材或其他经认可的材料进行有效的建造，并具备水密和气密性；

（f）　用于建造内部舱壁、天花板和衬板、地板和铺设的材料应适合于其自身功用并有益于保证健康环境；

（g）　应提供适当的照明和充分的排水系统；以及

（h）　起居舱室和娱乐设施及膳食服务设施应满足规则 4.3 以及守则的相关规定中关于保护健康和安全及防止事故的要求，充分考虑到防止海员被暴露于达到有害水平的噪声、振动和其他环境因素以及船上化学品中的风险，并为海员提供一个可接受的职业和船上生活环境。

7　关于通风和供暖的要求：

（a）　卧室和餐厅应通风良好；

（b）　除常年在温带地区航行不需要空调的船舶以外，应为船舶的海员起居舱室、任何独立的无线电报务室和任何中央机器控制室配备空调设备；

（c）　所有盥洗处所应有直接通向露天的通风装置，并与起居舱室的任何其他部分相独立；以及

（d）　除专门在热带气候中航行的船舶外，应通过适当的供暖系统提供充足的取暖。

8　就照明的要求而言，根据客船可能允许的特殊布置，卧室和餐厅应有合适的自然采光，并应配备足够的人工灯光。

9　如果要求船上有卧室，应适用以下关于卧室的要求：

（a）　在除客船以外的船舶上，应为每一海员提供单独的卧室，对于低于 3 000 总吨的船舶或特殊用途船舶，主管当局在与有关船东和海员组织协商后可准予免除此要求；

（b）　应为男海员和女海员提供分开的卧室；

（c）　卧室应有足够的尺寸并配备适当的陈设，以保证合理的舒适度及便于保持整洁；

(**d**)   a separate berth for each seafarer shall in all circumstances be provided;

(**e**)   the minimum inside dimensions of a berth shall be at least 198 centimetres by 80 centimetres;

(**f**)   in single berth seafarers' sleeping rooms the floor area shall not be less than:

   (**i**)   4. 5 square metres in ships of less than 3,000 gross tonnage;

   (**ii**)   5. 5 square metres in ships of 3,000 gross tonnage or over but less than 10,000 gross tonnage;

   (**iii**)   7 square metres in ships of 10,000 gross tonnage or over;

(**g**)   however, in order to provide single berth sleeping rooms on ships of less than 3,000 gross tonnage, passenger ships and special purpose ships, the competent authority may allow a reduced floor area;

(**h**)   in ships of less than 3,000 gross tonnage other than passenger ships and special purpose ships, sleeping rooms may be occupied by a maximum of two seafarers; the floor area of such sleeping rooms shall not be less than 7 square metres;

(**i**)   on passenger ships and special purpose ships the floor area of sleeping rooms for seafarers not performing the duties of ships' officers shall not be less than:

   (**i**)   7. 5 square metres in rooms accommodating two persons;

   (**ii**)   11. 5 square metres in rooms accommodating three persons;

   (**iii**)   14. 5 square metres in rooms accommodating four persons;

(**j**)   on special purpose ships sleeping rooms may accommodate more than four persons; the floor area of such sleeping rooms shall not be less than 3. 6 square metres per person;

(**k**)   on ships other than passenger ships and special purpose ships, sleeping rooms for seafarers who perform the duties of ships' officers, where no private sitting room or day room is provided, the floor area per person shall not be less than:

   (**i**)   7. 5 square metres in ships of less than 3,000 gross tonnage;

   (**ii**)   8. 5 square metres in ships of 3,000 gross tonnage or over but less than 10,000 gross tonnage;

   (**iii**)   10 square metres in ships of 10,000 gross tonnage or over;

(**l**)   on passenger ships and special purpose ships the floor area for seafarers performing the duties of ships' officers where no private sitting room or day room is provided, the floor area per person for junior officers shall not be less than 7. 5 square metres and for senior officers not less than 8. 5 square metres; junior officers are understood to be at the operational level, and senior officers at the management level;

(d)　在所有情况下都应为每个海员提供单独的床位;

(e)　每个床位的最小内部面积应至少为 198 厘米×80 厘米;

(f)　在单床位的海员卧室,地板面积应不小于:

　　(i)　在 3 000 总吨以下的船舶上,4.5 平方米;

　　(ii)　在 3 000 总吨或以上但低于 10,000 总吨的船舶上,5.5 平方米;

　　(iii)　在 10 000 总吨或以上的船舶上,7 平方米;

(g)　但是,为了在 3 000 总吨以下的船舶、客船和特殊用途船舶上提供单床位的卧室,主管当局可允许减少地板面积;

(h)　对于客船和特殊用途船舶以外的 3 000 总吨以下的船舶,卧室最多可容许两名海员居住;此类卧室的地板面积应不少于 7 平方米;

(i)　在客船和特殊用途船上,不担任高级船员职责的海员的卧室地板面积应不少于:

　　(i)　双人间,7.5 平方米;

　　(ii)　三人间,11.5 平方米;

　　(iii)　四人间,14.5 平方米;

(j)　在特殊用途船舶上,卧室可容纳 4 人以上,此类卧室的地板面积不得小于 3.6 平方米/人;

(k)　在客船和特殊用途船舶以外的船舶上,对于担任高级船员职责的海员的卧室,如果不提供专用起居室或休息室,地板面积每人应不少于:

　　(i)　在 3 000 总吨以下的船舶上,7.5 平方米;

　　(ii)　在 3 000 总吨或以上但低于 10 000 总吨的船舶上,8.5 平方米;

　　(iii)　在 10 000 总吨或以上的船舶上,10 平方米;

(l)　在客船和特殊用途船舶上,对担任高级船员职责的海员的卧室,如果不提供专用的起居室或休息室,每人所占的地板面积:对于低级别的高级船员应不少于 7.5 平方米,对于高级别的高级船员应不少于 8.5 平方米;低级别的高级船员指操作级,高级别的高级船员指管理级;

(**m**) the master, the chief engineer and the chief navigating officer shall have, in addition to their sleeping rooms, an adjoining sitting room, day room or equivalent additional space; ships of less than 3,000 gross tonnage may be exempted by the competent authority from this requirement after consultation with the shipowners' and seafarers' organizations concerned;

(**n**) for each occupant, the furniture shall include a clothes locker of ample space (minimum 475 litres) and a drawer or equivalent space of not less than 56 litres; if the drawer is incorporated in the clothes locker then the combined minimum volume of the clothes locker shall be 500 litres; it shall be fitted with a shelf and be able to be locked by the occupant so as to ensure privacy;

(**o**) each sleeping room shall be provided with a table or desk, which may be of the fixed, drop-leaf or slide-out type, and with comfortable seating accommodation as necessary.

10 With respect to requirements for mess rooms:

(**a**) mess rooms shall be located apart from the sleeping rooms and as close as practicable to the galley; ships of less than 3,000 gross tonnage may be exempted by the competent authority from this requirement after consultation with the shipowners' and seafarers' organizations concerned; and

(**b**) mess rooms shall be of adequate size and comfort and properly furnished and equipped (including ongoing facilities for refreshment), taking account of the number of seafarers likely to use them at any one time; provision shall be made for separate or common mess room facilities as appropriate.

11 With respect to requirements for sanitary facilities:

(**a**) all seafarers shall have convenient access on the ship to sanitary facilities meeting minimum standards of health and hygiene and reasonable standards of comfort, with separate sanitary facilities being provided for men and for women;

(**b**) there shall be sanitary facilities within easy access of the navigating bridge and the machinery space or near the engine room control centre; ships of less than 3,000 gross tonnage may be exempted by the competent authority from this requirement after consultation with the shipowners' and seafarers' organizations concerned;

(**c**) in all ships a minimum of one toilet, one washbasin and one tub or shower or both for every six persons or less who do not have personal facilities shall be provided at a convenient location;

(**d**) with the exception of passenger ships, each sleeping room shall be provided with a washbasin having hot and cold running fresh water, except where such a washbasin is situated in the private bathroom provided;

(**e**) in passenger ships normally engaged on voyages of not more than four hours' duration, consideration may be given by the competent authority to special arrangements or to a reduction in the number of facilities required; and

（**m**）　除卧室外，船长、轮机长和大副还应有相连的起居室、休息室或等效的额外空间。主管当局经与有关船东和海员组织协商后，可对 3 000 总吨以下的船舶免除此要求；

（**n**）　对于每个居住者，家具应包括一个宽敞的衣柜（至少为 475 升）和空间不小于 56 升的抽屉或等效空间；如果抽屉设在衣柜里面，则衣柜的合计容积至少应为 500 升；柜内应设搁板，并能够由居住者上锁以确保隐私；

（**o**）　每间卧室应备有一张桌子或书桌，可以为固定式、折叠式或可滑动式的，并按需要配备舒适的座位。

10　关于餐厅的要求：

（**a**）　餐厅的位置应与卧室隔开，并应尽可能靠近厨房；主管当局在与有关的船东和海员组织协商后可对低于 3 000 总吨的船舶免除此要求；以及

（**b**）　餐厅应足够大并且舒适，并在考虑到任一时间可能用餐的船员人数的基础上，配备适当的家具和设备（包括持续提供茶点的设施）；在适当时应配备分开或共用的餐厅设施。

11　关于卫生设施的要求：

（**a**）　船上的所有海员均应能够使用满足最低健康和卫生标准以及合理的舒适标准的卫生设施，为男海员和女海员应提供分开的卫生设施；

（**b**）　在驾驶台和机器处所容易到达之处或靠近机舱控制中心处应设有卫生设施；主管当局在与有关的船东和海员组织协商后可对低于 3 000 总吨的船舶免除此要求；

（**c**）　在所有船舶上，应在方便的位置为没有个人设施的海员每 6 名或以下至少提供一个厕所、一个洗脸池、一个浴盆和（或）淋浴室；

（**d**）　除了客船以外，船上每个卧室均应配备带有流动冷、热淡水的洗脸池，除非该洗脸池位于所提供的个人浴室中；

（**e**）　对于航行时间通常在 4 小时以内的客船，主管当局可考虑做出特殊安排或减少所要求的卫生设施数目；以及

(**f**)   hot and cold running fresh water shall be available in all wash places.

12   With respect to requirements for hospital accommodation, ships carrying 15 or more seafarers and engaged in a voyage of more than three days' duration shall provide separate hospital accommodation to be used exclusively for medical purposes; the competent authority may relax this requirement for ships engaged in coastal trade; in approving on-board hospital accommodation, the competent authority shall ensure that the accommodation will, in all weathers, be easy of access, provide comfortable housing for the occupants and be conducive to their receiving prompt and proper attention.

13   Appropriately situated and furnished laundry facilities shall be available.

14   All ships shall have a space or spaces on open deck to which the seafarers can have access when off duty, which are of adequate area having regard to the size of the ship and the number of seafarers on board.

15   All ships shall be provided with separate offices or a common ship's office for use by deck and engine departments; ships of less than 3,000 gross tonnage may be exempted by the competent authority from this requirement after consultation with the shipowners' and seafarers' organizations concerned.

16   Ships regularly trading to mosquito-infested ports shall be fitted with appropriate devices as required by the competent authority.

17   Appropriate seafarers' recreational facilities, amenities and services, as adapted to meet the special needs of seafarers who must live and work on ships, shall be provided on board for the benefit of all seafarers, taking into account Regulation 4.3 and the associated Code provisions on health and safety protection and accident prevention.

18   The competent authority shall require frequent inspections to be carried out on board ships, by or under the authority of the master, to ensure that seafarer accommodation is clean, decently habitable and maintained in a good state of repair. The results of each such inspection shall be recorded and be available for review.

19   In the case of ships where there is need to take account, without discrimination, of the interests of seafarers having differing and distinctive religious and social practices, the competent authority may, after consultation with the shipowners' and seafarers' organizations concerned, permit fairly applied variations in respect of this Standard on condition that such variations do not result in overall facilities less favourable than those which would result from the application of this Standard.

20   Each Member may, after consultation with the shipowners' and seafarers' organizations concerned, exempt ships of less than 200 gross tonnage where it is reasonable to do so, taking account of the size of the ship and the number of persons on board in relation to the requirements of the following provisions of this Standard:

(**a**)   paragraph 7(b), 11(d) and 13; and

(**b**)   paragraph 9(f) and (h) to (1) inclusive, with respect to floor area only.

(f) 所有盥洗场所均应有流动的冷热淡水。

12 就医务室的要求而言,航程时间超过 3 天、船上海员 15 人以上的船舶应设有独立的医务室,专供医疗使用。对从事沿岸航行的船舶,主管当局可放宽此项要求;在批准设立船上医务室时,主管当局应确保该处所在各种气候下都容易进出,能为使用者提供舒适的居住条件并有助于其获得迅速和适当的照料。

13 应提供所处位置合适并有适当设施的洗衣房。

14 所有船舶应根据其大小和船上海员的人数,在露天甲板上安排一块或数块面积充足的场地,供不当班的海员休息之用。

15 所有船舶应配备分开的或共用的船舶办公室,供甲板部和轮机部使用;主管当局在与有关的船东和海员组织协商后可对低于 3 000 总吨的船舶免除此要求。

16 经常停靠蚊虫猖獗的港口的船舶应按主管当局的要求安装适当的设施。

17 为了所有海员的利益,在船上应提供满足于必须在船上工作和生活的海员的特殊需求的适当海员娱乐设施、福利设施和服务,同时还应考虑规则 4.3 和相关守则中关于保护健康和安全及防止事故的规定。

18 主管当局应要求由船长或在船长的授权下,在船上开展经常性检查,以确保海员起居舱室干净、体面地适宜居住,并且维护良好。每次此类检查的结果均应记录并在审核时可用。

19 对于需要对不同宗教和社会习惯的海员的利益给予一视同仁考虑的船舶,主管当局经与有关船东和海员组织协商后,可以允许对本标准进行适当的变通适用,条件是这种变通不会导致总体设施劣于适用本标准的要求所配备的设施。

20 各成员国考虑到船舶的尺度和船上人员的数量,经与有关的船东和海员组织协商后,可以对 200 总吨以下的船舶免除本标准下述规定中的有关要求:

(a) 第 7(b)、11(d) 和 13 款;以及

(b) 第 9(f) 和(h)至(1)款,仅涉及地板面积。

21   Any exemptions with respect to the requirements of this Standard may be made only where they are expressly permitted in this Standard and only for particular circumstances in which such exemptions can be clearly justified on strong grounds and subject to protecting the seafarers' health and safety.

Guideline B3. 1   Accommodation and recreational facilities

Guideline B3. 1. 1   Design and construction

1   External bulkheads of sleeping rooms and mess rooms should be adequately insulated. All machinery casings and all boundary bulkheads of galleys and other spaces in which heat is produced should be adequately insulated where there is a possibility of resulting heat effects in adjoining accommodation or passageways. Measures should also be taken to provide protection from heat effects of steam or hot-water service pipes or both.

2   Sleeping rooms, mess rooms, recreation rooms and alleyways in the accommodation space should be adequately insulated to prevent condensation or overheating.

3   The bulkhead surfaces and deckheads should be of material with a surface easily kept clean. No form of construction likely to harbour vermin should be used.

4   The bulkhead surfaces and deckheads in sleeping rooms and mess rooms should be capable of being easily kept clean and light in colour with a durable, nontoxic finish.

5   The decks in all seafarer accommodation should be of approved material and construction and should provide a non-slip surface impervious to damp and easily kept clean.

6   Where the floorings are made of composite materials, the joints with the sides should be profiled to avoid crevices.

Guideline B3. 1. 2   Ventilation

1   The system of ventilation for sleeping rooms and mess rooms should be controlled so as to maintain the air in a satisfactory condition and to ensure a sufficiency of air movement in all conditions of weather and climate.

2   Air-conditioning systems, whether of a centralized or individual unit type, should be designed to:

   (a)   maintain the air at a satisfactory temperature and relative humidity as compared to outside air conditions, ensure a sufficiency of air changes in all air-conditioned spaces, take account of the particular characteristics of operations at sea and not produce excessive noises or vibrations; and

   (b)   facilitate easy cleaning and disinfection to prevent or control the spread of disease.

3   Power for the operation of the air conditioning and other aids to ventilation required by the preceding paragraphs of this Guideline should be available at all times when seafarers are living or working on board and conditions so require. However, this power need not be provided from an emergency source.

21 关于本标准的要求做出的任何免除只有在标准明确准许,且只有在特定的环境下此种免除有充分明显的理由时才可做出,并应以保护海员的健康和安全为前提。

导则 B3.1 起居舱室和娱乐设施

导则 B3.1.1 设计和建造

1 卧室和餐厅的外部舱壁应适当地隔热。如果有可能在毗邻起居舱室或过道处会产生发热影响,厨房和其他发热处所的所有机器外罩和所有界限舱壁应予充分隔热。还应采取措施防止蒸汽和(或)热水管道的发热影响。

2 卧室、餐厅、娱乐室和起居舱室内的通道应适当隔热,以防止蒸汽凝结或室温过高。

3 舱壁表面和舱室天花板的材料应为表面易于保持清洁的材料。不得使用容易隐藏害虫的构造方式。

4 卧室和餐厅的舱壁与天花板应能够易于保持清洁并应使用经久耐用、无毒的浅色涂料装饰。

5 所有海员起居舱室的甲板应为认可的材料和构造,其表面应能防滑、防潮并易于保持清洁。

6 如果地板用复合材料制成,其与侧面的搭接应该严密,避免留下缝隙。

导则 B3.1.2 通风

1 卧室和餐厅的通风系统应受到控制,以使空气的状况令人满意,并确保在任何季节和任何气候下都有充分的空气流通。

2 空调系统,无论其为中央空调还是单个空调,均应设计成:

（**a**） 根据户外大气条件使室内空气保持适宜的温度和相对湿度,并保证在使用空气调节的全部处所有充分的空气交换,并考虑海上作业的特点,避免产生过度的噪声或振动;以及

（**b**） 便于容易清洁和灭菌,以防止或控制疾病的传播。

3 如果海员在船上生活或工作且情况需要,本导则前面各款要求的空调和其他通风设施工作所需动力应随时可用。但是,此动力不应由应急电源提供。

Guideline B3.1.3   Heating

1   The system of heating the seafarer accommodation should be in operation at all times when seafarers are living or working on board and conditions require its use.

2   In all ships in which a heating system is required, the heating should be by means of hot water, warm air, electricity, steam or equivalent. However, within the accommodation area, steam should not be used as a medium for heat transmission. The heating system should be capable of maintaining the temperature in seafarer accommodation at a satisfactory level under normal conditions of weather and climate likely to be met within the trade in which the ship is engaged. The competent authority should prescribe the standard to be provided.

3   Radiators and other heating apparatus should be placed and, where necessary, shielded so as to avoid risk of fire or danger or discomfort to the occupants.

Guideline B3.1.4   Lighting

1   In all ships, electric light should be provided in the seafarer accommodation. If there are not two independent sources of electricity for lighting, additional lighting should be provided by properly constructed lamps or lighting apparatus for emergency use.

2   In sleeping rooms an electric reading lamp should be installed at the head of each berth.

3   Suitable standards of natural and artificial lighting should be fixed by the competent authority.

Guideline B3.1.5   Sleeping rooms

1   There should be adequate berth arrangements on board, making it as comfortable as possible for the seafarer and any partner who may accompany the seafarer.

2   Where the size of the ship, the activity in which it is to be engaged and its layout make it reasonable and practicable, sleeping rooms should be planned and equipped with a private bathroom, including a toilet, so as to provide reasonable comfort for the occupants and to facilitate tidiness.

3   As far as practicable, sleeping rooms of seafarers should be so arranged that watches are separated and that no seafarers working during the day share a room with watchkeepers.

4   In the case of seafarers performing the duty of petty officers there should be no more than two persons per sleeping room.

5   Consideration should be given to extending the facility referred to in Standard A3.1, paragraph 9(m), to the second engineer officer when practicable.

6   Space occupied by berths and lockers, chests of drawers and seats should be included in the measurement of the floor area. Small or irregularly shaped spaces which do not add effectively to the space available for free movement and cannot be used for installing furniture should be excluded.

导则 B3.1.3 供暖

1 如果海员在船上生活或工作且情况需要,海员起居舱室的供暖系统应一直开放。

2 在所有要求配备供暖系统的船上,可用热水、热气、电力、蒸汽或等效方式供暖。但是,在起居舱室区域,不应使用蒸汽作为传热媒介。供暖设备应能在船舶于航行中可能遇到的正常气候和天气状况时,使海员起居舱室的温度保持在适当水平;主管当局应对须达到的标准作出规定。

3 应设置取暖器和其他供暖装置,在必要时,应装保护罩以避免火灾,或者对居住者构成危险或带来不便。

导则 B3.1.4 照明

1 在所有船舶里,应为海员起居舱室配备电灯。如果没有两个独立的照明电源,应通过适当装设的灯具或照明装置提供应急使用的附加照明。

2 在卧室里,应在每个铺位的床头安装一个台灯。

3 自然和人工采光的适当标准应由主管当局确定。

导则 B3.1.5 卧室

1 船上应有充足的床位,使海员及可能与其同住的伴侣尽可能舒适。

2 在船舶的尺寸、其所从事的航行活动及其布置使这样做合理可行时,卧室的规划和配备应带有包括一个卫生间的单独浴室,从而为居住者提供合理的舒适性并便于保持整洁。

3 应尽可能在安排卧室时将值班人员分开,避免使日间工作的海员与值班人员同住一间。

4 对于担任见习高级船员职责的海员,每间卧室居住的人数不应超过 2 人。

5 凡可行时,应考虑将标准 A3.1 第 9(m) 款中的设施待遇扩展到大管轮。

6 在丈量地板面积时,应包括床铺位和储物柜、抽屉柜和座位所占空间。不应包括那些不能有效地增加供自由移动的可用空间和不能用来放置家具的小的和形状不规则的空间。

7   Berths should not be arranged in tiers of more than two; in the case of berths placed along the ship's side, there should be only a single tier where a sidelight is situated above a berth.

8   The lower berth in a double tier should be not less than 30 centimetres above the floor; the upper berth should be placed approximately midway between the bottom of the lower berth and the lower side of the deckhead beams.

9   The framework and the lee-board, if any, of a berth should be of approved material, hard, smooth, and not likely to corrode or to harbour vermin.

10   If tubular frames are used for the construction of berths, they should be completely sealed and without perforations which would give access to vermin.

11   Each berth should be fitted with a comfortable mattress with cushioning bottom or a combined cushioning mattress, including a spring bottom or a spring mattress. The mattress and cushioning material used should be made of approved material. Stuffing of material likely to harbour vermin should not be used.

12   When one berth is placed over another, a dust-proof bottom should be fitted beneath the bottom mattress or spring bottom of the upper berth.

13   The furniture should be of smooth, hard material not liable to warp or corrode.

14   Sleeping rooms should be fitted with curtains or equivalent for the sidelights.

15   Sleeping rooms should be fitted with a mirror, small cabinets for toilet requisites, a book rack and a sufficient number of coat hooks.

Guideline B3.1.6   Mess rooms

1   Mess room facilities may be either common or separate. The decision in this respect should be taken after consultation with seafarers' and shipowners' representatives and subject to the approval of the competent authority. Account should be taken of factors such as the size of the ship and the distinctive cultural, religious and social needs of the seafarers.

2   Where separate mess room facilities are to be provided to seafarers, then separate mess rooms should be provided for:

(a)   master and officers; and

(b)   petty officers and other seafarers.

3   On ships other than passenger ships, the floor area of mess rooms for seafarers should be not less than 1.5 square metres per person of the planned seating capacity.

4   In all ships, mess rooms should be equipped with tables and appropriate seats, fixed or movable, sufficient to accommodate the greatest number of seafarers likely to use them at any one time.

7 不应使用超过两层的床铺;如果床位靠船侧摆放,当床位上方有舷窗时,只应设置单层床位。

8 如安置双层床,则下床在地面上的高度不应小于30厘米;上床应大约位于下床床板与天花板甲板梁底部的中间位置。

9 床架及挡板(如果有的话)应使用经认可的材料,质地坚硬而光滑,不易腐蚀和隐藏害虫。

10 如床架为管状材料,应将它们完全封闭,不留孔穴,以免害虫进入。

11 每张床铺应配备带有缓冲底板的舒服床垫或包括弹簧底板或弹簧床绷在内的复合缓冲床垫。床垫和缓冲材料应采用经认可的材料。不得使用易于隐藏害虫的充填材料。

12 如使用双层床,上铺床垫下的弹簧床绷下方应垫上一层防灰尘的底板。

13 家具应使用光滑、坚硬、不易变形和被腐蚀的材料制作。

14 卧室内的舷窗应装有窗帘或等效物。

15 每间卧室应备有一面镜子、存放盥洗用具的小柜、一个书架和足够数量的衣服挂钩。

导则 B3.1.6 餐厅

1 餐厅既可以共用也可以分开。关于此事项的决定应在与海员和船东组织协商并经主管当局批准后做出。应考虑到诸如船舶的尺寸和海员不同的文化、宗教和社会需要等方面的因素。

2 如果向海员提供分开的餐厅设施,则分开的餐厅应提供给:

(**a**) 船长和高级船员;和

(**b**) 见习高级船员和其他海员。

3 在客船以外的船舶上,海员餐厅的地板面积应不少于按计划容纳人数每人1.5平方米。

4 所有船舶的餐厅均应配备固定式或移动式的餐桌和座位,足以容纳最大人数的海员同时用餐。

5   There should be available at all times when seafarers are on board:

   (**a**)   a refrigerator, which should be conveniently situated and of sufficient capacity for the number of persons using the mess room or mess rooms;

   (**b**)   facilities for hot beverages; and

   (**c**)   cool water facilities.

6   Where available pantries are not accessible to mess rooms, adequate lockers for mess utensils and proper facilities for washing utensils should be provided.

7   The tops of tables and seats should be of damp-resistant material.

Guideline B3. 1. 7   Sanitary accommodation

1   Washbasins and tub baths should be of adequate size and constructed of approved material with a smooth surface not liable to crack, flake or corrode.

2   All toilets should be of an approved pattern and provided with an ample flush of water or with some other suitable flushing means, such as air, which are available at all times and independently controllable.

3   Sanitary accommodation intended for the use of more than one person should comply with the following:

   (**a**)   floors should be of approved durable material, impervious to damp, and should be properly drained;

   (**b**)   bulkheads should be of steel or other approved material and should be watertight up to at least 23 centimetres above the level of the deck;

   (**c**)   the accommodation should be sufficiently lit, heated and ventilated;

   (**d**)   toilets should be situated convenient to, but separate from, sleeping rooms and wash rooms, without direct access from the sleeping rooms or from a passage between sleeping rooms and toilets to which there is no other access; this requirement does not apply where a toilet is located in a compartment between two sleeping rooms having a total of not more than four seafarers; and

   (**e**)   where there is more than one toilet in a compartment, they should be sufficiently screened to ensure privacy.

4   The laundry facilities provided for seafarers' use should include:

   (**a**)   washing machines;

   (**b**)   drying machines or adequately heated and ventilated drying rooms; and

   (**c**)   irons and ironing boards or their equivalent.

5 当海员在船上时,应随时提供:

（**a**）　一台所处位置方便使用且容量足够在该餐厅就餐的人使用的冰箱;

（**b**）　制作热饮料的设备;和

（**c**）　冷水设备。

6　如果可用的餐具室不与餐厅直接相通,应提供充足的餐具柜和洗涤餐具的适当设备。

7　桌面和椅面应为防潮材料。

导则 B3.1.7　卫生设施

1　洗脸池和浴缸应具有适当的尺寸,用具备光滑的表面,不易开裂、剥落或被腐蚀的认可材料制成。

2　所有厕所均应为经认可的样式,有足够的冲水力或其他一些适合的冲洗方式,例如空气,随时可用且能够独立控制。

3　一人以上使用的卫生设施应符合以下要求:

（**a**）　地板应为认可的耐久材料,防潮,并应配备有效排水;

（**b**）　隔板应选用钢材或其他经认可的材料,至少在甲板以上 23 厘米水密;

（**c**）　室内应有充分的照明、供暖和通风;

（**d**）　厕所应位于方便到达卧室和盥洗室之处,但又要与它们隔开,厕所门不应直接朝向卧室或卧室与厕所之间的唯一通道;但如果厕所位于总居住人数不到四人的两间卧室之间,则可不执行后一项规定;以及

（**e**）　如同一舱室有不止一个厕所,应予充分遮挡,确保隐私。

4　供海员使用的洗衣设施应包括:

（**a**）　洗衣机;

（**b**）　烘干机或具有足够加热和通风的烘干室;和

（**c**）　熨斗和熨衣板或其等效物。

Guideline B3.1.8 Hospital accommodation

1 The hospital accommodation should be designed so as to facilitate consultation and the giving of medical first aid and to help prevent the spread of infectious diseases.

2 The arrangement of the entrance, berths, lighting, ventilation, heating and water supply should be designed to ensure the comfort and facilitate the treatment of the occupants.

3 The number of hospital berths required should be prescribed by the competent authority.

4 Sanitary accommodation should be provided for the exclusive use of the occupants of the hospital accommodation, either as part of the accommodation or in close proximity thereto. Such sanitary accommodation should comprise a minimum of one toilet, one washbasin and one tub or shower.

Guideline B3.1.9 Other facilities

1 Where separate facilities for engine department personnel to change their clothes are provided, they should be:

  (**a**) located outside the machinery space but with easy access to it; and

  (**b**) fitted with individual clothes lockers as well as with tubs or showers or both and washbasins having hot and cold running fresh water.

Guideline B3.1.10 Bedding, mess utensils and miscellaneous provisions

1 Each Member should consider applying the following principles:

  (**a**) clean bedding and mess utensils should be supplied by the shipowner to all seafarers for use on board during service on the ship, and such seafarers should be responsible for their return at times specified by the master and on completion of service in the ship;

  (**b**) bedding should be of good quality, and plates, cups and other mess utensils should be of approved material which can be easily cleaned; and

  (**c**) towels, soap and toilet paper for all seafarers should be provided by the shipowner.

Guideline B3.1.11 Recreational facilities, mail and ship visit arrangements

1 Recreational facilities and services should be reviewed frequently to ensure that they are appropriate in the light of changes in the needs of seafarers resulting from technical, operational and other developments in the shipping industry.

2 Furnishings for recreational facilities should as a minimum include a bookcase and facilities for reading, writing and, where practicable, games.

3 In connection with the planning of recreation facilities, the competent authority should give consideration to the provision of a canteen.

导则 B3.1.8　医务室

1　医务室的设计应便于会诊和进行医疗急救,并有助于防止传染性疾病传播。

2　入口、床位、照明、通风、取暖及供水的设计安排,应以保证使用者的舒适度和便于治疗为目的。

3　所需病床的数量应由主管当局规定。

4　应为医务室的使用者提供专用的卫生间,既可作为医务室的一部分也可就近设置。此类卫生间至少应包括一个厕所、一个洗脸池、一个浴盆或淋浴室。

导则 B3.1.9　其他设施

1　如果为轮机部人员提供单独的更衣室,这些更衣室应:

　　（**a**）　设在机器处所之外但易于进入机器处所的位置;和

　　（**b**）　配备个人衣柜以及通有流动冷、热淡水的浴盆和(或)淋浴室与洗脸池。

导则 B3.1.10　床具、餐具和杂项规定

1　各成员国应考虑适用以下原则:

　　（**a**）　船东应向在船上工作的全体海员提供洁净的床具和餐具供其在船上服务期间使用,当海员完成该船上的服务时,有责任按船长规定的时间归还这些用品;

　　（**b**）　床具应质量好,盘子、杯子和其他餐具应为认可的材料制成,便于清洗;以及

　　（**c**）　船东应向全体海员提供毛巾、肥皂和卫生纸。

导则 B3.1.11　娱乐设施、邮件和上船探访安排

1　对娱乐设施和服务应予经常审查,以保证其适应因海运业技术、操作和其他方面的发展所带来的海员需求的改变。

2　娱乐设施的配备应至少包括书架和阅读与书写设施,实际可行时,还在包括游戏设施。

3　涉及娱乐设施的规划,主管当局应考虑开设一个小卖部。

4   Consideration should also be given to including the following facilities at no cost to the seafarer, where practicable:

(**a**)   a smoking room;

(**b**)   television viewing and the reception of radio broadcasts;

(**c**)   showing of films, the stock of which should be adequate for the duration of the voyage and, where necessary, changed at reasonable intervals;

(**d**)   sports equipment including exercise equipment, table games and deck games;

(**e**)   where possible, facilities for swimming;

(**f**)   a library containing vocational and other books, the stock of which should be adequate for the duration of the voyage and changed at reasonable intervals;

(**g**)   facilities for recreational handicrafts;

(**h**)   electronic equipment such as a radio, television, video recorders, DVD/CD player, personal computer and software and cassette recorder/player;

(**i**)   where appropriate, the provision of bars on board for seafarers unless these are contrary to national, religious or social customs; and

(**j**)   reasonable access to ship-to-shore telephone communications, and email and Internet facilities, where available, with any charges for the use of these services being reasonable in amount.

5   Every effort should be given to ensuring that the forwarding of seafarers' mail is as reliable and expeditious as possible. Efforts should also be considered for avoiding seafarers being required to pay additional postage when mail has to be readdressed owing to circumstances beyond their control.

6   Measures should be considered to ensure, subject to any applicable national or international laws or regulations, that whenever possible and reasonable seafarers are expeditiously granted permission to have their partners, relatives and friends as visitors on board their ship when in port. Such measures should meet any concerns for security clearances.

7   Consideration should be given to the possibility of allowing seafarers to be accompanied by their partners on occasional voyages where this is practicable and reasonable. Such partners should carry adequate insurance cover against accident and illness; the shipowners should give every assistance to the seafarer to effect such insurance.

Guideline B3. 1. 12   Prevention of noise and vibration

1   Accommodation and recreational and catering facilities should be located as far as practicable from the engines, steering gear rooms, deck winches, ventilation, heating and air-conditioning equipment and other noisy machinery and apparatus.

4 在可行时,还应考虑包括以下不向海员收费的设施:

（**a**） 吸烟室;

（**b**） 观看电视和收听广播;

（**c**） 放映电影,存片应足够航程期间使用,在必要时,每隔适当时间予以更换;

（**d**） 运动器械,包括锻炼器械、台式运动和甲板运动;

（**e**） 如可能,提供游泳设施;

（**f**） 藏有业务书籍和其他书籍的图书馆,其藏书量应够航程期间使用,并且每隔适当时间予以更换;

（**g**） 娱乐性手工艺设施;

（**h**） 电子设备,如收音机、电视机、录像机、DVD/CD 播放机、个人计算机和软件以及磁带录音机;

（**i**） 凡适宜,只要不违反国家、宗教或社会习俗,在船上为海员提供酒吧;和

（**j**） 提供合理的船—岸电话通信、电子邮件和互联网设施,如有这些设施,使用这些服务的任何收费金额应合理。

5 应尽力保证尽可能稳妥、迅速地投递海员邮件。还应努力避免使海员在不得已转寄邮件时加付邮资。

6 在国家和国际法律或法规允许的情况下,如果可能和合理,应考虑采取措施保证船舶在港口停留期间,从速批准海员的伴侣、亲属和朋友登船探视。此种措施应满足任何关于保安审查的考虑。

7 应考虑有无可能在合理及可行的情况下允许海员的伴侣偶尔陪伴其航海。这些伴侣应购买足够的意外事故和疾病保险;船东应为海员获得这种保险给予一切帮助。

导则 B3.1.12　防止噪声和振动

1 居住和娱乐及膳食服务设施的位置应尽可能远离主机、舵机室、甲板绞盘、通风设备、取暖设备和空调设备以及其他有噪声的机器和装置。

2   Acoustic insulation or other appropriate sound-absorbing materials should be used in the construction and finishing of bulkheads, deckheads and decks within the sound-producing spaces as well as self-closing noise-isolating doors for machinery spaces.

3   Engine rooms and other machinery spaces should be provided, wherever practicable, with soundproof centralized control rooms for engine-room personnel. Working spaces, such as the machine shop, should be insulated, as far as practicable, from the general engine-room noise and measures should be taken to reduce noise in the operation of machinery.

4   The limits for noise levels for working and living spaces should be in conformity with the ILO international guidelines on exposure levels, including those in the ILO code of practice entitled Ambient factors in the workplace, 2001, and, where applicable, the specific protection recommended by the International Maritime Organization, and with any subsequent amending and supplementary instruments for acceptable noise levels on board ships. A copy of the applicable instruments in English or the working language of the ship should be carried on board and should be accessible to seafarers.

5   No accommodation or recreational or catering facilities should be exposed to excessive vibration.

Regulation 3. 2

Food and catering

Purpose: To ensure that seafarers have access to good quality food and drinking water provided under regulated hygienic conditions

1   Each Member shall ensure that ships that fly its flag carry on board and serve food and drinking water of appropriate quality, nutritional value and quantity that adequately covers the requirements of the ship and takes into account the differing cultural and religious backgrounds.

2   Seafarers on board a ship shall be provided with food free of charge during the period of engagement.

3   Seafarers employed as ships' cooks with responsibility for food preparation must be trained and qualified for their position on board ship.

Standard A3. 2   Food and catering

1   Each Member shall adopt laws and regulations or other measures to provide minimum standards for the quantity and quality of food and drinking water and for the catering standards that apply to meals provided to seafarers on ships that fly its flag, and shall undertake educational activities to promote awareness and implementation of the standards referred to in this paragraph.

2 发出声音处所内的舱壁、天花板和甲板应使用隔音材料和其他适当的吸音材料制造和装修,并应为机器处所安装隔音的自动关闭门。

3 在可行时,应在机舱和其他机器处所为机舱人员设立隔音的中心控制室。工作场所,例如机修间,应尽实际可能隔离普通机舱的噪声,并应采取措施降低机器运转时的噪声。

4 工作和生活处所的噪声水平限制,应符合国际劳工组织关于暴露水平的国际导则,包括标题为《2001 年工作场所环境因素》的国际劳工组织实用守则,以及在适用时,国际海事组织建议的具体保护,以及任何关于船上可接受噪声水平的修正和补充文件。适用文件的英文或船上工作语言的副本应随船携带并使海员能够使用。

5 起居舱室或者娱乐或膳食服务设施不应暴露于过度振动中。

规则 3.2
食品和膳食服务

目的:确保海员获得依据规范的卫生条件提供的优质食品和饮用水

1 各成员国应确保悬挂其旗帜的船舶随船携带和供应充分满足船舶需求并同时考虑不同的文化和宗教背景要求的质量、营养价值和数量均合适的食品和饮用水。

2 在海员受雇期间,应为船上的海员免费提供食物。

3 受雇为船上厨师并负责配制食品的海员必须就其所担任的职位经过培训并取得资格。

标准 A3.2 食品和膳食服务

1 各成员国应通过法律法规或其他措施,为悬挂其旗帜的船舶供应给海员的食品和饮用水的数量与质量及适用于各餐的膳食标准规定最低标准,并应开展教育活动,促进对本款所述标准的认识和实施。

2   Each Member shall ensure that ships that fly its flag meet the following minimum standards:

(a)   food and drinking water supplies, having regard to the number of seafarers on board, their religious requirements and cultural practices as they pertain to food, and the duration and nature of the voyage, shall be suitable in respect of quantity, nutritional value, quality and variety;

(b)   the organization and equipment of the catering department shall be such as to permit the provision to the seafarers of adequate, varied and nutritious meals prepared and served in hygienic conditions; and

(c)   catering staff shall be properly trained or instructed for their positions.

3   Shipowners shall ensure that seafarers who are engaged as ships' cooks are trained, qualified and found competent for the position in accordance with requirements set out in the laws and regulations of the Member concerned.

4   The requirements under paragraph 3 of this Standard shall include a completion of a training course approved or recognized by the competent authority, which covers practical cookery, food and personal hygiene, food storage, stock control, and environmental protection and catering health and safety.

5   On ships operating with a prescribed manning of less than ten which, by virtue of the size of the crew or the trading pattern, may not be required by the competent authority to carry a fully qualified cook, anyone processing food in the galley shall be trained or instructed in areas including food and personal hygiene as well as handling and storage of food on board ship.

6   In circumstances of exceptional necessity, the competent authority may issue a dispensation permitting a non-fully qualified cook to serve in a specified ship for a specified limited period, until the next convenient port of call or for a period not exceeding one month, provided that the person to whom the dispensation is issued is trained or instructed in areas including food and personal hygiene as well as handling and storage of food on board ship.

7   In accordance with the ongoing compliance procedures under Title 5, the competent authority shall require that frequent documented inspections be carried out on board ships, by or under the authority of the master, with respect to:

(a)   supplies of food and drinking water;

(b)   all spaces and equipment used for the storage and handling of food and drinking water; and

(c)   galley and other equipment for the preparation and service of meals.

8   No seafarer under the age of 18 shall be employed or engaged or work as a ship's cook.

2 各成员国应确保悬挂其旗帜的船舶满足以下最低标准：

（**a**） 考虑到船上海员人数、他们饮食方面的宗教要求和文化习惯，以及航行的时间和性质，供应在数量、营养价值、质量和品种方面均为适当的食品和饮用水；

（**b**） 设置并配备膳食服务部门，以便为海员提供在良好卫生条件下准备和供应的充分、多品种和有营养的餐食；以及

（**c**） 膳食服务人员应就其职责接受过适当培训和指导。

3 船东应确保以船上厨师的身份受雇的海员必须按有关成员国的法律和法规所规定的要求接受过培训，培训合格并胜任其职位。

4 本标准第 3 款中的要求应包括完成主管当局批准或认可的培训课程，涉及实用厨艺、食品和个人卫生、食品储存、备料管理和环境保护以及膳食健康和安全。

5 在船舶营运的规定配员少于 10 人的船上，由于船员数目或航行特点，主管当局可能不要求配备完全具有正式资格的厨师，但要求在厨房加工食品的任何人员均应在包括食品和个人卫生以及船上处理和储存食品等方面受过培训或指导。

6 在极其必要的情况下，主管当局可签发特免证明，允许不具备正式资格的厨师在规定的有限时间内为某特定船舶服务，直到下一个方便的挂靠港或时间不超过一个月，条件是获发特免证明的人员在包括食品和个人卫生以及船上处理和储存食品方面受到过培训或指导。

7 根据标题五中的持续符合程序，主管当局应要求由船长或经船长授权的人员，在船舶上对以下方面开展有记录的经常性检查：

（**a**） 食品和饮用水供应；

（**b**） 用于储存和处理食物及饮用水的所有场所与设备；以及

（**c**） 用于准备和供应餐食的厨房或其他设备。

8 不得雇用或聘用 18 岁以下的海员担任船上的厨师。

Guideline B3. 2   Food and catering

Guideline B3. 2. 1   Inspection, education, research and publication

1   The competent authority should, in cooperation with other relevant agencies and organizations, collect up-to-date information on nutrition and on methods of purchasing, storing, preserving, cooking and serving food, with special reference to the requirements of catering on board a ship. This information should be made available, free of charge or at reasonable cost, to manufacturers of and traders in ships' food supplies and equipment, masters, stewards and cooks, and to shipowners' and seafarers' organizations concerned. Appropriate forms of publicity, such as manuals, brochures, posters, charts or advertisements in trade journals, should be used for this purpose.

2   The competent authority should issue recommendations to avoid wastage of food, facilitate the maintenance of a proper standard of hygiene, and ensure the maximum practicable convenience in working arrangements.

3   The competent authority should work with relevant agencies and organizations to develop educational materials and on-board information concerning methods of ensuring proper food supply and catering services.

4   The competent authority should work in close cooperation with the shipowners' and seafarers' organizations concerned and with national or local authorities dealing with questions of food and health, and may where necessary utilize the services of such authorities.

Guideline B3. 2. 2   Ships' cooks

1   Seafarers should only be qualified as ships' cooks if they have:

   (a)   served at sea for a minimum period to be prescribed by the competent authority, which could be varied to take into account existing relevant qualifications or experience;

   (b)   passed an examination prescribed by the competent authority or passed an equivalent examination at an approved training course for cooks.

2   The prescribed examination may be conducted and certificates granted either directly by the competent authority or, subject to its control, by an approved school for the training of cooks.

3   The competent authority should provide for the recognition, where appropriate, of certificates of qualification as ships' cooks issued by other Members, which have ratified this Convention or the Certification of Ships' Cooks Convention, 1946 (No. 69), or other approved body.

导则 B3.2 食品和膳食服务

导则 B3.2.1 检查、教育、研究和出版

1 主管当局应与其他相关机构和组织合作,收集有关食品营养和食品购买、储存、保存、烹调和服务的方法方面的最新信息,并特别注意船上膳食服务的要求。此类信息应免费或以合理的价格向专事供应船用食品或设备的生产厂和经销商,船长、管事和厨师以及有关船东和海员组织提供。为此目的,应利用手册、小册子、招贴画、图表或在专业期刊上登载广告等适当的宣传形式。

2 主管当局应发布建议,以避免浪费食物,促进保持良好的卫生标准,并确保工作安排的最大便利性。

3 主管当局应与有关组织和机构共同制定关于旨在保证适当的食品供应和膳食服务的方法的教育材料和船上信息。

4 主管当局应与涉及食品和健康问题的有关船东和海员组织以及有关国家和地方当局密切合作,并在必要时,可利用上述当局的服务。

导则 B3.2.2 船上厨师

1 海员应满足以下条件才有资格成为船上厨师:

（**a**） 在海上服务的时间达到了主管当局确定的最低期限,考虑到现有的相关资格和经验,此期限可有所变化;

（**b**） 通过了主管当局规定的考试或通过了经认可的厨师培训课程的等效考试。

2 可直接由主管当局或在其监督下由经认可的烹饪培训学校开展规定的考试并颁发证书。

3 主管当局应规定,在适宜时,承认由批准了本公约或《1946 年船上厨师发证公约》(第 69号)的其他成员国或其他认可机构签发的船上厨师资格证书。

Title 4
Health protection, medical care, welfare and social security protection

Regulation 4. 1
Medical care on board ship and ashore

Purpose: To protect the health of seafarers and ensure their prompt access to medical care on board ship and ashore

1   Each Member shall ensure that all seafarers on ships that fly its flag are covered by adequate measures for the protection of their health and that they have access to prompt and adequate medical care whilst working on board.

2   The protection and care under paragraph 1 of this Regulation shall, in principle, be provided at no cost to the seafarers.

3   Each Member shall ensure that seafarers on board ships in its territory who are in need of immediate medical care are given access to the Member's medical facilities on shore.

4   The requirements for on-board health protection and medical care set out in the Code include standards for measures aimed at providing seafarers with health protection and medical care as comparable as possible to that which is generally available to workers ashore.

Standard A4. 1   Medical care on board ship and ashore

1   Each Member shall ensure that measures providing for health protection and medical care, including essential dental care, for seafarers working on board a ship that flies its flag are adopted which:

  (a)   ensure the application to seafarers of any general provisions on occupational health protection and medical care relevant to their duties, as well as of special provisions specific to work on board ship;

  (b)   ensure that seafarers are given health protection and medical care as comparable as possible to that which is generally available to workers ashore, including prompt access to the necessary medicines, medical equipment and facilities for diagnosis and treatment and to medical information and expertise;

  (c)   give seafarers the right to visit a qualified medical doctor or dentist without delay in ports of call, where practicable;

  (d)   ensure that, to the extent consistent with the Member's national law and practice, medical care and health protection services while a seafarer is on board ship or landed in a foreign port are provided free of charge to seafarers; and

标题四
健康保护、医疗、福利和社会保障保护

规则 4.1
船上和岸上医疗

目的:保护海员健康并确保其能迅速得到船上和岸上医疗

1 各成员国应确保在悬挂其旗帜船舶上的所有海员均被保护其健康的充分措施所覆盖,并且他们在船上工作期间能够得到迅速和适当的医疗。

2 按本规则第 1 款所提供的保护和医疗原则上应向海员免费提供。

3 各成员国应确保在其领土内的船舶上需要紧急医疗的海员能够使用成员国的岸上医疗设施。

4 守则中规定的船上健康保护和医疗要求包括旨在向海员提供尽可能相当于岸上工人能够得到的健康保护和医疗的措施标准。

标准 A4.1　船上和岸上医疗

1 各成员国应确保采取措施向在悬挂其旗帜的船舶上工作的海员提供健康保护和医疗,包括必需的牙科治疗,这些措施应:

　（**a**）　保证将任何与海员职责相关的关于职业健康保护和医疗的一般规定以及专门针对船上工作的特殊规定适用于海员;

　（**b**）　保证向海员提供尽可能相当于岸上工人一般能够得到的健康保护和医疗,包括迅速使用诊断和治疗所必需的药品、医疗设备和设施,以及利用医疗信息和医疗专业技能;

　（**c**）　凡可行,在停靠港不延误地给予海员去看合格医生或牙医的权利;

　（**d**）　在与成员国国家法律和惯例一致的限度内,保证免费向船上海员或在外国港口下船的海员提供健康保护和医疗;以及

(**e**) are not limited to treatment of sick or injured seafarers but include measures of a preventive character such as health promotion and health education programmes.

2 The competent authority shall adopt a standard medical report form for use by the ships' masters and relevant onshore and on-board medical personnel. The form, when completed, and its contents shall be kept confidential and shall only be used to facilitate the treatment of seafarers.

3 Each Member shall adopt laws and regulations establishing requirements for on-board hospital and medical care facilities and equipment and training on ships that fly its flag.

4 National laws and regulations shall as a minimum provide for the following requirements:

(**a**) all ships shall carry a medicine chest, medical equipment and a medical guide, the specifics of which shall be prescribed and subject to regular inspection by the competent authority; the national requirements shall take into account the type of ship, the number of persons on board and the nature, destination and duration of voyages and relevant national and international recommended medical standards;

(**b**) ships carrying 100 or more persons and ordinarily engaged on international voyages of more than three days' duration shall carry a qualified medical doctor who is responsible for providing medical care; national laws or regulations shall also specify which other ships shall be required to carry a medical doctor, taking into account, inter alia, such factors as the duration, nature and conditions of the voyage and the number of seafarers on board;

(**c**) ships which do not carry a medical doctor shall be required to have either at least one seafarer on board who is in charge of medical care and administering medicine as part of their regular duties or at least one seafarer on board competent to provide medical first aid; persons in charge of medical care on board who are not medical doctors shall have satisfactorily completed training in medical care that meets the requirements of the International Convention on Standards of Training, Certification and Watchkeeping for Seafarers, 1978, as amended ("STCW"); seafarers designated to provide medical first aid shall have satisfactorily completed training in medical first aid that meets the requirements of STCW; national laws or regulations shall specify the level of approved training required taking into account, inter alia, such factors as the duration, nature and conditions of the voyage and the number of seafarers on board; and

(**d**) the competent authority shall ensure by a prearranged system that medical advice by radio or satellite communication to ships at sea, including specialist advice, is available 24 hours a day; medical advice, including the onward transmission of medical messages by radio or satellite communication between a ship and those ashore giving the advice, shall be available free of charge to all ships irrespective of the flag that they fly.

（e） 不局限于对患病或受伤海员的治疗,同时还应包括预防性措施,如促进健康和保健教育的计划。

2 主管当局应制定一个标准的海员医疗报告表格,供船长和相关的岸上和船上医疗人员使用。填好后的表格及其内容应予保密,只应用于方便海员的治疗。

3 各成员国应通过法律和法规对悬挂其旗帜的船舶规定船上医务室及医疗设施和设备以及培训的要求。

4 国家法律或法规最低限度应规定以下要求:

（a） 所有船舶均应携带医药箱、医疗设备和医疗指南,具体内容由主管当局规定并受到主管当局的定期检查;国家要求应考虑到船舶类型、船上人员的数量及航次性质、目的地和航程以及相关的国家和国际的建议医疗标准;

（b） 载员 100 人或以上,通常从事 3 天以上国际航行的船舶应配备一名医生负责提供医疗。国家法律或法规还应考虑到诸如航行的时间、性质和条件以及船上海员人数等因素,规定哪些其他船舶也应要求配备一名医生;

（c） 应要求不配备医生的船舶,要么在船上至少有一名海员的一部分正式职责是负责医疗和管理药品,要么船上至少有一名海员胜任提供医疗急救服务;不是专职医生但负责船上医疗的人员应该圆满完成符合经修正的《1978 年海员培训、发证和值班标准国际公约》(STCW 公约)要求的培训;被指定提供医疗急救的海员应圆满完成符合《STCW 公约》要求的医疗急救培训。国家法律或法规应规定所要求的认可培训水平,并特别注意到诸如航行时间、性质和条件以及船上海员的数量等因素;以及

（d） 主管当局应通过一个预先安排的机制,保证船舶在海上能够每天 24 小时均可得到通过无线电或卫星通信提供的医疗指导,包括专家指导。医疗指导,包括船舶与岸上提供医疗咨询的机构通过无线电台或卫星通信进行的医疗信息沟通,均应由所有船舶免费使用,无论其悬挂哪一国旗帜。

Guideline B4.1 Medical care on board ship and ashore

Guideline B4.1.1 Provision of medical care

1 When determining the level of medical training to be provided on board ships that are not required to carry a medical doctor, the competent authority should require that:

(**a**) ships which ordinarily are capable of reaching qualified medical care and medical facilities within eight hours should have at least one designated seafarer with the approved medical first-aid training required by STCW which will enable such persons to take immediate, effective action in case of accidents or illnesses likely to occur on board a ship and to make use of medical advice by radio or satellite communication; and

(**b**) all other ships should have at least one designated seafarer with approved training in medical care required by STCW, including practical training and training in life-saving techniques such as intravenous therapy, which will enable the persons concerned to participate effectively in coordinated schemes for medical assistance to ships at sea, and to provide the sick or injured with a satisfactory standard of medical care during the period they are likely to remain on board.

2 The training referred to in paragraph 1 of this Guideline should be based on the contents of the most recent editions of the International Medical Guide for Ships, the Medical First Aid Guide for Use in Accidents Involving Dangerous Goods, the Document for Guidance—An International Maritime Training Guide, and the medical section of the International Code of Signals as well as similar national guides.

3 Persons referred to in paragraph 1 of this Guideline and such other seafarers as may be required by the competent authority should undergo, at approximately five-year intervals, refresher courses to enable them to maintain and increase their knowledge and skills and to keep up-to-date with new developments.

4 The medicine chest and its contents, as well as the medical equipment and medical guide carried on board, should be properly maintained and inspected at regular intervals, not exceeding 12 months, by responsible persons designated by the competent authority, who should ensure that the labelling, expiry dates and conditions of storage of all medicines and directions for their use are checked and all equipment functioning as required. In adopting or reviewing the ship's medical guide used nationally, and in determining the contents of the medicine chest and medical equipment, the competent authority should take into account international recommendations in this field, including the latest edition of the International Medical Guide for Ships, and other guides mentioned in paragraph 2 of this Guideline.

导则 B4.1 船上和岸上医疗

导则 B4.1.1 医疗的提供

1 在确定不要求配备医生的船舶上将提供的医疗培训水平时,主管当局应要求:

（**a**） 通常能够在 8 小时内获得合格的医疗和医疗设施的船舶应至少有一名指定海员接受过 STCW 公约所要求的经认可的医疗急救培训,使其能够在船上可能发生事故或出现疾病时立即采取有效行动和采用通过无线电或卫星通信获得的医疗建议;以及

（**b**） 所有其他船舶应至少有一名指定的海员接受过 STCW 公约所要求的经认可的培训,包括实际训练以及诸如静脉注射等抢救技能的培训,这些培训使有关人员能有效参与船舶海上医疗援助协调活动,并能在病号或伤员可能继续留在船上期间,向他们提供符合标准的医疗。

2 本导则第 1 款所述的培训应建立在以下文件最新版本的内容的基础上:《国际船舶医疗指南》《用于涉及危险品事故的医疗急救指南》《指导文件——国际海事培训指南》,以及《国际信号规则》的医疗部分及类似的国家指南。

3 本导则第 1 款所述的人员和主管当局可能要求的其他海员每隔 5 年左右应参加进修课程,以保持和增加其知识与技能并适应新的发展。

4 船上医药箱及箱内药品,以及医疗设备和医疗指南应由主管当局指定负责人员妥善维护,并每隔不超过 12 个月进行定期检查。这些人员应确保核对全部药品的标签、失效日期和存放条件及其用法与用量,并确保所有设备功能合乎要求。在通过或审定国内使用的船舶医疗指南以及在确定医药箱内的药品和医疗设备时,主管当局应考虑此领域的国际建议,包括最新版本的《国际船舶医疗指南》和本导则第 2 款所述的其他指南。

5   Where a cargo which is classified dangerous has not been included in the most recent edition of the Medical First Aid Guide for Use in Accidents Involving Dangerous Goods, the necessary information on the nature of the substances, the risks involved, the necessary personal protective devices, the relevant medical procedures and specific antidotes should be made available to the seafarers. Such specific antidotes and personal protective devices should be on board whenever dangerous goods are carried. This information should be integrated with the ship's policies and programmes on occupational safety and health described in Regulation 4.3 and related Code provisions.

6   All ships should carry a complete and up-to-date list of radio stations through which medical advice can be obtained; and, if equipped with a system of satellite communication, carry an up-to-date and complete list of coast earth stations through which medical advice can be obtained. Seafarers with responsibility for medical care or medical first aid on board should be instructed in the use of the ship's medical guide and the medical section of the most recent edition of the International Code of Signals so as to enable them to understand the type of information needed by the advising doctor as well as the advice received.

Guideline B4.1.2   Medical report form

1   The standard medical report form for seafarers required under Part A of this Code should be designed to facilitate the exchange of medical and related information concerning individual seafarers between ship and shore in cases of illness or injury.

Guideline B4.1.3   Medical care ashore

1   Shore-based medical facilities for treating seafarers should be adequate for the purposes. The doctors, dentists and other medical personnel should be properly qualified.

2   Measures should be taken to ensure that seafarers have access when in port to:

(**a**)   outpatient treatment for sickness and injury;

(**b**)   hospitalization when necessary; and

(**c**)   facilities for dental treatment, especially in cases of emergency.

3   Suitable measures should be taken to facilitate the treatment of seafarers suffering from disease. In particular, seafarers should be promptly admitted to clinics and hospitals ashore, without difficulty and irrespective of nationality or religious belief, and, whenever possible, arrangements should be made to ensure, when necessary, continuation of treatment to supplement the medical facilities available to them.

Guideline B4.1.4   Medical assistance to other ships and international cooperation

1   Each Member should give due consideration to participating in international cooperation in the area of assistance, programmes and research in health protection and medical care. Such cooperation might cover:

5 如果属危险品的货物尚未列入最新版本的《用于涉及危险品事故的医疗急救指南》，应向海员提供关于该物质的性质、存在的风险、必要的个人保护装置、相关的医疗程序和专用解毒剂方面的必要信息。凡船舶载运危险品时，船上应备有此类专用解毒剂和个人保护装置。此信息应纳入规则 4.3 和相关守则规定所述的船舶职业安全和健康的政策与计划中。

6 所有船舶均应备有一份最新的能够获得医疗指导的无线电台的完整清单；并且，如果装备了卫星通信系统，则还应备有一份最新的能获得医疗指导的岸上地面站的完整清单。应指导负责船上医疗或医疗急救的海员使用船舶医疗指南以及最新版《国际信号规则》的医疗部分，以使他们明白提供指导的医生所需的信息类型以及所收到的指导意见。

导则 B4.1.2　医疗报告表格

1 本守则 A 部分所要求的标准海员医疗报告表格应设计成便于在海员生病或受伤时，在船舶与岸上之间交换有关该海员的医疗及相关信息的格式。

导则 B4.1.3　岸上医疗

1 用于治疗海员的岸上医疗设施应充分符合其目的。医生、牙医和其他医务人员应具备合适的资格。

2 应采取措施确保海员在港口时能够：

（**a**）　在患病或受伤时得到门诊治疗；

（**b**）　在必要时住院治疗；以及

（**c**）　得到牙病治疗的便利，特别是在紧急情况下。

3 应采取适当措施便利患病海员的治疗。特别是，应没有困难地立即接受海员进入岸上的诊室和医院，不论其国籍和宗教信仰，并在可能时，提供旨在保证必要的连续治疗安排，以补充海员可用的医疗设施。

导则 B4.1.4　对其他船舶的医疗援助和国际合作

1 各成员国应充分考虑参与健康保护和医疗的援助、项目和研究领域的国际合作。此种合作可包括：

(a) developing and coordinating search and rescue efforts and arranging prompt medical help and evacuation at sea for the seriously ill or injured on board a ship through such means as periodic ship position reporting systems, rescue coordination centres and emergency helicopter services, in conformity with the International Convention on Maritime Search and Rescue, 1979, as amended, and the International Aeronautical and Maritime Search and Rescue (IAMSAR) Manual;

(b) making optimum use of all ships carrying a doctor and stationing ships at sea which can provide hospital and rescue facilities;

(c) compiling and maintaining an international list of doctors and medical care facilities available worldwide to provide emergency medical care to seafarers;

(d) landing seafarers ashore for emergency treatment;

(e) repatriating seafarers hospitalized abroad as soon as practicable, in accordance with the medical advice of the doctors responsible for the case, which takes into account the seafarer's wishes and needs;

(f) arranging personal assistance for seafarers during repatriation, in accordance with the medical advice of the doctors responsible for the case, which takes into account the seafarer's wishes and needs;

(g) endeavouring to set up health centres for seafarers to:

(i) conduct research on the health status, medical treatment and preventive health care of seafarers; and

(ii) train medical and health service staff in maritime medicine;

(h) collecting and evaluating statistics concerning occupational accidents, diseases and fatalities of seafarers and integrating and harmonizing the statistics with any existing national system of statistics on occupational accidents and diseases covering other categories of workers;

(i) organizing international exchanges of technical information, training material and personnel, as well as international training courses, seminars and working groups;

(j) providing all seafarers with special curative and preventive health and medical services in port, or making available to them general health, medical and rehabilitation services; and

(k) arranging for the repatriation of the bodies or ashes of deceased seafarers, in accordance with the wishes of the next of kin and as soon as practicable.

2 International cooperation in the field of health protection and medical care for seafarers should be based on bilateral or multilateral agreements or consultations among Members.

（**a**） 按照经修订的《1979 年海上搜寻与救助国际公约》和《国际航空和海上搜寻与救助（IAMSAR）手册》,发展和协调搜寻与救助力量,并通过定期船位报告制度、救助协调中心和应急直升机服务等手段,迅速安排船上重病号或重伤员的海上治疗帮助和撤离;

（**b**） 充分利用载有医生的所有船舶并向海上派驻能够提供医院和救助设施的船舶;

（**c**） 汇编和保存一份世界范围内能向海员提供应急医疗的医生和医疗设施的国际名录;

（**d**） 安排海员上岸进行紧急治疗;

（**e**） 根据负责医生的医疗建议并考虑海员本人的愿望和需要,尽可能将在国外住院的海员遣返回国;

（**f**） 根据负责医生的医疗建议并考虑海员本人的愿望和需要,在遣返期间为海员提供个人帮助;

（**g**） 努力建立海员健康中心,以便:

　　（**i**） 对海员的健康状况、医疗和预防性保健问题开展研究;以及

　　（**ii**） 培训从事海事医学的医疗和健康服务人员;

（**h**） 收集和评估有关海员职业事故、疾病和伤亡的统计资料,把这些统计资料纳入国家现行的包括其他各类工人的职业事故和疾病的统计资料系统中并与之相协调;

（**i**） 组织技术情报、培训材料和教学人员的国际交流,以及国际培训课程、研讨会和工作组;

（**j**） 在港口向所有海员提供专门的治疗和预防性健康和医疗服务,或使他们能得到一般性的保健、医疗和康复服务;以及

（**k**） 根据已故海员最近亲属的意愿,视情况尽早安排将已故海员遗体或骨灰运回。

2 海员健康保护和医疗领域的国际合作应以成员国间的双边或多边协议或者协商为基础。

Guideline B4.1.5   Dependants of seafarers

1   Each Member should adopt measures to secure proper and sufficient medical care for the dependants of seafarers domiciled in its territory pending the development of a medical care service which would include within its scope workers generally and their dependants where such services do not exist and should inform the International Labour Office concerning the measures taken for this purpose.

Regulation 4.2
Shipowners' liability

Purpose: To ensure that seafarers are protected from the financial consequences of sickness, injury or death occurring in connection with their employment

1   Each Member shall ensure that measures, in accordance with the Code, are in place on ships that fly its flag to provide seafarers employed on the ships with a right to material assistance and support from the shipowner with respect to the financial consequences of sickness, injury or death occurring while they are serving under a seafarers' employment agreement or arising from their employment under such agreement.

2   This Regulation does not affect any other legal remedies that a seafarer may seek.

Standard A4.2.1   Shipowners' liability

1   Each Member shall adopt laws and regulations requiring that shipowners of ships that fly its flag are responsible for health protection and medical care of all seafarers working on board the ships in accordance with the following minimum standards:

(a)   shipowners shall be liable to bear the costs for seafarers working on their ships in respect of sickness and injury of the seafarers occurring between the date of commencing duty and the date upon which they are deemed duly repatriated, or arising from their employment between those dates;

(b)   shipowners shall provide financial security to assure compensation in the event of the death or long-term disability of seafarers due to an occupational injury, illness or hazard, as set out in national law, the seafarers' employment agreement or collective agreement;

(c)   shipowners shall be liable to defray the expense of medical care, including medical treatment and the supply of the necessary medicines and therapeutic appliances, and board and lodging away from home until the sick or injured seafarer has recovered, or until the sickness or incapacity has been declared of a permanent character; and

(d)   shipowners shall be liable to pay the cost of burial expenses in the case of death occurring on board or ashore during the period of engagement.

2   National laws or regulations may limit the liability of the shipowner to defray the expense of medical care and board and lodging to a period which shall not be less than 16 weeks from the day of the injury or the commencement of the sickness.

导则 B4.1.5　海员的受赡养人

1　若不存在其范围总体上包括工人及其受赡养人的医疗服务,在开展此种服务之前,各成员国应采取措施保障海员在其领土内居住的受赡养人得到妥善和充分的医疗服务,并应将其为此目的而采取的措施通报国际劳工局。

规则 4.2
船东的责任

目的:确保在因就业而产生的疾病、受伤或死亡导致的经济后果方面对海员予以保护

1　针对海员根据其就业协议在船上服务期间发生的或在此种协议下就业所引起的疾病、伤害或死亡导致的经济后果,各成员国应根据守则确保悬挂其旗帜的船舶上存在措施,向在船上就业的海员提供从船东处获得物质援助和支持的权利。

2　本规则不影响海员可能寻求的任何其他法律救济。

标准 A4.2.1　船东的责任

1　各成员国应通过法律和法规,要求悬挂其旗帜的船舶的船东根据以下最低标准,对船上工作的所有海员的健康保护和医疗负责:

（**a**）　对于在其船上工作的海员,船东应有责任对海员从开始履行职责之日起到其被视为妥善遣返之日期间所发生的或源自这些时日的在就业期间所患疾病和所受伤害承担费用;

（**b**）　船东应提供财务担保,以确保在发生国家法律、海员就业协议或集体协议中规定的海员因工伤、疾病或危险而死亡或者长期残疾的情况获得赔偿;

（**c**）　船东应有责任支付医疗费用,包括治疗及提供必要的药品和治疗设备,以及在外的膳宿,直到该患病或受伤海员康复,或直到该疾病或机能丧失被宣布为永久性的;以及

（**d**）　如果发生海员受雇期间在船上或岸上死亡的情况,船东应有责任支付丧葬费用。

2　国家法律或法规可以把船东支付医疗和膳宿费用的责任限制在从受伤或患病之日起不少于 16 周的期限内。

3 Where the sickness or injury results in incapacity for work the shipowner shall be liable:

   (**a**)   to pay full wages as long as the sick or injured seafarers remain on board or until the seafarers have been repatriated in accordance with this Convention; and

   (**b**)   to pay wages in whole or in part as prescribed by national laws or regulations or as provided for in collective agreements from the time when the seafarers are repatriated or landed until their recovery or, if earlier, until they are entitled to cash benefits under the legislation of the Member concerned.

4 National laws or regulations may limit the liability of the shipowner to pay wages in whole or in part in respect of a seafarer no longer on board to a period which shall not be less than 16 weeks from the day of the injury or the commencement of the sickness.

5 National laws or regulations may exclude the shipowner from liability in respect of:

   (**a**)   injury incurred otherwise than in the service of the ship;

   (**b**)   injury or sickness due to the wilful misconduct of the sick, injured or deceased seafarer; and

   (**c**)   sickness or infirmity intentionally concealed when the engagement is entered into.

6 National laws or regulations may exempt the shipowner from liability to defray the expense of medical care and board and lodging and burial expenses in so far as such liability is assumed by the public authorities.

7 Shipowners or their representatives shall take measures for safeguarding property left on board by sick, injured or deceased seafarers and for returning it to them or to their next of kin.

8 National laws and regulations shall provide that the system of financial security to assure compensation as provided by paragraph 1(b) of this Standard for contractual claims, as defined in Standard A4.2.2, meet the following minimum requirements:

   (**a**)   the contractual compensation, where set out in the seafarer's employment agreement and without prejudice to subparagraph (c) of this paragraph, shall be paid in full and without delay;

   (**b**)   there shall be no pressure to accept a payment less than the contractual amount;

   (**c**)   where the nature of the long-term disability of a seafarer makes it difficult to assess the full compensation to which the seafarer may be entitled, an interim payment or payments shall be made to the seafarer so as to avoid undue hardship;

   (**d**)   in accordance with Regulation 4.2, paragraph 2, the seafarer shall receive payment without prejudice to other legal rights, but such payment may be offset by the shipowner against any damages resulting from any other claim made by the seafarer against the shipowner and arising from the same incident; and

3 如果因疾病或受伤造成海员工作能力的丧失,船东应有责任:

（**a**） 只要患病或受伤海员还留在船上或者在海员根据本公约得到遣返以前,向其支付全额工资;以及

（**b**） 从海员被遣返或到达上岸之时起直到身体康复,或者直到有权根据有关成员国的法律获得保险金(如果早于康复的话),按照国内法律或法规或集体协议的规定向其支付全额或部分工资。

4 国家法律或法规可将船东向一名离船海员支付全部或部分工资的责任限制在从患病或受伤之日起不少于 16 周的期限内。

5 国家法律或法规可在以下情况下排除船东的责任:

（**a**） 在船舶服务之外发生的其他受伤;

（**b**） 受伤或患病是因患病、受伤或死亡海员的故意不当行为所致;以及

（**c**） 在接受雇用时故意隐瞒的疾病或病症。

6 只要此种责任由公共当局承担,国家法律或法规可免除船东支付船上医疗费用及膳宿和丧葬费用的责任。

7 船东或其代表应采取措施保护患病、受伤或死亡海员留在船上的财物并将其归还给海员或其最近亲属。

8 国家法律和法规应规定,本标准第 1(b) 款所规定的确保对本标准 A4.2.2 定义的合同索赔做出赔偿的财务担保制度应符合以下最低要求:

（**a**） 应足额、毫不迟延地支付海员就业协议中规定的、不妨碍本款第(c)段的合同赔偿;

（**b**） 不得施加压力,要求接受低于合同数额的付款额;

（**c**） 若海员长期残疾的性质导致难以评估海员可能应得的全部赔偿,应一次或多次向海员支付临时赔偿,以避免海员面对不应有的困难。

（**d**） 根据规则 4.2 第 2 款,海员收到支付款项后并不妨碍海员行使其他合法权利,但船东可将此类付款额与海员就同一事故向船东提出的任何其他索赔所导致的损害赔偿金相抵销;及

(e) the claim for contractual compensation may be brought directly by the seafarer concerned, or their next of kin, or a representative of the seafarer or designated beneficiary.

9 National laws and regulations shall ensure that seafarers receive prior notification if a shipowner's financial security is to be cancelled or terminated.

10 National laws and regulations shall ensure that the competent authority of the flag State is notified by the provider of the financial security if a shipowner's financial security is cancelled or terminated.

11 Each Member shall require that ships that fly its flag carry on board a certificate or other documentary evidence of financial security issued by the financial security provider. A copy shall be posted in a conspicuous place on board where it is available to the seafarers. Where more than one financial security provider provides cover, the document provided by each provider shall be carried on board.

12 The financial security shall not cease before the end of the period of validity of the financial security unless the financial security provider has given prior notification of at least 30 days to the competent authority of the flag State.

13 The financial security shall provide for the payment of all contractual claims covered by it which arise during the period for which the document is valid.

14 The certificate or other documentary evidence of financial security shall contain the information required in Appendix A4- I . It shall be in English or accompanied by an English translation.

Standard A4. 2. 2 Treatment of contractual claims

1 For the purposes of Standard A4. 2. 1, paragraph 8, and the present Standard, the term "contractual claim" means any claim which relates to death or long-term disability of seafarers due to an occupational injury, illness or hazard as set out in national law, the seafarers' employment agreement or collective agreement.

2 The system of financial security, as provided for in Standard A4. 2. 1, paragraph 1 (b) , may be in the form of a social security scheme or insurance or fund or other similar arrangements. Its form shall be determined by the Member after consultation with the shipowners' and seafarers' organizations concerned.

3 National laws and regulations shall ensure that effective arrangements are in place to receive, deal with and impartially settle contractual claims relating to compensation referred to in Standard A4. 2. 1, paragraph 8, through expeditious and fair procedures.

Guideline B4. 2. 1 Shipowners' liability

1 The payment of full wages required by Standard A4. 2. 1, paragraph 3 (a) , may be exclusive of bonuses.

（e） 对合同赔偿的索赔可由相关海员,或其直系亲属,或海员的代表或者指定受益人直接提出。

9 国家法律和法规应确保,若一个船东的财务担保将被取消或终止,海员应事先收到通知。

10 国家法律和法规应确保,若一个船东的财务担保将被取消或终止,财务担保提供方应事先通知船旗国主管当局。

11 各成员国应要求悬挂其旗帜的船舶在船上携带一份由财务担保提供方签发的财务担保证书或其他财务担保证明文件。应在船上的醒目位置张贴一份副本,供海员知悉。若有不止一个财务担保提供方提供保障,应在船上携带每个财务担保提供方所提供的文件。

12 在财务担保有效期结束之前不得停止财务担保,除非财务担保提供方提前至少 30 天通知船旗国主管当局。

13 财务担保应预备支付所覆盖的在该文件有效期内产生的所有合同索赔。

14 财务担保证书或其他证明文件应包含附件 A4-I 所要求的信息。它应为英文版或附英文译文。

标准 A4.2.2 合同索赔的处理

1 就标准 A4.2.1 第 8 款和本标准而言,“合同索赔”一词系指按照国家法律、海员就业协议或集体协议的规定,与任何因职业伤害、疾病或风险而引起的海员死亡或长期残疾相关的索赔。

2 标准 A4.2.1 第 1(b)款所规定的财务担保制度可采取社会保障计划、保险或基金或其他类似安排的形式。成员国应当经与相关船东组织和海员组织协商后,确定财务担保制度的形式。

3 国家法律和法规应确保做出有效安排,通过迅速和公平的程序受理、处理和公正解决与标准 A4.2.1 第 8 款中提及的赔偿相关的合同索赔。

导则 B4.2.1 船东的责任

1 标准 A4.2.1 第 3(a)款所要求的支付全额工资可不包括奖金。

2   National laws or regulations may provide that a shipowner shall cease to be liable to bear the costs of a sick or injured seafarer from the time at which that seafarer can claim medical benefits under a scheme of compulsory sickness insurance, compulsory accident insurance or workers' compensation for accidents.

3   National laws or regulations may provide that burial expenses paid by the shipowner shall be reimbursed by an insurance institution in cases in which funeral benefit is payable in respect of the deceased seafarer under laws or regulations relating to social insurance or workers' compensation.

Guideline B4.2.2   Treatment of contractual claims

1   National laws or regulations should provide that the parties to the payment of a contractual claim may use the Model Receipt and Release Form set out in Appendix B4-I.

Regulation 4.3
Health and safety protection and accident prevention

Purpose: To ensure that seafarers' work environment on board ships promotes occupational safety and health

1   Each Member shall ensure that seafarers on ships that fly its flag are provided with occupational health protection and live, work and train on board ship in a safe and hygienic environment.

2   Each Member shall develop and promulgate national guidelines for the management of occupational safety and health on board ships that fly its flag, after consultation with representative shipowners' and seafarers' organizations and taking into account applicable codes, guidelines and standards recommended by international organizations, national administrations and maritime industry organizations.

3   Each Member shall adopt laws and regulations and other measures addressing the matters specified in the Code, taking into account relevant international instruments, and set standards for occupational safety and health protection and accident prevention on ships that fly its flag.

Standard A4.3   Health and safety protection and accident prevention

1   The laws and regulations and other measures to be adopted in accordance with Regulation 4.3, paragraph 3, shall include the following subjects:

(**a**)   the adoption and effective implementation and promotion of occupational safety and health policies and programmes on ships that fly the Member's flag, including risk evaluation as well as training and instruction of seafarers;

(**b**)   reasonable precautions to prevent occupational accidents, injuries and diseases on board ship, including measures to reduce and prevent the risk of exposure to harmful levels of ambient factors and chemicals as well as the risk of injury or disease that may arise from the use of equipment and machinery on board ships;

2 国家法律或法规可以规定：从患病或受伤海员能够根据疾病强制保险计划、事故强制保险计划或工人事故赔偿计划索取医疗保险之日起，船东不再对支付其费用的事宜负有责任。

3 如果根据有关社会保险和工人赔偿的法律或法规可对死亡海员支付丧葬补助，国家法律或法规可规定由一保险机构偿付船东已支付的费用。

导则 4.2.2　合同索赔的处理

1 国家法律或法规应规定涉及支付合同索赔的各方可使用附录 B4-I 提供的收据和解除责任书范本。

规则 4.3
保护健康和安全及防止事故

目的：确保海员的船上工作环境有利于职业安全和健康

1 各成员国应确保悬挂其旗帜的船舶上的海员得到职业健康保护，并且在一个安全和卫生的环境下在船上生活、工作和参加培训。

2 各成员国应在与代表船东的组织和代表海员的组织协商后，并考虑到国际组织、国家管理机关和海运业的组织所建议的适用守则、导则和标准，为悬挂其旗帜的船舶的职业安全和健康管理制定和颁布国家导则。

3 各成员国应通过国家法律和法规及其他措施处理守则中规定的事项，同时考虑到相关的国际文件，并为悬挂其旗帜的船舶规定职业安全和健康保护及防止事故的标准。

标准 A4.3　保护健康和安全及防止事故

1 根据规则 4.3 第 3 款通过的法律和法规或其他措施应包括以下主题：

（**a**）　在悬挂其旗帜的船舶上通过和有效实施并促进职业安全和健康政策和计划，包括风险评估及培训和指导海员；

（**b**）　采取合理预防措施，防止船上的职业事故及伤害和疾病，包括减少和防止置身于有害水平的环境因素和化学品中的风险以及由于使用船上设备和机械而可能引起的伤害和疾病的风险；

(**c**) on-board programmes for the prevention of occupational accidents, injuries and diseases and for continuous improvement in occupational safety and health protection, involving seafarers' representatives and all other persons concerned in their implementation, taking account of preventive measures, including engineering and design control, substitution of processes and procedures for collective and individual tasks, and the use of personal protective equipment; and

(**d**) requirements for inspecting, reporting and correcting unsafe conditions and for investigating and reporting on-board occupational accidents.

2 The provisions referred to in paragraph 1 of this Standard shall:

(**a**) take account of relevant international instruments dealing with occupational safety and health protection in general and with specific risks, and address all matters relevant to the prevention of occupational accidents, injuries and diseases that may be applicable to the work of seafarers and particularly those which are specific to maritime employment;

(**b**) clearly specify the obligation of shipowners, seafarers and others concerned to comply with the applicable standards and with the ship's occupational safety and health policy and programme with special attention being paid to the safety and health of seafarers under the age of 18;

(**c**) specify the duties of the master or a person designated by the master, or both, to take specific responsibility for the implementation of and compliance with the ship's occupational safety and health policy and programme; and

(**d**) specify the authority of the ship's seafarers appointed or elected as safety representatives to participate in meetings of the ship's safety committee. Such a committee shall be established on board a ship on which there are five or more seafarers.

3 The laws and regulations and other measures referred to in Regulation 4.3, paragraph 3, shall be regularly reviewed in consultation with the representatives of the shipowners' and seafarers' organizations and, if necessary, revised to take account of changes in technology and research in order to facilitate continuous improvement in occupational safety and health policies and programmes and to provide a safe occupational environment for seafarers on ships that fly the Member's flag.

4 Compliance with the requirements of applicable international instruments on the acceptable levels of exposure to workplace hazards on board ships and on the development and implementation of ships' occupational safety and health policies and programmes shall be considered as meeting the requirements of this Convention.

5 The competent authority shall ensure that:

(**a**) occupational accidents, injuries and diseases are adequately reported, taking into account the guidance provided by the International Labour Organization with respect to the reporting and recording of occupational accidents and diseases;

（**c**）　船上防止职业事故、伤害和疾病及确保不断改善职业安全和健康保护的计划,让海员代表和所有其他有关人员参与其实施,同时考虑到预防性的措施,包括工程和设计控制、对成组或独立的任务采取替代工序或程序以及使用个人保护设备等;以及

（**d**）　关于检查、报告和纠正不安全的状况的要求以及关于调查和报告船上安全事故的要求。

2　本标准第 1 款所述的规定应:

（**a**）　考虑到涉及一般性和具有特殊风险的职业安全和健康保护的相关国际文件,并应针对那些可能适用于海员工作,特别是那些海上就业所特有的与防止职业事故、伤害和疾病有关的所有事项;

（**b**）　明确规定船东、海员和其他有关人员遵守适用的标准和船上职业安全与健康政策和计划的义务并特别注意 18 岁以下海员的安全和健康;

（**c**）　规定船长和(或)船长指定的人员的职责,以承担履行和实施船舶的职业安全和健康方针和计划的具体责任;以及

（**d**）　规定船上被任命或选举为安全代表参与船舶安全委员会的海员的权威。在有 5 名或以上海员的船上应成立此委员会。

3　规则 4.3 第 3 款中所述的法律和法规及其他措施,应与有关船东和海员组织的代表协商予以定期审查,并在必要时加以修订,以便考虑到技术和研究方面的变化,从而促进对职业安全和健康政策和计划的不断改善,并为悬挂其旗帜船舶上的海员提供一个安全的职业环境。

4　符合适用的国际文件中关于船上工作场所中危害的可接受水平的要求以及关于制定和实施船上职业安全和健康政策和计划的要求,应被视为满足了本公约的要求。

5　主管当局应确保:

（**a**）　考虑到国际劳工组织关于报告和记录职业事故和疾病的指导,使职业事故、伤害和疾病得到充分报告;

(**b**) comprehensive statistics of such accidents and diseases are kept, analysed and published and, where appropriate, followed up by research into general trends and into the hazards identified; and

(**c**) occupational accidents are investigated.

6 Reporting and investigation of occupational safety and health matters shall be designed to ensure the protection of seafarers' personal data, and shall take account of the guidance provided by the International Labour Organization on this matter.

7 The competent authority shall cooperate with shipowners' and seafarers' organizations to take measures to bring to the attention of all seafarers information concerning particular hazards on board ships, for instance, by posting official notices containing relevant instructions.

8 The competent authority shall require that shipowners conducting risk evaluation in relation to management of occupational safety and health refer to appropriate statistical information from their ships and from general statistics provided by the competent authority.

Guideline B4. 3   Health and safety protection and accident prevention

Guideline B4. 3. 1   Provisions on occupational accidents, injuries and diseases

1 The provisions required under Standard A4. 3 should take into account the ILO code of practice entitled Accident Prevention on Board Ship at Sea and in Port, 1996, and subsequent versions and other related ILO and other international standards and guidelines and codes of practice regarding occupational safety and health protection, including any exposure levels that they may identify. Account should also be taken of the latest version of the Guidance on Eliminating Shipboard Harassment and Bullying jointly published by the International Chamber of Shipping and the International Transport Workers' Federation.

2 The competent authority should ensure that the national guidelines for the management of occupational safety and health address the following matters, in particular:

(**a**)   general and basic provisions;

(**b**)   structural features of the ship, including means of access and asbestos-related risks;

(**c**)   machinery;

(**d**)   the effects of the extremely low or high temperature of any surfaces with which seafarers may be in contact;

(**e**)   the effects of noise in the workplace and in shipboard accommodation;

(**f**)   the effects of vibration in the workplace and in shipboard accommodation;

(**g**)   the effects of ambient factors, other than those referred to in subparagraphs (e) and (f), in the workplace and in shipboard accommodation, including tobacco smoke;

(**h**)   special safety measures on and below deck;

(**i**)   loading and unloading equipment;

144

（**b**） 此类事故和疾病的全面统计材料得以保持、分析和公布，并且在适宜时，对总体趋势和所确定的危害进行跟踪研究；以及

（**c**） 对职业事故开展调查。

6 职业安全和健康事项的报告与调查的安排应确保海员的个人资料得到保护，并应考虑到国际劳工组织关于此事项提供的指南。

7 主管当局应与船东和海员组织合作，采取措施使所有海员注意有关船上特殊危险的信息，例如通过张贴包含相关指导的正式通知。

8 主管当局应要求船东利用来自其船舶的统计资料和主管当局提供的一般性统计资料开展职业安全与健康管理的风险评估。

导则 B4.3 保护健康和安全及防止事故

导则 B4.3.1 关于职业事故、伤害和疾病的规定

1 标准 A4.3 中的规定应考虑到标题为《1996 年海上和港口防止船上事故》的 ILO 实用守则及其以后的版本，以及关于职业安全和健康保护的其他相关的 ILO 和其他国际标准、指南和行为守则，包括这些规定中可能确定的任何工作场所环境暴露水平。还应考虑到由国际航运公会和国际运输工人联合会联合出版的最新版《关于消除船上骚扰和欺凌的指南》。

2 主管当局应确保关于职业安全和健康管理的国家指南要特别涉及以下事项：

（**a**） 一般和基本规定；

（**b**） 船舶结构特征，包括出入通道和与石棉有关的风险；

（**c**） 机器；

（**d**） 海员可能会接触到的任何高温或低温表面的影响；

（**e**） 工作场所和船上起居舱室中的噪声影响；

（**f**） 工作场所和船上起居舱室中的振动影响；

（**g**） 工作场所和船上起居舱室内除（e）和（f）项中所述以外的环境因素的影响，包括吸烟的影响；

（**h**） 甲板上和甲板下的特别安全措施；

（**i**） 装卸设备；

(j)   fire prevention and fire-fighting;

(k)   anchors, chains and lines;

(l)   dangerous cargo and ballast;

(m)   personal protective equipment for seafarers;

(n)   work in enclosed spaces;

(o)   physical and mental effects of fatigue;

(p)   the effects of drug and alcohol dependency;

(q)   HIV/AIDS protection and prevention; and

(r)   emergency and accident response.

3   The assessment of risks and reduction of exposure on the matters referred to in paragraph 2 of this Guideline should take account of the physical occupational health effects, including manual handling of loads, noise and vibration, the chemical and biological occupational health effects, the mental occupational health effects, the physical and mental health effects of fatigue, and occupational accidents. The necessary measures should take due account of the preventive principle according to which, among other things, combating risk at the source, adapting work to the individual, especially as regards the design of workplaces, and replacing the dangerous by the non-dangerous or the less dangerous, have precedence over personal protective equipment for seafarers.

4   In addition, the competent authority should ensure that the implications for health and safety are taken into account, particularly in the following areas:

(a)   emergency and accident response;

(b)   the effects of drug and alcohol dependency;

(c)   HIV/AIDS protection and prevention; and

(d)   harassment and bullying.

Guideline B4. 3. 2   Exposure to noise

1   The competent authority, in conjunction with the competent international bodies and with representatives of shipowners' and seafarers' organizations concerned, should review on an ongoing basis the problem of noise on board ships with the objective of improving the protection of seafarers, in so far as practicable, from the adverse effects of exposure to noise.

2   The review referred to in paragraph 1 of this Guideline should take account of the adverse effects of exposure to excessive noise on the hearing, health and comfort of seafarers and the measures to be prescribed or recommended to reduce shipboard noise to protect seafarers. The measures to be considered should include the following:

（**j**） 防火和灭火；

（**k**） 锚、锚链和绳索；

（**l**） 危险货物和压载；

（**m**） 海员个人保护设备；

（**n**） 在封闭处所工作；

（**o**） 疲劳对身心的影响；

（**p**） 毒品和酒精依赖的影响；

（**q**） 艾滋病病毒/艾滋病的防护；以及

（**r**） 应急和事故反应。

3 关于本导则第 2 款所述项目的风险评估和减少危险的措施应考虑到：身体因素对职业健康的影响，包括人工装卸货物、噪声和振动；化学因素和生物因素对职业健康的影响；心理因素对职业健康的影响；疲劳对身心健康的影响以及职业事故。必要的措施应充分考虑到预防性原则，根据这一原则，最重要的是从源头降低风险，使工作适合于个人，特别是关于工作场所的设计，优先考虑用无危险或危险性小的设计来取代危险的设计，然后再考虑海员的个人保护设备。

4 此外，主管当局应确保特别考虑以下方面对健康和安全的影响：

（**a**） 应急和事故反应；

（**b**） 毒品和酒精依赖的影响；

（**c**） 艾滋病病毒/艾滋病的防护；以及

（**d**） 骚扰和欺凌。

导则 B4.3.2 噪声问题

1 主管当局应与主管的国际机构和有关船东组织的代表和海员组织的代表一起，以尽实际可能改善对海员保护，使其免受置身于噪声环境中的不利影响为目标，不断审议船上的噪声问题。

2 本导则第 1 款中所述的审议应考虑到置身于过度的噪声中对海员的听觉、健康和舒适感产生的不利影响，以及为减少船上噪声、保护海员需规定或建议的措施。需要考虑的措施应包括：

(**a**) instruction of seafarers in the dangers to hearing and health of prolonged exposure to high noise levels and in the proper use of noise protection devices and equipment;

(**b**) provision of approved hearing protection equipment to seafarers where necessary; and

(**c**) assessment of risk and reduction of exposure levels to noise in all accommodation and recreational and catering facilities, as well as engine rooms and other machinery spaces.

Guideline B4.3.3   Exposure to vibration

1   The competent authority, in conjunction with the competent international bodies and with representatives of shipowners' and seafarers' organizations concerned, and taking into account, as appropriate, relevant international standards, should review on an ongoing basis the problem of vibration on board ships with the objective of improving the protection of seafarers, in so far as practicable, from the adverse effects of vibration.

2   The review referred to in paragraph 1 of this Guideline should cover the effect of exposure to excessive vibration on the health and comfort of seafarers and the measures to be prescribed or recommended to reduce shipboard vibration to protect seafarers. The measures to be considered should include the following:

(**a**) instruction of seafarers in the dangers to their health of prolonged exposure to vibration;

(**b**) provision of approved personal protective equipment to seafarers where necessary; and

(**c**) assessment of risks and reduction of exposure to vibration in all accommodation and recreational and catering facilities by adopting measures in accordance with the guidance provided by the ILO code of practice entitled Ambient Factors in the Workplace, 2001, and any subsequent revisions, taking account of the difference between exposure in those areas and in the workplace.

Guideline B4.3.4   Obligations of shipowners

1   Any obligation on the shipowner to provide protective equipment or other accident prevention safeguards should, in general, be accompanied by provisions requiring their use by seafarers and by a requirement for seafarers to comply with the relevant accident prevention and health protection measures.

2   Account should also be taken of Articles 7 and 11 of the Guarding of Machinery Convention, 1963 (No. 119), and the corresponding provisions of the Guarding of Machinery Recommendation, 1963 (No. 118), under which the obligation to ensure compliance with the requirement that machinery in use is properly guarded, and its use without appropriate guards prevented, rests on the employer, while there is an obligation on the worker not to use machinery without the guards being in position nor to make inoperative the guards provided.

（**a**）　向海员讲解长时间置身于高分贝噪声中可能对听觉和健康造成的危害,以及噪声防护装置和器材的妥善使用;

（**b**）　凡必要时向海员提供经认可的听觉保护设备;以及

（**c**）　进行风险分析并减少所有起居舱室及娱乐和膳食服务设施以及机舱和其他机器处所的噪声水平。

导则 B4.3.3　振动问题

1　主管当局应与主管的国际机构和有关船东和海员组织的代表一起,并适当考虑相关的国际标准,以尽实际可能保护海员免受振动的不利影响为目标,不断审议船上的振动问题。

2　本导则第 1 款所述的审议应包括置身于过度的振动环境中对海员健康和舒适感的影响,以及为减少船上振动以保护海员需规定或建议的措施。需要考虑的措施应包括:

（**a**）　向海员讲解长时间置身于振动环境中对其健康的危害;

（**b**）　如必要,向海员提供经认可的个人保护设备;以及

（**c**）　进行风险分析并根据标题为《2001 年工作场所的环境因素》的 ILO 实用守则及其任何后续修订本采取措施,减少所有起居舱室及娱乐和膳食服务设施内的振动程度,并考虑到置身于这些场所内的振动和置身于生活场所内的振动之间的区别。

导则 B4.3.4　船东的责任

1　一般而言,任何关于船东须提供防护性设备或其他防止事故的保障措施的义务,都应配套以要求海员使用此设备和要求海员遵守有关防止事故和健康保护措施的规定。

2　还应考虑《1963 年机器防护公约》（第 119 号）第 7、11 条以及《1963 年机器防护建议书》（第 118 号）的相应规定,根据这些规定,雇主有责任确保符合对使用的机器进行适当的防护、防止使用无保护装置机器的要求;而工人则有不使用未安保护装置的机器的责任,亦不得损坏这些保护装置。

Guideline B4. 3. 5   Reporting and collection of statistics

1   All occupational accidents and occupational injuries and diseases should be reported so that they can be investigated and comprehensive statistics can be kept, analysed and published, taking account of protection of the personal data of the seafarers concerned. Reports should not be limited to fatalities or to accidents involving the ship.

2   The statistics referred to in paragraph 1 of this Guideline should record the numbers, nature, causes and effects of occupational accidents and occupational injuries and diseases, with a clear indication, as applicable, of the department on board a ship, the type of accident and whether at sea or in port.

3   Each Member should have due regard to any international system or model for recording accidents to seafarers which may have been established by the International Labour Organization.

Guideline B4. 3. 6   Investigations

1   The competent authority should undertake investigations into the causes and circumstances of all occupational accidents and occupational injuries and diseases resulting in loss of life or serious personal injury, and such other cases as may be specified in national laws or regulations.

2   Consideration should be given to including the following as subjects of investigation:

(a)   working environment, such as working surfaces, layout of machinery, means of access, lighting and methods of work;

(b)   incidence in different age groups of occupational accidents and occupational injuries and diseases;

(c)   special physiological or psychological problems created by the shipboard environment;

(d)   problems arising from physical stress on board a ship, in particular as a consequence of increased workload;

(e)   problems arising from and effects of technical developments and their influence on the composition of crews;

(f)   problems arising from any human failures; and

(g)   problems arising from harassment and bullying.

Guideline B4. 3. 7   National protection and prevention programmes

1   In order to provide a sound basis for measures to promote occupational safety and health protection and prevention of accidents, injuries and diseases which are due to particular hazards of maritime employment, research should be undertaken into general trends and into such hazards as are revealed by statistics.

导则 B4.3.5 报告和统计数据收集

1 一切职业事故以及职业伤害和疾病均应报告,从而能够对其开展调查以及保存、分析和公布完整的统计数据,并应考虑到保护有关海员的个人资料。报告不应局限于伤亡事故或涉及船舶的事故。

2 本导则第 1 款中所述的统计资料应包括职业事故及职业伤害和疾病的次数、性质、原因和影响,并如果可行,应明确指出事故发生在船上的岗位、事故的类型以及在海上还是在港口。

3 各成员国应充分考虑到国际劳工组织可能业已确立的任何记录海员事故的国际制度或模式。

导则 B4.3.6 调查

1 主管当局应对所有造成人命损失或严重人身伤害的职业事故及职业伤害和疾病,以及国家法律或法规可能规定的其他事件的原因和当时的情况进行调查。

2 应考虑将以下内容列入调查项目:

(**a**) 工作环境,如作业场地、机器布置、出入通道、照明和工作方法;

(**b**) 不同年龄组发生职业事故及职业伤害和疾病的发生率;

(**c**) 船上环境产生的特殊的生理或心理问题;

(**d**) 船上的体力消耗,特别是工作量增加引起的体力消耗所产生的问题;

(**e**) 技术进步带来的问题和后果及其对船员组成的影响;

(**f**) 任何人为失误产生的问题;和

(**g**) 骚扰和欺凌引起的问题。

导则 B4.3.7 国家保护和预防计划

1 为了给促进职业安全和健康保护并防止由于海上就业的特有危害而发生的事故、伤害和疾病的措施打下坚实的基础,应对统计结果所揭示的总趋势以及各种危害进行研究。

2 The implementation of protection and prevention programmes for the promotion of occupational safety and health should be so organized that the competent authority, shipowners and seafarers or their representatives and other appropriate bodies may play an active role, including through such means as information sessions, on-board guidelines on maximum exposure levels to potentially harmful ambient workplace factors and other hazards or outcomes of a systematic risk evaluation process. In particular, national or local joint occupational safety and health protection and accident prevention committees or ad hoc working parties and on-board committees, on which shipowners' and seafarers' organizations concerned are represented, should be established.

3 Where such activity takes place at company level, the representation of seafarers on any safety committee on board that shipowner's ships should be considered.

Guideline B4.3.8 Content of protection and prevention programmes

1 Consideration should be given to including the following in the functions of the committees and other bodies referred to in Guideline B4.3.7, paragraph 2:

(**a**) the preparation of national guidelines and policies for occupational safety and health management systems and for accident prevention provisions, rules and manuals;

(**b**) the organization of occupational safety and health protection and accident prevention training and programmes;

(**c**) the organization of publicity on occupational safety and health protection and accident prevention, including films, posters, notices and brochures; and

(**d**) the distribution of literature and information on occupational safety and health protection and accident prevention so that it reaches seafarers on board ships.

2 Relevant provisions or recommendations adopted by the appropriate national authorities or organizations or international organizations should be taken into account by those preparing texts of occupational safety and health protection and accident prevention measures or recommended practices.

3 In formulating occupational safety and health protection and accident prevention programmes, each Member should have due regard to any code of practice concerning the safety and health of seafarers which may have been published by the International Labour Organization.

Guideline B4.3.9 Instruction in occupational safety and health protection and the prevention of occupational accidents

1 The curriculum for the training referred to in Standard A4.3, paragraph 1(a), should be reviewed periodically and brought up to date in the light of development in types and sizes of ships and in their equipment, as well as changes in manning practices, nationality, language and the organization of work on board ships.

2 在组织实施促进职业安全和健康保护的防护计划时,主管当局、船东和海员或其代表及其他适当部门应发挥积极作用,包括采用诸如召开信息通报会,制定关于有潜在危害的工作场所环境因素和其他危害的最高接触水平的船上指南,或考虑系统性风险评估过程的结果等方式。特别是应成立由有关船东组织和海员组织的代表参加的全国性或地方性职业安全和健康保护及防止事故联合委员会或特设工作组和船上委员会。

3 如果在公司的层面上开展此类活动,应考虑在该船东的船舶上的任何安全委员会中都有海员的代表参加。

导则 B4.3.8　保护和预防计划的内容

1 应考虑在导则 B4.3.7 第 2 款中所述委员会和其他机构的职能中包括以下内容:

（**a**）　制定职业安全和健康管理系统及防止事故发生的规定、规章和手册的国家指南与政策;

（**b**）　组织职业安全、健康保护及事故防止的培训和计划;

（**c**）　通过电影、宣传画、通知和小册子等形式,组织对职业安全和健康保护及事故防止进行宣传;以及

（**d**）　散发有关职业安全和健康保护及事故防止的材料和信息,以方便在船上工作的海员们获取。

2 负责起草有关职业安全和健康保护及防止事故发生的措施或建议做法的人员应考虑国内有关当局或组织或者国际组织所通过的有关规定或建议。

3 在制订关于职业安全和健康保护及防止事故发生的计划时,各成员国应充分考虑国际劳工组织可能业已出版的关于海员安全和健康的任何实用守则。

导则 B4.3.9　职业安全和健康保护及防止职业事故的指导

1 应根据船舶类型和尺度及其设备的发展,以及在配员实践、国籍、语言和船上工作组织等方面发生的变化,定期审议标准 A4.3 第 1(a) 款中所述的培训大纲,对其加以更新。

2   There should be continuous occupational safety and health protection and accident prevention publicity. Such publicity might take the following forms:

(**a**)   educational audiovisual material, such as films, for use in vocational training centres for seafarers and where possible shown on board ships;

(**b**)   display of posters on board ships;

(**c**)   inclusion in periodicals read by seafarers of articles on the hazards of maritime employment and on occupational safety and health protection and accident prevention measures; and

(**d**)   special campaigns using various publicity media to instruct seafarers, including campaigns on safe working practices.

3   The publicity referred to in paragraph 2 of this Guideline should take account of the different nationalities, languages and cultures of seafarers on board ships.

Guideline B4.3.10   Safety and health education of young seafarers

1   Safety and health regulations should refer to any general provisions on medical examinations before and during employment and on the prevention of accidents and the protection of health in employment, which may be applicable to the work of seafarers. Such regulations should specify measures which will minimize occupational dangers to young seafarers in the course of their duties.

2   Except where a young seafarer is recognized as fully qualified in a pertinent skill by the competent authority, the regulations should specify restrictions on young seafarers undertaking, without appropriate supervision and instruction, certain types of work presenting special risk of accident or of detrimental effect on their health or physical development, or requiring a particular degree of maturity, experience or skill. In determining the types of work to be restricted by the regulations, the competent authority might consider in particular work involving:

(**a**)   the lifting, moving or carrying of heavy loads or objects;

(**b**)   entry into boilers, tanks and cofferdams;

(**c**)   exposure to harmful noise and vibration levels;

(**d**)   operating hoisting and other power machinery and tools, or acting as signallers to operators of such equipment;

(**e**)   handling mooring or tow lines or anchoring equipment;

(**f**)   rigging;

(**g**)   work aloft or on deck in heavy weather;

(**h**)   nightwatch duties;

(**i**)   servicing of electrical equipment;

2 有关职业安全和健康保护及防止事故发生的宣传应持续不断。宣传可采取如下形式：

（**a**） 在海员职业培训中心或可能时在船上放映诸如电影等视听教育材料；

（**b**） 在船上张贴宣传画；

（**c**） 在海员阅读的期刊上刊登关于海上就业中的危害以及关于职业安全和健康保护及防止事故发生的措施的文章；以及

（**d**） 组织专题宣传运动利用各种宣传媒体来教育海员，包括对安全工作实践的宣传推广。

3 本导则第 2 款所述的宣传工作应考虑船上海员的不同民族、语言和文化。

导则 B4.3.10　未成年海员的安全和健康教育

1 安全和健康的法规应参考有关上岗之前和工作期间须进行体格检查以及可能适用于海员工作的有关工作中防止事故发生和健康保护的任何一般规定。这些法规还应明确规定尽量减少未成年海员在履行职责过程中遇到的职业危险的措施。

2 除非未成年海员经主管当局认可充分具备相关的技能资格，法规应规定一些限制条件，防止未成年海员在没有适当的监督和教育的情况下从事某些存在特别事故风险或对其健康或者发育有不利影响，或对成熟程度、工作经验和技能有特殊要求的工作。在确定法规中需要加以限制的工作类型时，主管当局可特别考虑涉及以下方面的工作：

（**a**） 搬起、挪动或运送重荷或者重物；

（**b**） 进入锅炉、液舱和隔离舱；

（**c**） 置身于达到有害水平的噪声和振动中；

（**d**） 操作起重机械或其他动力设备或者器械，或向操作此类机械的人员发信号；

（**e**） 操作系泊或拖缆或锚具；

（**f**） 索具作业；

（**g**） 恶劣天气中在高处或甲板上工作；

（**h**） 夜间值班；

（**i**） 电气设备维护；

(j)   exposure to potentially harmful materials, or harmful physical agents such as dangerous or toxic substances and ionizing radiations;

(k)   the cleaning of catering machinery; and

(l)   the handling or taking charge of ships' boats.

3   Practical measures should be taken by the competent authority or through the appropriate machinery to bring to the attention of young seafarers information concerning the prevention of accidents and the protection of their health on board ships. Such measures could include adequate instruction in courses, official accident prevention publicity intended for young persons and professional instruction and supervision of young seafarers.

4   Education and training of young seafarers both ashore and on board ships should include guidance on the detrimental effects on their health and well-being of the abuse of alcohol and drugs and other potentially harmful substances, and the risk and concerns relating to HIV/ AIDS and of other health risk related activities.

Guideline B4. 3. 11   International cooperation

1   Members, with the assistance as appropriate of intergovernmental and other international organizations, should endeavour, in cooperation with each other, to achieve the greatest possible uniformity of action for the promotion of occupational safety and health protection and prevention of accidents.

2   In developing programmes for promoting occupational safety and health protection and prevention of accidents under Standard A4. 3, each Member should have due regard to relevant codes of practice published by the International Labour Organization and the appropriate standards of international organizations.

3   Members should have regard to the need for international cooperation in the continuous promotion of activity related to occupational safety and health protection and prevention of occupational accidents. Such cooperation might take the form of:

(a)   bilateral or multilateral arrangements for uniformity in occupational safety and health protection and accident prevention standards and safeguards;

(b)   exchange of information on particular hazards affecting seafarers and on means of promoting occupational safety and health protection and preventing accidents;

(c)   assistance in testing of equipment and inspection according to the national regulations of the flag State;

(d)   collaboration in the preparation and dissemination of occupational safety and health protection and accident prevention provisions, rules or manuals;

(e)   collaboration in the production and use of training aids; and

(f)   joint facilities for, or mutual assistance in, the training of seafarers in occupational safety and health protection, accident prevention and safe working practices.

（**j**） 接触有潜在危害的物质,或诸如危险或者有毒物质等有害的物理试剂,及受到电离辐射;

（**k**） 清洗厨房机械;和

（**l**） 操作或负责小艇。

3 主管当局应采取或通过适当机制采取切实措施使未成年海员注意关于船上防止事故发生和保护其健康的信息。这些措施可包括适当的课程讲授、针对未成年海员的防止事故发生的宣传、以及对未成年海员的专业指导和监督。

4 在陆地和船上对未成年海员的教育和培训应包括关于酗酒和吸毒及其他潜在有害物质对其身心健康的危害以及与艾滋病病毒/艾滋病病有关的风险和担忧及其他存在健康风险的活动的指导。

导则 B4.3.11 国际合作

1 在政府间和其他国际组织的适当帮助下,各成员国应相互合作,在促进职业安全和健康保护及防止事故方面尽最大可能采取统一行动。

2 在根据标准 A4.3 制订促进职业安全和健康保护及防止事故的计划时,各成员国应充分考虑到国际劳工组织出版的行为守则和国际组织的适当标准。

3 各成员国应注意到在不断促进与职业安全和健康保护及防止职业事故有关的活动方面进行国际合作的必要性。此类合作可采取以下形式:

（**a**） 为统一有关职业安全和健康保护及防止事故发生的标准和保障而做出的双边或多边安排;

（**b**） 交换关于影响海员的特殊风险和关于职业安全和健康保护及防止事故发生的方法方面的信息;

（**c**） 根据船旗国的国家规定,在设备测试以及检查方面提供帮助;

（**d**） 在编制与传播职业安全和健康及防止事故发生的规定、规则或手册的过程中开展合作;

（**e**） 在培训材料的制作和使用方面开展合作;以及

（**f**） 在对海员进行职业安全和健康保护及防止事故发生和安全工作实践方面的培训方面,共享设施或相互提供帮助。

Regulation 4. 4

Access to shore-based welfare facilities

Purpose: To ensure that seafarers working on board a ship have access to shore-based facilities and services to secure their health and well-being

1　Each Member shall ensure that shore-based welfare facilities, where they exist, are easily accessible. The Member shall also promote the development of welfare facilities, such as those listed in the Code, in designated ports to provide seafarers on ships that are in its ports with access to adequate welfare facilities and services.

2　The responsibilities of each Member with respect to shore-based facilities, such as welfare, cultural, recreational and information facilities and services, are set out in the Code.

Standard A4. 4　Access to shore-based welfare facilities

1　Each Member shall require, where welfare facilities exist on its territory, that they are available for the use of all seafarers, irrespective of nationality, race, colour, sex, religion, political opinion or social origin and irrespective of the flag State of the ship on which they are employed or engaged or work.

2　Each Member shall promote the development of welfare facilities in appropriate ports of the country and determine, after consultation with the shipowners' and seafarers' organizations concerned, which ports are to be regarded as appropriate.

3　Each Member shall encourage the establishment of welfare boards which shall regularly review welfare facilities and services to ensure that they are appropriate in the light of changes in the needs of seafarers resulting from technical, operational and other developments in the shipping industry.

Guideline B4. 4　Access to shore-based welfare facilities

Guideline B4. 4. 1　Responsibilities of Members

1　Each Member should:

　（a）　take measures to ensure that adequate welfare facilities and services are provided for seafarers in designated ports of call and that adequate protection is provided to seafarers in the exercise of their profession; and

　（b）　take into account, in the implementation of these measures, the special needs of seafarers, especially when in foreign countries and when entering war zones, in respect of their safety, health and spare-time activities.

2　Arrangements for the supervision of welfare facilities and services should include participation by representative shipowners' and seafarers' organizations concerned.

规则 4.4
获得使用岸上福利设施

目的:确保在船上工作的海员能使用岸上设施和服务,以确保其健康和福利

1 各成员国应确保如果存在岸上福利设施,应易于供海员使用。成员国还应促进在指定的港口发展本守则中所列的福利设施,为挂靠其港口的船舶上的海员提供充分的福利设施与服务。

2 各成员国关于岸上设施的责任,如福利、文化、娱乐和信息等设施和服务,在守则中规定。

标准 A4.4 获得使用岸上福利设施

1 各成员国应要求,如果在其领土内存在福利设施,这些设施应向所有海员开放,无论其国籍、种族、肤色、性别、宗教信仰、政治见解或社会出身,也无论他们受雇、受聘或工作的船舶的船旗国。

2 各成员国应促进其国内适当的港口发展港口福利设施,并应在与有关的船东和海员组织协商后,确定哪些港口应被视为适当的港口。

3 各成员国应鼓励设立福利委员会,该委员会应经常性地审查福利设施与服务,以保证其适应因海运业技术、运营和其他方面发展所带来的海员需求的改变。

导则 B4.4 获得使用岸上福利设施

导则 B4.4.1 成员国的责任

1 各成员国应:

(**a**) 采取措施确保在指定的挂靠港口向海员提供充分的福利设施与服务,并对从事其职业的海员提供充分的保护;以及

(**b**) 在实施这些措施时,应考虑海员的安全、健康和业余活动方面的特殊需求,特别是在外国和进入战争地区时。

2 对福利设施与服务的监督安排应包括有代表性的船东组织和海员组织的参与。

3   Each Member should take measures designed to expedite the free circulation among ships, central supply agencies and welfare establishments of welfare materials such as films, books, newspapers and sports equipment for use by seafarers on board their ships and in welfare centres ashore.

4   Members should cooperate with one another in promoting the welfare of seafarers at sea and in port. Such cooperation should include the following:

(**a**)   consultations among competent authorities aimed at the provision and improvement of seafarers' welfare facilities and services, both in port and on board ships;

(**b**)   agreements on the pooling of resources and the joint provision of welfare facilities in major ports so as to avoid unnecessary duplication;

(**c**)   organization of international sports competitions and encouragement of the participation of seafarers in sports activities; and

(**d**)   organization of international seminars on the subject of welfare of seafarers at sea and in port.

Guideline B4. 4. 2   Welfare facilities and services in ports

1   Each Member should provide or ensure the provision of such welfare facilities and services as may be required, in appropriate ports of the country.

2   Welfare facilities and services should be provided, in accordance with national conditions and practice, by one or more of the following:

(**a**)   public authorities;

(**b**)   shipowners' and seafarers' organizations concerned under collective agreements or other agreed arrangements; and

(**c**)   voluntary organizations.

3   Necessary welfare and recreational facilities should be established or developed in ports. These should include:

(**a**)   meeting and recreation rooms as required;

(**b**)   facilities for sports and outdoor facilities, including competitions;

(**c**)   educational facilities; and

(**d**)   where appropriate, facilities for religious observances and for personal counselling.

4   These facilities may be provided by making available to seafarers in accordance with their needs facilities designed for more general use.

3 各成员国应采取措施,加速福利产品在船舶、中央供应机构和福利部门之间的自由周转,例如影片、图书、报纸和体育器材,供海员在其船舶上和岸上福利中心使用。

4 成员国应相互合作,促进海员在海上和港口的福利。这种合作应包括以下内容:

（**a**） 为提供和改善海员在港口和船上的福利设施与服务,在各主管当局之间进行协商;

（**b**） 就集中资源及在主要港口联合提供福利设施达成协议,以避免不必要的重复;

（**c**） 组织国际体育竞赛,并鼓励海员参加体育活动;以及

（**d**） 组织以海员在海上和港口的福利为主题的国际研讨会。

导则 B4.4.2 港口的福利设施与服务

1 各成员国应在其国内的适当港口提供或确保提供可能要求的福利设施和服务。

2 应根据国家条件和惯例,由下列一方或几方提供福利设施与服务:

（**a**） 公共当局;

（**b**） 有关的船东和海员组织,按照集体协议或其他协议安排来提供;以及

（**c**） 志愿组织。

3 应在港口建立或发展必要的福利和娱乐设施,这些设施应包括:

（**a**） 必要的会议室和娱乐室;

（**b**） 运动设施和户外活动设施,包括比赛设施;

（**c**） 教育设施;以及

（**d**） 凡适当时,举行宗教仪式和进行个人咨询的场所。

4 在提供这些设施时,可以按海员的需要向其提供设计成更针对一般性使用的设施。

5   Where large numbers of seafarers of different nationalities require facilities such as hotels, clubs and sports facilities in a particular port, the competent authorities or bodies of the countries of origin of the seafarers and of the flag States, as well as the international associations concerned, should consult and cooperate with the competent authorities and bodies of the country in which the port is situated and with one another, with a view to the pooling of resources and to avoiding unnecessary duplication.

6   Hotels or hostels suitable for seafarers should be available where there is need for them. They should provide facilities equal to those found in a good-class hotel, and should wherever possible be located in good surroundings away from the immediate vicinity of the docks. Such hotels or hostels should be properly supervised, the prices charged should be reasonable in amount and, where necessary and possible, provision should be made for accommodating seafarers' families.

7   These accommodation facilities should be open to all seafarers, irrespective of nationality, race, colour, sex, religion, political opinion or social origin and irrespective of the flag State of the ship on which they are employed or engaged or work. Without in any way infringing this principle, it may be necessary in certain ports to provide several types of facilities, comparable in standard but adapted to the customs and needs of different groups of seafarers.

8   Measures should be taken to ensure that, as necessary, technically competent persons are employed full time in the operation of seafarers' welfare facilities and services, in addition to any voluntary workers.

Guideline B4. 4. 3   Welfare boards

1   Welfare boards should be established, at the port, regional and national levels, as appropriate. Their functions should include:

(a)   keeping under review the adequacy of existing welfare facilities and monitoring the need for the provision of additional facilities or the withdrawal of underutilized facilities; and

(b)   assisting and advising those responsible for providing welfare facilities and ensuring coordination between them.

2   Welfare boards should include among their members representatives of shipowners' and seafarers' organizations, the competent authorities and, where appropriate, voluntary organizations and social bodies.

3   As appropriate, consuls of maritime States and local representatives of foreign welfare organizations should, in accordance with national laws and regulations, be associated with the work of port, regional and national welfare boards.

Guideline B4. 4. 4   Financing of welfare facilities

1   In accordance with national conditions and practice, financial support for port welfare facilities should be made available through one or more of the following:

5 如果在某特定港口有人数众多的不同国籍海员需要旅馆、俱乐部和体育设施等设施,海员本国和船旗国的各主管当局或机构以及有关国际协会应与港口所在国的各主管当局和机构协商与合作,并进行相互间的协商与合作,以集中资源并避免不必要的重复。

6 在需要的地方,应有适合于海员住宿的旅馆或招待所。这些旅馆或招待所应提供与一流宾馆相同的设施,并在可能时,位于周边环境良好的区域,避开紧靠码头的位置。这些旅馆和招待所应受到适当的监督,收费应合理,并在需要和可能时,应为海员家庭供应食宿。

7 这些居住设施应向所有海员开放,无论其国籍、种族、肤色、性别、信仰、政治观点或社会出身,也不论他们受雇、受聘或工作的船舶的船旗国。在绝不违背此原则的前提下,可能有必要在某些港口提供一些不同类型的设施,标准相当但适合于不同海员群体的习惯和需要。

8 除志愿工作者外,还应采取必要的措施保证雇用全职、合格的技术人员从事海员的福利设施的经营与服务工作。

导则 B4.4.3　福利委员会

1 如适宜,应在港口、地区和国家层次上成立福利委员会。其职能应包括:

（a） 经常审查现有福利设施是否适当,监督有无需要提供更多设施或撤销利用率不足的设施;以及

（b） 帮助提供福利设施的主管人员,并向他们提出建议,保证他们之间的协调。

2 福利委员会的成员应包括船东组织和海员组织的代表、各主管当局的代表以及在适当时,志愿组织和社会机构的代表。

3 在适当时,应根据国家法律和法规,使海运国家的领事和外国福利组织的当地代表参与港口、地区和国家福利委员会的工作。

导则 B4.4.4　福利设施的资金来源

1 根据国家条件和做法,应通过以下一种或几种途径为港口福利设施提供财政支持:

(**a**)   grants from public funds;

(**b**)   levies or other special dues from shipping sources;

(**c**)   voluntary contributions from shipowners, seafarers, or their organizations; and

(**d**)   voluntary contributions from other sources.

2   Where welfare taxes, levies and special dues are imposed, they should be used only for the purposes for which they are raised.

Guideline B4. 4. 5   Dissemination of information and facilitation measures

1   Information should be disseminated among seafarers concerning facilities open to the general public in ports of call, particularly transport, welfare, entertainment and educational facilities and places of worship, as well as facilities provided specifically for seafarers.

2   Adequate means of transport at moderate prices should be available at any reasonable time in order to enable seafarers to reach urban areas from convenient locations in the port.

3   All suitable measures should be taken by the competent authorities to make known to shipowners and to seafarers entering port any special laws and customs, the contravention of which may jeopardize their freedom.

4   Port areas and access roads should be provided by the competent authorities with adequate lighting and signposting and regular patrols for the protection of seafarers.

Guideline B4. 4. 6   Seafarers in a foreign port

1   For the protection of seafarers in foreign ports, measures should be taken to facilitate:

(**a**)   access to consuls of their State of nationality or State of residence; and

(**b**)   effective cooperation between consuls and the local or national authorities.

2   Seafarers who are detained in a foreign port should be dealt with promptly under due process of law and with appropriate consular protection.

3   Whenever a seafarer is detained for any reason in the territory of a Member, the competent authority should, if the seafarer so requests, immediately inform the flag State and the State of nationality of the seafarer. The competent authority should promptly inform the seafarer of the right to make such a request. The State of nationality of the seafarer should promptly notify the seafarer's next of kin. The competent authority should allow consular officers of these States immediate access to the seafarer and regular visits thereafter so long as the seafarer is detained.

4   Each Member should take measures, whenever necessary, to ensure the safety of seafarers from aggression and other unlawful acts while ships are in their territorial waters and especially in approaches to ports.

5   Every effort should be made by those responsible in port and on board a ship to facilitate shore leave for seafarers as soon as possible after a ship's arrival in port.

（**a**）　公共基金拨款；

（**b**）　航运征税或其他专项收费；

（**c**）　船东、海员或其组织的自愿捐款；以及

（**d**）　其他渠道的自愿捐款。

2　如果征收福利税、税费和专项费，它们应仅用于其筹款之初衷。

导则 B4.4.5　信息传播和便利措施

1　应在海员中传播有关挂靠港内向普通公众开放的设施的信息，特别是交通、福利、娱乐和教育设施与礼拜场所，以及专门为海员提供的设施的信息。

2　为使海员能从港口里方便的地点进入市区，应在任何合理时间内提供充足的廉价交通工具。

3　主管当局应采取所有适当措施使进入港口的船东和海员了解那些倘若违反即可能危及其自由的法律和习俗。

4　主管当局应在港口区域和进出港通道提供充分的照明和路标，并定期巡逻，以保护海员。

导则 B4.4.6　在外国港口的海员

1　为保护在外国港口的海员，应采取措施以便于：

（**a**）　接触其国籍国或居住国的领事；以及

（**b**）　领事与地方或国家当局的有效合作。

2　应按照适当的法律程序迅速处理被滞留在外国港口的海员并给予充分的领事保护。

3　不论出于何种原因，如果海员在一成员国领土上被滞留，若该海员提出要求，主管当局应立即通知船旗国和海员的国籍国。主管当局应即通知海员有提出此种要求的权利。海员的国籍国应即通知海员最近的亲属。如海员被拘禁，主管当局应允许这些国家的领事官员立即会见该海员，并在此后允许定期会见该海员。

4　当船舶位于一成员国的领海，特别是港口的引航道时，该成员国应在必要时采取措施以保证海员安全，使他们不受侵袭和其他非法行为的侵害。

5　港口和船上的负责人员应尽一切努力在船舶抵达港口后，方便海员尽快上岸休假。

Regulation 4. 5

Social security

Purpose: To ensure that measures are taken with a view to providing seafarers with access to social security protection

1 Each Member shall ensure that all seafarers and, to the extent provided for in its national law, their dependants have access to social security protection in accordance with the Code without prejudice however to any more favourable conditions referred to in paragraph 8 of Article 19 of the Constitution.

2 Each Member undertakes to take steps, according to its national circumstances, individually and through international cooperation, to achieve progressively comprehensive social security protection for seafarers.

3 Each Member shall ensure that seafarers who are subject to its social security legislation, and, to the extent provided for in its national law, their dependants, are entitled to benefit from social security protection no less favourable than that enjoyed by shoreworkers.

Standard A4. 5 Social security

1 The branches to be considered with a view to achieving progressively comprehensive social security protection under Regulation 4. 5 are: medical care, sickness benefit, unemployment benefit, old-age benefit, employment injury benefit, family benefit, maternity benefit, invalidity benefit and survivors' benefit, complementing the protection provided for under Regulations 4. 1, on medical care, and 4. 2, on shipowners' liability, and under other titles of this Convention.

2 At the time of ratification, the protection to be provided by each Member in accordance with Regulation 4. 5, paragraph 1, shall include at least three of the nine branches listed in paragraph 1 of this Standard.

3 Each Member shall take steps according to its national circumstances to provide the complementary social security protection referred to in paragraph 1 of this Standard to all seafarers ordinarily resident in its territory. This responsibility could be satisfied, for example, through appropriate bilateral or multilateral agreements or contribution-based systems. The resulting protection shall be no less favourable than that enjoyed by shoreworkers resident in their territory.

4 Notwithstanding the attribution of responsibilities in paragraph 3 of this Standard, Members may determine, through bilateral and multilateral agreements and through provisions adopted in the framework of regional economic integration organizations, other rules concerning the social security legislation to which seafarers are subject.

5 Each Member's responsibilities with respect to seafarers on ships that fly its flag shall include those provided for by Regulations 4. 1 and 4. 2 and the related provisions of the Code, as well as those that are inherent in its general obligations under international law.

规则 4.5

社会保障

目的:确保采取措施向海员提供社会保障的保护

1 各成员国应确保所有海员,以及按其国家法律的规定,其受赡养人,能够获得符合守则的社会保障的保护,但不得妨碍《国际劳工组织章程》第十九条第八款中所述的任何更优厚条件。

2 各成员国承诺根据其本国情况采取措施,独自或通过国际合作逐步为海员提供全面的社会保障的保护。

3 各成员国应确保受到其社会保障法律管辖的海员,以及在其国家法律规定的范围内,其受赡养人,有权享受不低于岸上工人所享受的社会保障的保护。

标准 A4.5 社会保障

1 为逐步完成规则 4.5 中的全面社会保障保护而需要考虑的分项包括:医疗、疾病津贴、失业津贴、老年津贴、工伤津贴、家庭津贴、生育津贴、病残津贴和遗属津贴,并由规则 4.1 规定的医疗、规则 4.2 规定的船东责任、以及本公约其他标题所提供的保护来补充。

2 在批准本公约时,各成员国根据规则 4.5 第 1 款所提供的保护应至少包括本标准第 1 款所列 9 个分项中的 3 个。

3 各成员国应根据其本国情况采取措施,向通常在其领土内居住的海员提供本标准第 1 款所述的补充社会保障的保护。例如,此义务可通过适当的双边或多边协定或者建立在付费基础上的制度来履行。所构成的保护应不低于居住在其领土上的岸上工人。

4 尽管有本标准第 3 款中的责任归属,成员国仍可以通过双边或多边协定并通过区域经济一体化组织框架中通过的规定,来决定关于海员社会保障立法的其他规定。

5 各成员国对悬挂其旗帜的船舶上的海员的责任应包括规则 4.1 和规则 4.2 及守则相关条款所规定的内容,以及他们根据国际法要履行的一般义务中的固有内容。

6 Each Member shall give consideration to the various ways in which comparable benefits will, in accordance with national law and practice, be provided to seafarers in the absence of adequate coverage in the branches referred to in paragraph 1 of this Standard.

7 The protection under Regulation 4. 5, paragraph 1, may, as appropriate, be contained in laws or regulations, in private schemes or in collective bargaining agreements or in a combination of these.

8 To the extent consistent with their national law and practice, Members shall cooperate, through bilateral or multilateral agreements or other arrangements, to ensure the maintenance of social security rights, provided through contributory or noncontributory schemes, which have been acquired, or are in the course of acquisition, by all seafarers regardless of residence.

9 Each Member shall establish fair and effective procedures for the settlement of disputes.

10 Each Member shall at the time of ratification specify the branches for which protection is provided in accordance with paragraph 2 of this Standard. It shall subsequently notify the Director-General of the International Labour Office when it provides social security protection in respect of one or more other branches stated in paragraph 1 of this Standard. The Director-General shall maintain a register of this information and shall make it available to all interested parties.

11 The reports to the International Labour Office pursuant to article 22 of the Constitution, shall also include information regarding steps taken in accordance with Regulation 4. 5, paragraph 2, to extend protection to other branches.

Guideline B4. 5   Social security

1 The protection to be provided at the time of ratification in accordance with Standard A4. 5, paragraph 2, should at least include the branches of medical care, sickness benefit and employment injury benefit.

2 In the circumstances referred to in Standard A4. 5, paragraph 6, comparable benefits may be provided through insurance, bilateral and multilateral agreements or other effective means, taking into consideration the provisions of relevant collective bargaining agreements. Where such measures are adopted, seafarers covered by such measures should be advised of the means by which the various branches of social security protection will be provided.

3 Where seafarers are subject to more than one national legislation covering social security, the Members concerned should cooperate in order to determine by mutual agreement which legislation is to apply, taking into account such factors as the type and level of protection under the respective legislations which is more favourable to the seafarer concerned as well as the seafarer's preference.

4 The procedures to be established under Standard A4. 5, paragraph 9, should be designed to cover all disputes relevant to the claims of the seafarers concerned, irrespective of the manner in which the coverage is provided.

6 各成员国应考虑在没有本标准第 1 款所述分项险种的充分覆盖情况下,根据国家法律和惯例向海员提供类似福利的各种不同方法。

7 规则 4.5 第 1 款下的保护可视情况包含在法律或法规、私立机制或集体谈判协议中或者几种情况的组合中。

8 在与国家法律和惯例一致的范围内,成员国应通过双边或多边协定或其他安排进行合作,保证维持所有海员已经获得或正在获得的通过缴费或不缴费的机制所提供的社会保障权利,无论其居住地在哪里。

9 各成员国应建立公平而有效的争议解决程序。

10 各成员国在批准公约时应明确指出其根据本标准第 2 款所提供保护的分项险种。在其提供本标准第 1 款中所述的一种或几种其他分项的社会保障保护时应随即通知国际劳工局局长。局长应保存一份关于此信息的记录,以备所有相关各方索取。

11 按照《国际劳工组织章程》第二十二条向国际劳工局提交的报告还应包括关于根据规则 4.5 第 2 款采取措施将保护扩展到其他分项的信息。

导则 B4.5　社会保障

1 在批准公约时根据标准 A4.5 第 2 款所提供的保护分项应至少包括医疗、疾病津贴和工伤津贴。

2 在标准 A4.5 第 6 款所述的情况下,考虑到有关集体谈判协议的规定,可以通过保险、双边和多边协议或其他有效方式来提供类似的福利。如果采取了此种措施,应将各种社会保险保护分项的提供方式告知被此种措施所覆盖的海员。

3 如果海员受到不止一个国家的社会保障法律的管辖,有关成员国应开展合作,以便通过相互间的协议确定适用哪一国法律,并应考虑到在各自法律中,哪一个能向有关海员提供更优越的保护种类和水平以及海员的个人选择等因素。

4 根据标准 A4.5 第 9 款建立的程序应设计成涵盖与有关海员的追偿请求有关的所有争议,无论有关保障以何种方式提供。

5   Each Member which has national seafarers, non-national seafarers or both serving on ships that fly its flag should provide the social security protection in the Convention as applicable, and should periodically review the branches of social security protection in Standard A4. 5, paragraph 1, with a view to identifying any additional branches appropriate for the seafarers concerned.

6   The seafarers' employment agreement should identify the means by which the various branches of social security protection will be provided to the seafarer by the shipowner as well as any other relevant information at the disposal of the shipowner, such as statutory deductions from the seafarers' wages and shipowners' contributions which may be made in accordance with the requirements of identified authorized bodies pursuant to relevant national social security schemes.

7   The Member whose flag the ship flies should, in effectively exercising its jurisdiction over social matters, satisfy itself that the shipowners' responsibilities concerning social security protection are met, including making the required contributions to social security schemes.

Title 5
Compliance and enforcement

1   The Regulations in this Title specify each Member's responsibility to fully implement and enforce the principles and rights set out in the Articles of this Convention as well as the particular obligations provided for under its Titles 1, 2, 3 and 4.

2   Paragraphs 3 and 4 of Article VI, which permit the implementation of Part A of the Code through substantially equivalent provisions, do not apply to Part A of the Code in this Title.

3   In accordance with paragraph 2 of Article VI, each Member shall implement its responsibilities under the Regulations in the manner set out in the corresponding Standards of Part A of the Code, giving due consideration to the corresponding Guidelines in Part B of the Code.

4   The provisions of this Title shall be implemented bearing in mind that seafarers and shipowners, like all other persons, are equal before the law and are entitled to the equal protection of the law and shall not be subject to discrimination in their access to courts, tribunals or other dispute resolution mechanisms. The provisions of this Title do not determine legal jurisdiction or a legal venue.

Regulation 5. 1
Flag State responsibilities

Purpose: To ensure that each Member implements its responsibilities under this Convention with respect to ships that fly its flag

5 有本国海员和(或)非本国海员在悬挂其旗帜的船舶上服务的各成员国,应提供公约中适用的社会保障保护,并应定期审查标准 A4.5 第 1 款中的社会保障保护分项,以确定适合于有关海员的任何附加分项。

6 海员就业协议应明确由船东向海员提供各分项的社会保障保护的方式以及船东掌握的任何其他相关信息,例如根据有关的国家社会保障制度,按指定的经授权机构的要求可能从海员工资中法定扣减以及船东缴费的情况。

7 船舶所悬旗帜之成员国在对社会事项有效行使其管辖时,应确认船东履行了其关于社会保障的义务,包括向社会保障制度交纳了所要求的保险费。

标题五
遵守与执行

1 本标题下的规则确定了各成员国充分实施和执行本公约正文所规定之原则和权利及其标题一、二、三和四所规定之具体义务的责任。

2 允许通过实质上等效的规定来实施守则 A 部分的第六条第 3 和 4 款不适用于本标题下的守则 A 部分。

3 根据本公约第六条第 2 款,各成员国应以守则 A 部分的相应标准所规定的方式实施其在规则下的责任,并充分考虑到守则 B 部分的相关导则。

4 实施本标题中的规定时应切记,同任何其他人一样,海员和船东在法律面前平等,有权受到法律的同等保护,不得在诉诸法院、仲裁庭或其他争议解决机制方面受到歧视。本标题中的规定并不决定法律管辖权和法院所在地的选择。

规则 5.1
船旗国责任

目的:确保各成员国就悬挂其旗帜的船舶履行其在本公约下的责任

Regulation 5.1.1   General principles

1   Each Member is responsible for ensuring implementation of its obligations under this Convention on ships that fly its flag.

2   Each Member shall establish an effective system for the inspection and certification of maritime labour conditions, in accordance with Regulations 5.1.3 and 5.1.4 ensuring that the working and living conditions for seafarers on ships that fly its flag meet, and continue to meet, the standards in this Convention.

3   In establishing an effective system for the inspection and certification of maritime labour conditions, a Member may, where appropriate, authorize public institutions or other organizations (including those of another Member, if the latter agrees) which it recognizes as competent and independent to carry out inspections or to issue certificates or to do both. In all cases, the Member shall remain fully responsible for the inspection and certification of the working and living conditions of the seafarers concerned on ships that fly its flag.

4   A maritime labour certificate, complemented by a declaration of maritime labour compliance, shall constitute prima facie evidence that the ship has been duly inspected by the Member whose flag it flies and that the requirements of this Convention relating to working and living conditions of the seafarers have been met to the extent so certified.

5   Information about the system referred to in paragraph 2 of this Regulation, including the method used for assessing its effectiveness, shall be included in the Member's reports to the International Labour Office pursuant to article 22 of the Constitution.

Standard A5.1.1   General principles

1   Each Member shall establish clear objectives and standards covering the administration of its inspection and certification systems, as well as adequate overall procedures for its assessment of the extent to which those objectives and standards are being attained.

2   Each Member shall require all ships that fly its flag to have a copy of this Convention available on board.

Guideline B5.1.1   General principles

1   The competent authority should make appropriate arrangements to promote effective cooperation between public institutions and other organizations, referred to in Regulations 5.1.1 and 5.1.2, concerned with seafarers' shipboard working and living conditions.

2   In order to better ensure cooperation between inspectors and shipowners, seafarers and their respective organizations, and to maintain or improve seafarers' working and living conditions, the competent authority should consult the representatives of such organizations at regular intervals as to the best means of attaining these ends. The manner of such consultation should be determined by the competent authority after consulting with shipowners' and seafarers' organizations.

规则 5.1.1 一般原则

1 各成员国有责任确保悬挂其旗帜的船舶实施本公约为其规定的义务。

2 各成员国应根据规则 5.1.3 和 5.1.4 建立一个有效的海事劳工条件检查和发证系统,确保悬挂其旗帜船舶上的海员工作和生活条件符合并持续符合本公约中的标准。

3 在建立有效的海事劳工条件检查和发证系统时,凡适宜,成员国可以授权经其认可具备能力和独立性的公共机构或其他组织(包括另一成员国的机构或组织,如果其同意)开展检查和(或)发证工作。在所有情况下,成员国仍应对悬挂其旗帜船舶的有关海员的工作和生活条件的检查与发证负全部责任。

4 辅以一项海事劳工符合声明的海事劳工证书,应构成船舶已经过其船旗国正规检查,且本公约关于海员工作和生活条件的要求已在其所证明的范围内得到满足的表面证据。

5 关于本规则第 2 款所述系统的信息,包括用来评估其有效性的方法的信息,应包括在成员国根据《国际劳工组织章程》第二十二条提交给国际劳工局的报告中。

标准 A5.1.1 一般原则

1 各成员国应建立关于其检查和发证系统管理的明确目标和标准,以及对达到这些目标和标准的程度进行总体评估的适当程序。

2 各成员国应要求悬挂其旗帜的所有船舶均携带一份本公约。

导则 B5.1.1 一般原则

1 主管当局应作出适当的安排以促进规则 5.1.1 和 5.1.2 中所述的关注船上海员工作和生活条件的公共机构与其他组织之间的有效合作。

2 为了更好地确保检查员与船东、海员及其各自组织之间的合作,并且为了保持和改善海员的工作和生活条件,主管当局应定期与上述组织的代表就达到这些目标的最佳途径进行协商。此种协商的方式应由主管当局在与船东和海员组织协商后确定。

Regulation 5. 1. 2   Authorization of recognized organizations

1   The public institutions or other organizations referred to in paragraph 3 of Regulation 5. 1. 1 ("recognized organizations") shall have been recognized by the competent authority as meeting the requirements in the Code regarding competency and independence. The inspection or certification functions which the recognized organizations may be authorized to carry out shall come within the scope of the activities that are expressly mentioned in the Code as being carried out by the competent authority or a recognized organization.

2   The reports referred to in paragraph 5 of Regulation 5. 1. 1 shall contain information regarding any recognized organization, the extent of authorizations given and the arrangements made by the Member to ensure that the authorized activities are carried out completely and effectively.

Standard A5. 1. 2   Authorization of recognized organizations

1   For the purpose of recognition in accordance with paragraph 1 of Regulation 5. 1. 2, the competent authority shall review the competency and independence of the organization concerned and determine whether the organization has demonstrated, to the extent necessary for carrying out the activities covered by the authorization conferred on it, that the organization:

(**a**)   has the necessary expertise in the relevant aspects of this Convention and an appropriate knowledge of ship operations, including the minimum requirements for seafarers to work on a ship, conditions of employment, accommodation, recreational facilities, food and catering, accident prevention, health protection, medical care, welfare and social security protection;

(**b**)   has the ability to maintain and update the expertise of its personnel;

(**c**)   has the necessary knowledge of the requirements of this Convention as well as of applicable national laws and regulations and relevant international instruments; and

(**d**)   is of the appropriate size, structure, experience and capability commensurate with the type and degree of authorization.

2   Any authorizations granted with respect to inspections shall, as a minimum, empower the recognized organization to require the rectification of deficiencies that it identifies in seafarers' working and living conditions and to carry out inspections in this regard at the request of a port State.

3   Each Member shall establish:

(**a**)   a system to ensure the adequacy of work performed by recognized organizations, which includes information on all applicable national laws and regulations and relevant international instruments; and

(**b**)   procedures for communication with and oversight of such organizations.

规则 5.1.2　对认可组织的授权

1 规则 5.1.1 第 3 款所述的公共机构或其他组织("认可组织")应经主管当局认可满足本守则关于能力和独立性的要求。认可组织可以被授权从事的检查和发证职能应在本守则明确规定由主管当局或认可组织从事的活动范围之内。

2 规则 5.1.1 第 5 款所述之报告应包含关于任何认可组织的信息、所授权范围的信息和成员国为确保所授权的活动得以完整和有效地实施所做安排的信息。

标准 A5.1.2　对认可组织的授权

1 为根据规则 5.1.2 第 1 款的认可之目的,主管当局应审查有关组织的能力和独立性并确定该组织在开展经授权的活动所必要的限度内是否能够表明该组织:

（**a**）　在本公约的相关方面具备必要的专业知识和船舶营运的适当知识,包括对海员上船工作的最低要求、就业条件、起居舱室、娱乐设施、食品和膳食服务、防止事故、健康保护、医疗、福利和社会保障保护方面的知识;

（**b**）　具备维持和更新其人员专业水平的能力;

（**c**）　具备关于公约的要求以及适用的国家法律和法规及相关国际文件方面的必要知识;以及

（**d**）　规模、结构、经验和能力与其所被授权的类型和级别相当。

2 所准予的关于检查的任何授权,在最低限度上应授予该组织对发现的海员工作和生活条件方面的缺陷有要求纠正的权利,以及应港口国的要求开展这方面检查的权力。

3 各成员国应建立:

（**a**）　一个确保认可组织所做工作之恰当性的机制,包括所有关于适用的国家法律和法规及相关国际文件的信息;以及

（**b**）　与此类组织进行通信和对其进行监督的程序。

4   Each Member shall provide the International Labour Office with a current list of any recognized organizations authorized to act on its behalf and it shall keep this list up to date. The list shall specify the functions that the recognized organizations have been authorized to carry out. The Office shall make the list publicly available.

Guideline B5. 1. 2   Authorization of recognized organizations

1   The organization seeking recognition should demonstrate the technical, administrative and managerial competence and capacity to ensure the provision of timely service of satisfactory quality.

2   In evaluating the capability of an organization, the competent authority should determine whether the organization:

(a)   has adequate technical, managerial and support staff;

(b)   has sufficient qualified professional staff to provide the required service, representing an adequate geographical coverage;

(c)   has proven ability to provide a timely service of satisfactory quality; and

(d)   is independent and accountable in its operations.

3   The competent authority should conclude a written agreement with any organization that it recognizes for purposes of an authorization. The agreement should include the following elements:

(a)   scope of application;

(b)   purpose;

(c)   general conditions;

(d)   the execution of functions under authorization;

(e)   legal basis of the functions under authorization;

(f)   reporting to the competent authority;

(g)   specification of the authorization from the competent authority to the recognized organization; and

(h)   the competent authority's supervision of activities delegated to the recognized organization.

4   Each Member should require the recognized organizations to develop a system for qualification of staff employed by them as inspectors to ensure the timely updating of their knowledge and expertise.

5   Each Member should require the recognized organizations to maintain records of the services performed by them such that they are able to demonstrate achievement of the required standards in the items covered by the services.

4 各成员国应向国际劳工局提供一份关于目前授权代表其行事的任何认可组织的清单，并保持对清单的更新。该清单应明确认可组织经授权将履行的职能。国际劳工局应将该清单对公众开放。

导则 B5.1.2 对认可组织的授权

1 寻求认可的组织应表明其在技术、行政和管理方面的资质和能力，确保提供及时的优质服务。

2 在评估某一机构的能力时，主管当局应确定该组织是否：

（**a**） 具备充足的技术、管理和支持性工作人员；

（**b**） 具备充足的合格专业人员提供所要求的服务，有足够的地理覆盖范围；

（**c**） 具备经证实的提供及时的优质服务的能力；以及

（**d**） 其运作独立可靠。

3 主管当局应与其为授权之目的所认可的任何组织达成一份书面协议。该协议应包括以下要素：

（**a**） 适用范围；

（**b**） 目的；

（**c**） 一般条件；

（**d**） 行使授权的职能；

（**e**） 经授权职能的法律基础；

（**f**） 向主管当局报告；

（**g**） 主管当局向认可组织授权的具体内容；和

（**h**） 主管当局对认可组织代为行事活动的监督。

4 各成员国应要求认可组织制定一项关于被该组织雇用为检查员的人员的资格体系，以确保及时更新其知识和专业技能。

5 各成员国应要求认可组织保留其所做服务的记录，从而使它们能够表明在服务所涉及的项目中达到所要求的标准。

6 In establishing the oversight procedures referred to in Standard A5. 1. 2, paragraph 3 (b) , each Member should take into account the Guidelines for the Authorization of Organizations Acting on Behalf of the Administration, adopted in the framework of the International Maritime Organization.

Regulation 5. 1. 3   Maritime labour certificate and declaration of maritime labour compliance

1 This Regulation applies to ships of :

    (**a**)   500 gross tonnage or over, engaged in international voyages; and

    (**b**)   500 gross tonnage or over, flying the flag of a Member and operating from a port, or between ports, in another country.

For the purpose of this Regulation, "international voyage" means a voyage from a country to a port outside such a country.

2 This Regulation also applies to any ship that flies the flag of a Member and is not covered by paragraph 1 of this Regulation, at the request of the shipowner to the Member concerned.

3 Each Member shall require ships that fly its flag to carry and maintain a maritime labour certificate certifying that the working and living conditions of seafarers on the ship, including measures for ongoing compliance to be included in the declaration of maritime labour compliance referred to in paragraph 4 of this Regulation, have been inspected and meet the requirements of national laws or regulations or other measures implementing this Convention.

4 Each Member shall require ships that fly its flag to carry and maintain a declaration of maritime labour compliance stating the national requirements implementing this Convention for the working and living conditions for seafarers and setting out the measures adopted by the shipowner to ensure compliance with the requirements on the ship or ships concerned.

5 The maritime labour certificate and the declaration of maritime labour compliance shall conform to the model prescribed by the Code.

6 Where the competent authority of the Member or a recognized organization duly authorized for this purpose has ascertained through inspection that a ship that flies the Member's flag meets or continues to meet the standards of this Convention, it shall issue or renew a maritime labour certificate to that effect and maintain a publicly available record of that certificate.

7 Detailed requirements for the maritime labour certificate and the declaration of maritime labour compliance, including a list of the matters that must be inspected and approved, are set out in Part A of the Code.

6 在建立标准 A5.1.2 第 3(b) 款所述的监督程序时,各成员国应考虑在国际海事组织的框架内通过的《向代表主管当局行事的组织授权导则》。

规则 5.1.3 海事劳工证书和海事劳工符合声明

1 本规则适用于以下船舶:

(a) 从事国际航行的 500 总吨及以上船舶;以及

(b) 悬挂一成员国的旗帜并从另一成员国港口或在另一成员国港口之间航行的 500 总吨及以上船舶。

就本规则而言,"国际航行"系指从一国到该国以外的一个港口的航行。

2 如果船东向有关成员国提出请求,本规则还适用于悬挂该成员国的旗帜但未被本规则第 1 款所覆盖的船舶。

3 各成员国应要求悬挂其旗帜的船舶携带和保有一份海事劳工证书,证明该船舶上的海员工作和生活条件,包括本规则第 4 款所述的海事劳工符合声明中所提及的持续符合措施,已经过检查并满足国家法律或者法规或其他实施本公约之措施的要求。

4 各成员国应要求悬挂其旗帜的船舶携带和保有一份海事劳工符合声明,陈述在海员的工作和生活条件方面实施本公约的国家要求,并列明船东为确保符合对有关船舶的要求所采取的措施。

5 海事劳工证书和海事劳工符合声明应与守则所规定的范本相符。

6 如果成员国主管当局或为此目的正式授权的认可组织通过检查确定悬挂成员国旗帜的一艘船舶符合并持续符合本公约的标准,应就此向其签发或换新海事劳工证书并保持一份对公众开放的证书记录。

7 有关海事劳工证书和海事劳工符合声明的详细要求,包括必须检查和批准事项的清单,在守则的 A 部分中规定。

Standard A5. 1. 3   Maritime labour certificate and declaration of maritime labour compliance

1   The maritime labour certificate shall be issued to a ship by the competent authority, or by a recognized organization duly authorized for this purpose, for a period which shall not exceed five years. A list of matters that must be inspected and found to meet national laws and regulations or other measures implementing the requirements of this Convention regarding the working and living conditions of seafarers on ships before a maritime labour certificate can be issued is found in Appendix A5- I .

2   The validity of the maritime labour certificate shall be subject to an intermediate inspection by the competent authority, or by a recognized organization duly authorized for this purpose, to ensure continuing compliance with the national requirements implementing this Convention. If only one intermediate inspection is carried out and the period of validity of the certificate is five years, it shall take place between the second and third anniversary dates of the certificate. Anniversary date means the day and month of each year which will correspond to the date of expiry of the maritime labour certificate. The scope and depth of the intermediate inspection shall be equal to an inspection for renewal of the certificate. The certificate shall be endorsed following satisfactory intermediate inspection.

3   Notwithstanding paragraph 1 of this Standard, when the renewal inspection has been completed within three months before the expiry of the existing maritime labour certificate, the new maritime labour certificate shall be valid from the date of completion of the renewal inspection for a period not exceeding five years from the date of expiry of the existing certificate. When the renewal inspection is completed more than three months before the expiry date of the existing maritime labour certificate, the new maritime labour certificate shall be valid for a period not exceeding five years starting from the date of completion of the renewal inspection.

4   Notwithstanding paragraph 1 of this Standard, where, after a renewal inspection completed prior to the expiry of a maritime labour certificate, the ship is found to continue to meet national laws and regulations or other measures implementing the requirements of this Convention, but a new certificate cannot immediately be issued to and made available on board that ship, the competent authority, or the recognized organization duly authorized for this purpose, may extend the validity of the certificate for a further period not exceeding five months from the expiry date of the existing certificate, and endorse the certificate accordingly. The new certificate shall be valid for a period not exceeding five years starting from the date provided for in paragraph 3 of this Standard.

5   A maritime labour certificate may be issued on an interim basis:

  (**a**)   to new ships on delivery;

  (**b**)   when a ship changes flag; or

  (**c**)   when a shipowner assumes responsibility for the operation of a ship which is new to that shipowner.

标准 A5.1.3 海事劳工证书和海事劳工符合声明

1 海事劳工证书应由主管当局或主管当局为此目的而正式授权的认可组织签发给船舶，有效期不得超过 5 年。在签发海事劳工证书之前，在船上海员工作和生活条件方面必须予以检查并表明满足国家法律和法规或其他实施本公约要求之措施的项目清单见附录 A5-Ⅰ 。

2 海事劳工证书的有效性应取决于主管当局或主管当局为此目的而正式授权的认可组织所进行的一次中期检查，以确保持续符合实施本公约的国家要求。如果仅开展一次中期检查且证书的有效期为 5 年，该检查应安排在证书的第二和第三个周年日之间。周年日系指每年对应于海事劳工证书到期日的月份和日期。中期检查的范围和深度应与证书换证检查相同。在中期检查通过后应对证书进行签注。

3 尽管有本标准第 1 款的规定，如果在现有海事劳工证书到期之前三个月内完成了换证检查，新海事劳工证书应从完成换证检查之日起有效，有效期自现有证书到期之日起不超过五年。如果早于现有证书到期之前三个月完成了换证检查，新海事劳工证书的有效期从完成换证检查之日起不超过五年。

4 尽管有本标准第 1 款之规定，若在海事劳工证书到期之前完成了换证检查，船舶被认定为继续符合国家法律和法规或其他实施本公约要求的措施，但不能立即签发新证书给该船舶并随船携带该证书，主管当局或者为此目的而经正式授权的认可组织可延长现有证书的有效期，期限为自现有证书到期之日起不超过五个月，并据此认可该证书。新证书自本标准第 3 款所规定之日起有效，有效期不超过 5 年。

5 如有以下情形，海事劳工证书可以在临时的基础上签发：

（**a**） 刚交付的新船；

（**b**） 当船舶改换船旗时；或

（**c**） 当船东承担了其以前未经营过的某一船舶的经营责任时。

6   An interim maritime labour certificate may be issued for a period not exceeding six months by the competent authority or a recognized organization duly authorized for this purpose.

7   An interim maritime labour certificate may only be issued following verification that:

    (a)   the ship has been inspected, as far as reasonable and practicable, for the matters listed in Appendix A5- I , taking into account verification of items under subparagraphs (b), (c) and (d) of this paragraph;

    (b)   the shipowner has demonstrated to the competent authority or recognized organization that the ship has adequate procedures to comply with this Convention;

    (c)   the master is familiar with the requirements of this Convention and the responsibilities for implementation; and

    (d)   relevant information has been submitted to the competent authority or recognized organization to produce a declaration of maritime labour compliance.

8   A full inspection in accordance with paragraph 1 of this Standard shall be carried out prior to expiry of the interim certificate to enable issue of the full-term maritime labour certificate. No further interim certificate may be issued following the initial six months referred to in paragraph 6 of this Standard. A declaration of maritime labour compliance need not be issued for the period of validity of the interim certificate.

9   The maritime labour certificate, the interim maritime labour certificate and the declaration of maritime labour compliance shall be drawn up in the form corresponding to the models given in Appendix A5- II .

10   The declaration of maritime labour compliance shall be attached to the maritime labour certificate. It shall have two parts:

    (a)   Part I shall be drawn up by the competent authority which shall: (i) identify the list of matters to be inspected in accordance with paragraph 1 of this Standard; (ii) identify the national requirements embodying the relevant provisions of this Convention by providing a reference to the relevant national legal provisions as well as, to the extent necessary, concise information on the main content of the national requirements; (iii) refer to ship-type specific requirements under national legislation; (iv) record any substantially equivalent provisions adopted pursuant to paragraph 3 of Article VI; and (v) clearly indicate any exemption granted by the competent authority as provided in Title 3; and

    (b)   Part II shall be drawn up by the shipowner and shall identify the measures adopted to ensure ongoing compliance with the national requirements between inspections and the measures proposed to ensure that there is continuous improvement.

The competent authority or recognized organization duly authorized for this purpose shall certify Part II and shall issue the declaration of maritime labour compliance.

6 临时海事劳工证书可由主管当局或主管当局为此目的而正式授权的认可组织签发,有效期不超过 6 个月。

7 只有在核实了以下情况后才可签发临时海事劳工证书:

（**a**） 考虑到本款（b）、（c）和（d）中各个项目的核验,对船舶进行了附录 A5- Ⅰ 所列事项的合理可行的检查;

（**b**） 船东已向主管当局或认可组织表明,船舶具备适当程序来符合本公约的要求;

（**c**） 船长熟悉公约的要求和实施责任;以及

（**d**） 有关信息已提交给主管当局或认可组织来制作海事劳工符合声明。

8 在临时证书到期前,应根据本标准第 1 款进行全面检查,以便签发正式的海事劳工证书。在本标准第 6 款所述的最初 6 个月后不得再续发临时证书。在临时证书有效期内不必签发海事劳工符合声明。

9 海事劳工证书、临时海事劳工证书和海事劳工符合声明的格式应与附录 A5 - Ⅱ 中所列的范本相符。

10 海事劳工符合声明应附在海事劳工证书之后。声明应有两个部分:

（**a**） 第 Ⅰ 部分应由主管当局编制,该部分应:(i)明确根据本标准第 1 款将检查的事项清单;(ii)通过援引有关的国内法的规定来明确那些体现了公约有关规定的国内要求,以及在必要时提供关于国内要求主要内容的准确信息;(iii)提及国内立法中针对具体船舶类型的要求;(iv) 记录任何根据第六条第 3 款所采用的实质上等效的规定;并且(v) 明确指出标题三中规定的由主管当局准许的任何免除;以及

（**b**） 第 Ⅱ 部分应由船东编制并应明确所采取的确保在两次检验之间持续符合国内要求的措施和为确保不断改进而建议的措施。

主管机关或为此目的而正式授权的认可组织应对第 Ⅱ 部分予以认证并应签发海事劳工符合声明。

11   The results of all subsequent inspections or other verifications carried out with respect to the ship concerned and any significant deficiencies found during any such verification shall be recorded, together with the date when the deficiencies were found to have been remedied. This record, accompanied by an English-language translation where it is not in English, shall, in accordance with national laws or regulations, be inscribed upon or appended to the declaration of maritime labour compliance or made available in some other way to seafarers, flag State inspectors, authorized officers in port States and shipowners' and seafarers' representatives.

12   A current valid maritime labour certificate and declaration of maritime labour compliance, accompanied by an English-language translation where it is not in English, shall be carried on the ship and a copy shall be posted in a conspicuous place on board where it is available to the seafarers. A copy shall be made available in accordance with national laws and regulations, upon request, to seafarers, flag State inspectors, authorized officers in port States, and shipowners' and seafarers' representatives.

13   The requirement for an English-language translation in paragraphs 11 and 12 of this Standard does not apply in the case of a ship not engaged in an international voyage.

14   A certificate issued under paragraph 1 or 5 of this Standard shall cease to be valid in any of the following cases:

(a)   if the relevant inspections are not completed within the periods specified under paragraph 2 of this Standard;

(b)   if the certificate is not endorsed in accordance with paragraph 2 of this Standard;

(c)   when a ship changes flag;

(d)   when a shipowner ceases to assume the responsibility for the operation of a ship; and

(e)   when substantial changes have been made to the structure or equipment covered in Title 3.

15   In the case referred to in paragraph 14(c), (d) or (e) of this Standard, a new certificate shall only be issued when the competent authority or recognized organization issuing the new certificate is fully satisfied that the ship is in compliance with the requirements of this Standard.

16   A maritime labour certificate shall be withdrawn by the competent authority or the recognized organization duly authorized for this purpose by the flag State, if there is evidence that the ship concerned does not comply with the requirements of this Convention and any required corrective action has not been taken.

17   When considering whether a maritime labour certificate should be withdrawn in accordance with paragraph 16 of this Standard, the competent authority or the recognized organization shall take into account the seriousness or the frequency of the deficiencies.

11 对有关船舶的所有后续检查或其他核实的结果以及在任何此种核实过程中发现的重大缺陷都应予以记录,并记录所发现的缺陷得以纠正的日期。该记录,如果不是英文则连同英译文一起,应根据国家法律或法规写入或附在海事劳工符合声明之后,或采用一些其他方式提供给海员、船旗国检查员、港口国的授权官员及船东和海员的代表。

12 一份当前有效的海事劳工证书和海事劳工符合声明,在非英语的情况下辅以英译文,应随船携带,并将证书的一份副本张贴在船上海员明显可见的位置。如有要求,应根据国家法律和法规向海员、船旗国检查员、港口国授权官员、以及船东和海员的代表提供一份副本。

13 本标准第 11 和 12 款关于英译文的要求不适用于不从事国际航行的船舶。

14 根据本标准第 1 或 5 款签发的证书应在以下任何情况下终止效力:

（**a**）　如果在本标准第 2 款规定的期限内没有完成相关检查;

（**b**）　如果证书没有根据本标准第 2 款予以签注;

（**c**）　船舶转挂另一国旗帜;

（**d**）　如果船东不再承担某一船舶的经营责任;以及

（**e**）　如果对标题三所包括的结构和设备做出了实质性改变。

15 在本标准第 14(c)、(d)或(e)款所述的情况下,只有在签发新证书的主管当局或认可组织对船舶符合本标准要求的情况完全满意时才应签发新证书。

16 如果有证据表明有关船舶不符合本公约的要求且没有采取所要求的任何纠正措施,海事劳工证书应由主管当局或船旗国为此目的而正式授权的认可组织予以撤销。

17 在考虑是否应根据本标准第 16 款撤销一海事劳工证书时,主管当局或认可组织应考虑到缺陷的严重性或频发程度。

Guideline B5.1.3   Maritime labour certificate and declaration of maritime labour compliance

1   The statement of national requirements in Part I of the declaration of maritime labour compliance should include or be accompanied by references to the legislative provisions relating to seafarers' working and living conditions in each of the matters listed in Appendix A5-I. Where national legislation precisely follows the requirements stated in this Convention, a reference may be all that is necessary. Where a provision of the Convention is implemented through substantial equivalence as provided under Article VI, paragraph 3, this provision should be identified and a concise explanation should be provided. Where an exemption is granted by the competent authority as provided in Title 3, the particular provision or provisions concerned should be clearly indicated.

2   The measures referred to in Part II of the declaration of maritime labour compliance, drawn up by the shipowner, should, in particular, indicate the occasions on which ongoing compliance with particular national requirements will be verified, the persons responsible for verification, the records to be taken, as well as the procedures to be followed where non-compliance is noted. Part II may take a number of forms. It could make reference to other more comprehensive documentation covering policies and procedures relating to other aspects of the maritime sector, for example documents required by the International Safety Management (ISM) Code or the information required by Regulation 5 of the SOLAS Convention, Chapter XI-1 relating to the ship's Continuous Synopsis Record.

3   The measures to ensure ongoing compliance should include general international requirements for the shipowner and master to keep themselves informed of the latest advances in technology and scientific findings concerning workplace design, taking into account the inherent dangers of seafarers' work, and to inform the seafarers' representatives accordingly, thereby guaranteeing a better level of protection of the seafarers' working and living conditions on board.

4   The declaration of maritime labour compliance should, above all, be drafted in clear terms designed to help all persons concerned, such as flag State inspectors, authorized officers in port States and seafarers, to check that the requirements are being properly implemented.

5   An example of the kind of information that might be contained in a declaration of maritime labour compliance is given in Appendix B5-I.

6   When a ship changes flag as referred to in Standard A5.1.3, paragraph 14(c), and where both States concerned have ratified this Convention, the Member whose flag the ship was formerly entitled to fly should, as soon as possible, transmit to the competent authority of the other Member copies of the maritime labour certificate and the declaration of maritime labour compliance carried by the ship before the change of flag and, if applicable, copies of the relevant inspection reports if the competent authority so requests within three months after the change of flag has taken place.

导则 B5.1.3 海事劳工证书和海事劳工符合声明

1 海事劳工符合声明第 I 部分中关于国家要求的陈述应包括或后附对附录 A5-I 中所列各事项中与海员工作和生活条件有关的法律规定的引用。如果国家立法严格遵循了本公约中规定的要求,只需做出必要的参阅即可。如果公约的规定是通过第六条第 3 款规定的实质上等效来实施的,应明确该规定,并应提供简明的解释。如果主管机关准许了标题三中所规定的免除,应明确指出有关的具体规定。

2 船东所编写的海事劳工符合声明第 II 部分中所述的措施应特别指明对持续符合特定的国家要求进行核实的情景、负责核实的人员、将做出的记录以及发现不符合情况时须遵循的程序。第 II 部分可采用多种格式。它可以提及其他涵盖与海运行业其他方面有关的政策和程序的更全面性的文件,例如《国际安全管理(ISM)规则》所要求的证书或 SOLAS 公约第 XI-1 章第 5 条关于船舶《连续概要记录》所要求的信息。

3 确保持续符合的措施应包括一般性的国际要求,要求船东和船长自己不断了解关于工作场所设计的科技成果的最新进展,并考虑到海员工作固有的危险,并相应告知海员代表,从而保证船上海员工作和生活条件的更好保护水平。

4 最重要的是,海事劳工符合声明的编写应用词明确,以帮助所有相关人员,如船旗国检查员、港口国的授权官员和海员来核查各项要求正在得到妥善实施。

5 附录 B5-I 给出了一个海事劳工符合声明中可能包含的信息种类的范例。

6 如果船舶按标准 A5.1.3 第 14(c)款所述更换了船旗,并且两个有关国家均批准了本公约,如果另一成员国主管当局在换旗发生后三个月内提出此要求,船舶原来有权悬挂旗帜之成员国应尽快将换旗前该船舶所携带的海事劳工证书和海事劳工符合声明的副本以及,如果可行,所有与之相关的检查报告的副本转交给接受该船的另一成员国主管当局。

Regulation 5. 1. 4   Inspection and enforcement

1   Each Member shall verify, through an effective and coordinated system of regular inspections, monitoring and other control measures, that ships that fly its flag comply with the requirements of this Convention as implemented in national laws and regulations.

2   Detailed requirements regarding the inspection and enforcement system referred to in paragraph 1 of this Regulation are set out in Part A of the Code.

Standard A5. 1. 4   Inspection and enforcement

1   Each Member shall maintain a system of inspection of the conditions for seafarers on ships that fly its flag which shall include verification that the measures relating to working and living conditions as set out in the declaration of maritime labour compliance, where applicable, are being followed, and that the requirements of this Convention are met.

2   The competent authority shall appoint a sufficient number of qualified inspectors to fulfil its responsibilities under paragraph 1 of this Standard. Where recognized organizations have been authorized to carry out inspections, the Member shall require that personnel carrying out the inspection are qualified to undertake these duties and shall provide them with the necessary legal authority to perform their duties.

3   Adequate provision shall be made to ensure that the inspectors have the training, competence, terms of reference, powers, status and independence necessary or desirable so as to enable them to carry out the verification and ensure the compliance referred to in paragraph 1 of this Standard.

4   Inspections shall take place at the intervals required by Standard A5. 1. 3, where applicable. The interval shall in no case exceed three years.

5   If a Member receives a complaint which it does not consider manifestly unfounded or obtains evidence that a ship that flies its flag does not conform to the requirements of this Convention or that there are serious deficiencies in the implementation of the measures set out in the declaration of maritime labour compliance, the Member shall take the steps necessary to investigate the matter and ensure that action is taken to remedy any deficiencies found.

6   Adequate rules shall be provided and effectively enforced by each Member in order to guarantee that inspectors have the status and conditions of service to ensure that they are independent of changes of government and of improper external influences.

7   Inspectors, issued with clear guidelines as to the tasks to be performed and provided with proper credentials, shall be empowered:

(**a**)   to board a ship that flies the Member's flag;

(**b**)   to carry out any examination, test or inquiry which they may consider necessary in order to satisfy themselves that the standards are being strictly observed; and

规则 A5.1.4 检查和执行

1 各成员国应通过一个定期检查、监督和其他控制措施的有效与协调的系统,核实悬挂其旗帜的船舶符合由其国家法律和法规所实施的本公约的要求。

2 关于本规则第 1 款所述的检查和执行系统的详细要求在守则 A 部分中规定。

标准 A5.1.4 检查和执行

1 各成员国应维持一个对悬挂其旗帜船舶上的海员条件进行检查的系统,其中应包括凡适用时核实海事劳工符合声明中所列的与工作和生活条件有关的措施得以遵守,且满足本公约的要求。

2 主管当局应任命数量充足的合格检查员来履行其在本标准第 1 款下的责任。如果认可组织经授权实施检查,成员国应要求实施检查的人员有资格承担这些职责,并应向其提供行使其职责所必要的法定权力。

3 应做出充分的安排确保检查员具备必要或令人满意的培训、胜任能力、职责范围、权力、地位和独立性,从而使其能够开展核查并确保本标准第 1 款所述的符合情况。

4 如适用,检查应按标准 A5.1.3 所要求的间隔进行。在任何情况下该间隔不得超过 3 年。

5 如果成员国收到了其认为不是明显无根据的控诉,或者获得了证据,表明一艘悬挂其旗帜的船舶不符合本公约的要求,或在实施海事劳工符合声明中所列的措施方面有严重缺陷,该成员国应采取必要的步骤对该事项开展调查,确保采取行动纠正所发现的任何缺陷。

6 各成员国应制定适当的法规并加以有效执行,以保证检查员具有确保其独立于政府更迭和不当外部影响的地位与服务条件。

7 已获得关于所执行任务的明确指导并持有适当委任证书的检查员应被授权:

（**a**） 登上悬挂成员国旗帜的船舶;

（**b**） 为确定标准正在得到严格遵守,开展其可能认为必要的任何检查、测试或质询;以及

(**c**) to require that any deficiency is remedied and, where they have grounds to believe that deficiencies constitute a serious breach of the requirements of this Convention (including seafarers' rights), or represent a significant danger to seafarers' safety, health or security, to prohibit a ship from leaving port until necessary actions are taken.

8 Any action taken pursuant to paragraph 7(c) of this Standard shall be subject to any right of appeal to a judicial or administrative authority.

9 Inspectors shall have the discretion to give advice instead of instituting or recommending proceedings when there is no clear breach of the requirements of this Convention that endangers the safety, health or security of the seafarers concerned and where there is no prior history of similar breaches.

10 Inspectors shall treat as confidential the source of any grievance or complaint alleging a danger or deficiency in relation to seafarers' working and living conditions or a violation of laws and regulations and give no intimation to the shipowner, the shipowner's representative or the operator of the ship that an inspection was made as a consequence of such a grievance or complaint.

11 Inspectors shall not be entrusted with duties which might, because of their number or nature, interfere with effective inspection or prejudice in any way their authority or impartiality in their relations with shipowners, seafarers or other interested parties. In particular, inspectors shall:

(**a**) be prohibited from having any direct or indirect interest in any operation which they are called upon to inspect; and

(**b**) subject to appropriate sanctions or disciplinary measures, not reveal, even after leaving service, any commercial secrets or confidential working processes or information of a personal nature which may come to their knowledge in the course of their duties.

12 Inspectors shall submit a report of each inspection to the competent authority. One copy of the report in English or in the working language of the ship shall be furnished to the master of the ship and another copy shall be posted on the ship's notice board for the information of the seafarers and, upon request, sent to their representatives.

13 The competent authority of each Member shall maintain records of inspections of the conditions for seafarers on ships that fly its flag. It shall publish an annual report on inspection activities within a reasonable time, not exceeding six months, after the end of the year.

14 In the case of an investigation pursuant to a major incident, the report shall be submitted to the competent authority as soon as practicable, but not later than one month following the conclusion of the investigation.

15 When an inspection is conducted or when measures are taken under this Standard, all reasonable efforts shall be made to avoid a ship being unreasonably detained or delayed.

（c） 要求对任何缺陷予以纠正,并且,如果他们有理由相信某些缺陷构成了对本公约要求(包括海员的权利)的严重违反,或对海员的安全、健康或保安构成重大威胁,禁止船舶在采取必要措施前离港。

8 对于根据本标准第 7(c)款所采取的任何措施,均有向法院和行政当局上诉的权利。

9 如果没有对有关海员的安全、健康或保安构成危害的明显违反本公约要求的情况,且在过去没有类似违反的历史,检查员应有只提出劝诫但不提出或建议起诉的决定权。

10 检查员对指出有关海员工作和生活条件的危险或缺陷或者法律或法规被违反的任何抱怨或投诉来源应予保密,不向船东、船东代表或船舶经营人暗示进行某检查缘起于此类抱怨或投诉。

11 不得委托检查员行使因其数量或性质可能会干扰有效检查或以任何方式影响其对于船东、海员或其他利益方的权威或公正的职责。检查员特别应:

（a） 禁止在其被要求检查的任何活动中有任何直接或间接的利益;以及

（b） 受到适当的制裁或纪律措施的约束,不泄露在其行使职责中可能了解到的任何商业秘密或秘密工作程序或具有个人性质的信息,即使在离开岗位以后。

12 检查员应就每一次检查向主管当局提交一份报告。应将报告的一份英文或船上工作语言的副本提供给船舶的船长,同时将另一份副本张贴在船舶的布告栏内供海员知晓并应要求送给他们的代表。

13 各成员国的主管当局应保持关于悬挂其旗帜船舶上的海员条件检查的记录。其应在合理的时间内发布关于检查活动的年度报告,且该报告应在年终之后的 6 个月以内发布。

14 如系重大事故后的调查,应视可能尽快地提交报告,但不得晚于调查结束之后一个月。

15 当根据本标准进行检查或采取措施时,应做出一切合理努力,避免船舶被无理滞留或延误。

16 Compensation shall be payable in accordance with national laws and regulations for any loss or damage suffered as a result of the wrongful exercise of the inspectors' powers. The burden of proof in each case shall be on the complainant.

17 Adequate penalties and other corrective measures for breaches of the requirements of this Convention (including seafarers' rights) and for obstructing inspectors in the performance of their duties shall be provided for and effectively enforced by each Member.

Guideline B5. 1. 4 Inspection and enforcement

1 The competent authority and any other service or authority wholly or partly concerned with the inspection of seafarers' working and living conditions should have the resources necessary to fulfil their functions. In particular:

(**a**) each Member should take the necessary measures so that duly qualified technical experts and specialists may be called upon, as needed, to assist in the work of inspectors; and

(**b**) inspectors should be provided with conveniently situated premises, equipment and means of transport adequate for the efficient performance of their duties.

2 The competent authority should develop a compliance and enforcement policy to ensure consistency and otherwise guide inspection and enforcement activities related to this Convention. Copies of this policy should be provided to all inspectors and relevant law-enforcement officials and should be made available to the public and shipowners and seafarers.

3 The competent authority should establish simple procedures to enable it to receive information in confidence concerning possible breaches of the requirements of this Convention (including seafarers' rights) presented by seafarers directly or by representatives of the seafarers, and permit inspectors to investigate such matters promptly, including:

(**a**) enabling masters, seafarers or representatives of the seafarers to request an inspection when they consider it necessary; and

(**b**) supplying technical information and advice to shipowners and seafarers and organizations concerned as to the most effective means of complying with the requirements of this Convention and of bringing about a continual improvement in seafarers' on-board conditions.

4 Inspectors should be fully trained and sufficient in numbers to secure the efficient discharge of their duties with due regard to:

(**a**) the importance of the duties which the inspectors have to perform, in particular the number, nature and size of ships subject to inspection and the number and complexity of the legal provisions to be enforced;

(**b**) the resources placed at the disposal of the inspectors; and

16 对于因检查员错误地行使权利而遭受的任何损失或破坏,应根据国家法律和法规予以赔偿。在每种情况下均应由投诉者负责提供证据。

17 各成员国应规定并有效执行对于违反本公约要求(包括海员权利)及妨碍检查员履行其职责的行为的适当惩处和其他纠正措施。

导则 B5.1.4 检查和执行

1 主管当局和与海员工作和生活条件检查全部或部分有关的任何其他部门或当局应有履行其职能的所必需的资源。特别是:

(**a**) 各成员国应采取必要措施,使完全有资格的技术专家和专业人员可在需要时被请来协助检查员的工作;以及

(**b**) 应为所有的检查员配备地点方便的办公室、设备和交通手段,使其能高效地行使职责。

2 主管当局应制定一项遵守与执行政策,以确保一贯性并在其他方面指导与本公约有关的检查和执行活动。本政策的副本应提供给所有检查员和相关执法官员,并应使公众及船东和海员能够得到。

3 主管当局应建立简便的程序,使其能够秘密接收海员直接或由其代表提出的关于可能违反本公约要求(包括海员权利)的信息,并允许检查员迅速调查此类事项,包括:

(**a**) 使船长、海员或海员代表能在他们认为必要时要求进行检查;以及

(**b**) 就遵守本公约的要求和不断改善海员的船上条件的最有效的方法,向船东和海员及有关组织提供技术信息和建议。

4 对检查员应予全面培训,检查员的人数应足以保证其有效地履行其职责,并应充分考虑到:

(**a**) 检查员必须履行的职责的重要性,特别是应受检查的船舶数目、性质和大小以及需要执行的法律条款的数量和复杂性;

(**b**) 可供检查员使用的资源;和

(c) the practical conditions under which inspections must be carried out in order to be effective.

5 Subject to any conditions for recruitment to the public service which may be prescribed by national laws and regulations, inspectors should have qualifications and adequate training to perform their duties and where possible should have a maritime education or experience as a seafarer. They should have adequate knowledge of seafarers' working and living conditions and of the English language.

6 Measures should be taken to provide inspectors with appropriate further training during their employment.

7 All inspectors should have a clear understanding of the circumstances in which an inspection should be carried out, the scope of the inspection to be carried out in the various circumstances referred to and the general method of inspection.

8 Inspectors provided with proper credentials under the national law should at a minimum be empowered:

(a) to board ships freely and without previous notice; however, when commencing the ship inspection, inspectors should provide notification of their presence to the master or person in charge and, where appropriate, to the seafarers or their representatives;

(b) to question the master, seafarer or any other person, including the shipowner or the shipowner's representative, on any matter concerning the application of the requirements under laws and regulations, in the presence of any witness that the person may have requested;

(c) to require the production of any books, log books, registers, certificates or other documents or information directly related to matters subject to inspection, in order to verify compliance with the national laws and regulations implementing this Convention;

(d) to enforce the posting of notices required under the national laws and regulations implementing this Convention;

(e) to take or remove, for the purpose of analysis, samples of products, cargo, drinking water, provisions, materials and substances used or handled;

(f) following an inspection, to bring immediately to the attention of the shipowner, the operator of the ship or the master, deficiencies which may affect the health and safety of those on board ship;

(g) to alert the competent authority and, if applicable, the recognized organization to any deficiency or abuse not specifically covered by existing laws or regulations and submit proposals to them for the improvement of the laws or regulations; and

(h) to notify the competent authority of any occupational injuries or diseases affecting seafarers in such cases and in such manner as may be prescribed by laws and regulations.

（**c**） 有效开展检查所必备的实际条件。

5 以国家法律或法规可能规定的公共部门的任何招聘条件为前提,检查员应具备行使其职责的资格和受过这方面的适当培训,并且在可能时,应受过海事教育或有过当海员的经历。他们应充分了解海员的工作和生活条件并掌握英语。

6 应采取措施使检查员在就业期间接受适当的进一步培训。

7 所有检查员应清楚理解在何种情形下应该开展检查、在所提到的各种情形中开展检查的范围和检查的一般方法。

8 根据国家法律持有适当委任证书的检查员应至少被授权:

（**a**） 自由地和在不事先通知的情况下登船。但是,在开始对船舶进行检查时,检查员应将他们的到来通知船长或负责人,并在适宜时通知海员或其代表;

（**b**） 在当事人可能要求的任何证人在场的情况下,就涉及实施法律和法规的要求的任何事项询问船长、海员或任何其他人员,包括船东或船东的代表;

（**c**） 要求提供任何记录、航海日志、花名册、证书或其他与需要检查的事项直接相关的文件或资料,以便核实对实施本公约的国家法律和法规的符合情况;

（**d**） 根据实施本公约的国家法律和法规的要求规定张贴通知;

（**e**） 以进行分析为目的,提取或拿走曾使用过或者处理过的产品、货物、饮用水、给养、材料和物质的样品;

（**f**） 在检查后立即提请船东、船舶经营人或船长注意那些可能会影响到船上人员的健康与安全的缺陷;

（**g**） 提醒主管当局并在适用时提醒认可组织注意现行法律或法规没有明确包括的任何缺陷或弊病,并向其提出改善法律或法规的建议;以及

（**h**） 按照法律和法规可能规定的情况和方式,将影响海员的任何职业伤害或疾病通知主管当局。

9 When a sample referred to in paragraph 8(e) of this Guideline is being taken or removed, the shipowner or the shipowner's representative, and where appropriate a seafarer, should be notified or should be present at the time the sample is taken or removed. The quantity of such a sample should be properly recorded by the inspector.

10 The annual report published by the competent authority of each Member, in respect of ships that fly its flag, should contain:

(**a**) a list of laws and regulations in force relevant to seafarers' working and living conditions and any amendments which have come into effect during the year;

(**b**) details of the organization of the system of inspection;

(**c**) statistics of ships or other premises subject to inspection and of ships and other premises actually inspected;

(**d**) statistics on all seafarers subject to its national laws and regulations;

(**e**) statistics and information on violations of legislation, penalties imposed and cases of detention of ships; and

(**f**) statistics on reported occupational injuries and diseases affecting seafarers.

Regulation 5.1.5 On-board complaint procedures

1 Each Member shall require that ships that fly its flag have on-board procedures for the fair, effective and expeditious handling of seafarer complaints alleging breaches of the requirements of this Convention (including seafarers' rights).

2 Each Member shall prohibit and penalize any kind of victimization of a seafarer for filing a complaint.

3 The provisions in this Regulation and related sections of the Code are without prejudice to a seafarer's right to seek redress through whatever legal means the seafarer considers appropriate.

Standard A5.1.5 On-board complaint procedures

1 Without prejudice to any wider scope that may be given in national laws or regulations or collective agreements, the on-board procedures may be used by seafarers to lodge complaints relating to any matter that is alleged to constitute a breach of the requirements of this Convention (including seafarers' rights).

2 Each Member shall ensure that, in its laws or regulations, appropriate onboard complaint procedures are in place to meet the requirements of Regulation 5.1.5. Such procedures shall seek to resolve complaints at the lowest level possible. However, in all cases, seafarers shall have a right to complain directly to the master and, where they consider it necessary, to appropriate external authorities.

9 如果提取或拿走本导则第 8(e)款中所述的样品,应通知船东或船东代表,并在适宜时通知海员,或者当提取或拿走样品时他们应在现场。检查员对此类样品的数量应予妥善记录。

10 各成员国主管当局就悬挂其旗帜的船舶而发布的年度报告应包括:

（**a**） 与海员的工作和生活条件有关的现行有效的法律和法规清单,以及在该年度中生效的任何修改;

（**b**） 关于检查系统的组织细节;

（**c**） 有关应受检查和实受检查的船舶或其他场所的统计资料;

（**d**） 关于受其国家法律和法规管辖的所有海员的统计资料;

（**e**） 关于违反法律、所给予的惩处以及滞留船舶案例的统计资料和信息;以及

（**f**） 关于所报告的影响海员的职业伤害和疾病的统计资料。

规则 5.1.5 船上投诉程序

1 各成员国应要求悬挂其旗帜的船舶具备公平、有效和迅速处理海员指控违反本公约要求(包括海员权利)的投诉的船上程序。

2 各成员国应禁止和惩处以任何形式对提出投诉的海员进行迫害的行为。

3 本规则和守则的相关部分的规定不得妨碍海员通过其认为适当的任何法律手段寻求纠正的权利。

标准 A5.1.5 船上投诉程序

1 在不妨碍国家法律或法规或者集体协议可能规定更宽的范围的情况下,海员可以使用船上程序提出关于任何被指称为构成违反本公约要求(包括海员权利) 之事项的投诉。

2 各成员国应在其法律或法规中确保存在适当的船上投诉程序以满足规则 5.1.5 的要求。此类程序应寻求在尽可能最低的层次解决投诉。但是,在任何情况下,海员均有权直接向船长或在其认为必要时,向适当的外部当局投诉。

3   The on-board complaint procedures shall include the right of the seafarer to be accompanied or represented during the complaints procedure, as well as safeguards against the possibility of victimization of seafarers for filing complaints. The term "victimization" covers any adverse action taken by any person with respect to a seafarer for lodging a complaint which is not manifestly vexatious or maliciously made.

4   In addition to a copy of their seafarers' employment agreement, all seafarers shall be provided with a copy of the on-board complaint procedures applicable on the ship. This shall include contact information for the competent authority in the flag State and, where different, in the seafarers' country of residence, and the name of a person or persons on board the ship who can, on a confidential basis, provide seafarers with impartial advice on their complaint and otherwise assist them in following the complaint procedures available to them on board the ship.

Guideline B5.1.5   On-board complaint procedures

1   Subject to any relevant provisions of an applicable collective agreement, the competent authority should, in close consultation with shipowners' and seafarers' organizations, develop a model for fair, expeditious and well-documented on-board complaint-handling procedures for all ships that fly the Member's flag. In developing these procedures the following matters should be considered:

(**a**)   many complaints may relate specifically to those individuals to whom the complaint is to be made or even to the master of the ship. In all cases seafarers should also be able to complain directly to the master and to make a complaint externally; and

(**b**)   in order to help avoid problems of victimization of seafarers making complaints about matters under this Convention, the procedures should encourage the nomination of a person on board who can advise seafarers on the procedures available to them and, if requested by the complainant seafarer, also attend any meetings or hearings into the subject matter of the complaint.

2   At a minimum the procedures discussed during the consultative process referred to in paragraph 1 of this Guideline should include the following:

(**a**)   complaints should be addressed to the head of the department of the seafarer lodging the complaint or to the seafarer's superior officer;

(**b**)   the head of department or superior officer should then attempt to resolve the matter within prescribed time limits appropriate to the seriousness of the issues involved;

(**c**)   if the head of department or superior officer cannot resolve the complaint to the satisfaction of the seafarer, the latter may refer it to the master, who should handle the matter personally;

(**d**)   seafarers should at all times have the right to be accompanied and to be represented by another seafarer of their choice on board the ship concerned;

3 船上投诉程序应包括海员在投诉程序期间由人陪同或由人代表的权利,并保证不出现海员因提出投诉而受迫害的可能性。"受迫害"一词包括由任何人因海员提出投诉而对其采取的任何不利行动,只要该投诉不是明显的刁难或恶意而为。

4 除海员就业协议的副本以外,还应向所有海员提供一份适用于该船的船上投诉程序的副本,该副本应包括船旗国主管当局和海员居住国(如果与船旗国不同)主管当局的联络信息,以及能够在保密的基础上就海员的投诉向其提供公正的建议并在其他方面帮助他们遵循船上可用的投诉程序的船上人员的姓名。

导则 B5.1.5 船上投诉程序

1 根据适用的集体协议的任何相关规定,主管当局应与船东和海员组织密切协商,为悬挂该成员国旗帜的所有船舶制定公平、迅速和妥善记录的船上投诉处理程序的范本。在制定这些程序时,应考虑以下事项:

(**a**) 许多投诉可能与船上接收投诉的人或甚至与船长具体相关。在各种情况下,海员均应能够直接向船长投诉,或者向外部投诉;以及

(**b**) 为了帮助避免就本公约事项提出投诉的海员受到迫害的问题,程序应鼓励指定一名能够就海员可用的程序向海员提出建议的船上人员,并且,如果提出投诉的海员要求,该指定人员还应能参与关于该投诉事项的任何会议或听证。

2 本导则第 1 款所述的协商过程中所讨论的程序至少应包括以下内容:

(**a**) 投诉应提交给提出投诉的海员的部门负责人或该海员的上级高级船员;

(**b**) 部门负责人或上级高级船员应努力在与所涉问题的严重性相适应的规定时限内解决有关问题;

(**c**) 如果部门负责人或上级高级船员不能以海员满意的方式解决其投诉,该海员可以去找船长,船长则应亲自处理该事项;

(**d**) 海员应总是有权由其在相关船上选择的另一名海员陪同或代表;

(e) all complaints and the decisions on them should be recorded and a copy provided to the seafarer concerned;

(f) if a complaint cannot be resolved on board, the matter should be referred ashore to the shipowner, who should be given an appropriate time limit for resolving the matter, where appropriate, in consultation with the seafarers concerned or any person they may appoint as their representative; and

(g) in all cases seafarers should have a right to file their complaints directly with the master and the shipowner and competent authorities.

Regulation 5. 1. 6   Marine casualties

1   Each Member shall hold an official inquiry into any serious marine casualty, leading to injury or loss of life, that involves a ship that flies its flag. The final report of an inquiry shall normally be made public.

2   Members shall cooperate with each other to facilitate the investigation of serious marine casualties referred to in paragraph 1 of this Regulation.

Standard A5. 1. 6   Marine casualties

(No provisions)

Guideline B5. 1. 6   Marine casualties

(No provisions)

Regulation 5. 2
Port State responsibilities

Purpose: To enable each Member to implement its responsibilities under this Convention regarding international cooperation in the implementation and enforcement of the Convention standards on foreign ships

Regulation 5. 2. 1   Inspections in port

1   Every foreign ship calling, in the normal course of its business or for operational reasons, in the port of a Member may be the subject of inspection in accordance with paragraph 4 of Article V for the purpose of reviewing compliance with the requirements of this Convention (including seafarers' rights) relating to the working and living conditions of seafarers on the ship.

2   Each Member shall accept the maritime labour certificate and the declaration of maritime labour compliance required under Regulation 5. 1. 3 as prima facie evidence of compliance with the requirements of this Convention (including seafarers' rights). Accordingly, the inspection in its ports shall, except in the circumstances specified in the Code, be limited to a review of the certificate and declaration.

（e）　所有投诉和对于投诉所做的结论应予记录,记录的一份副本应提供给有关海员;

（f）　如果投诉不能在船上得到解决,该事项应交给岸上的船东,并应规定该船东解决该事项的时限,凡适宜时,与有关海员或可能被他们指定为代表的人协商;以及

（g）　在所有情况下海员均应有权直接向船长和船东及主管当局提出投诉。

规则 5.1.6　海上事故

1　各成员国应对悬挂其旗帜的船舶涉及的任何导致人员伤亡的严重海上事故开展官方调查。这种调查的最后报告通常应予公布。

2　成员国应相互合作,以便利本规则第 1 款所述的严重海上事故的调查。

标准 A5.1.6　海上事故

（无规定）

导则 B5.1.6　海上事故

（无规定）

规则 5.2
港口国的责任

目的:使各成员国能够履行本公约关于在外国船舶上实施和执行公约标准方面进行国际合作的责任

规则 5.2.1　在港口的检查

1　任何外国船舶在正常的业务航行中或出于操作性原因挂靠一成员国的港口时,可能受到根据第五条第 4 款所进行的目的在于核查该船符合本公约有关海员工作和生活条件要求(包括海员权利)情况的检查。

2　成员国应接受规则 5.1.3 所要求的海事劳工证书和海事劳工符合声明为符合本公约要求(包括海员权利)的表面证据;因此,除本守则中规定的情况外,其港口内的检查应仅限于核查证书和声明。

3 Inspections in a port shall be carried out by authorized officers in accordance with the provisions of the Code and other applicable international arrangements governing port State control inspections in the Member. Any such inspection shall be limited to verifying that the matter inspected is in conformity with the relevant requirements set out in the Articles and Regulations of this Convention and in Part A only of the Code.

4 Inspections that may be carried out in accordance with this Regulation shall be based on an effective port State inspection and monitoring system to help ensure that the working and living conditions for seafarers on ships entering a port of the Member concerned meet the requirements of this Convention (including seafarers' rights).

5 Information about the system referred to in paragraph 4 of this Regulation, including the method used for assessing its effectiveness, shall be included in the Member's reports pursuant to article 22 of the Constitution.

Standard A5. 2. 1 Inspections in port

1 Where an authorized officer, having come on board to carry out an inspection and requested, where applicable, the maritime labour certificate and the declaration of maritime labour compliance, finds that:

(**a**)   the required documents are not produced or maintained or are falsely maintained or that the documents produced do not contain the information required by this Convention or are otherwise invalid; or

(**b**)   there are clear grounds for believing that the working and living conditions on the ship do not conform to the requirements of this Convention; or

(**c**)   there are reasonable grounds to believe that the ship has changed flag for the purpose of avoiding compliance with this Convention; or

(**d**)   there is a complaint alleging that specific working and living conditions on the ship do not conform to the requirements of this Convention; a more detailed inspection may be carried out to ascertain the working and living conditions on board the ship. Such inspection shall in any case be carried out where the working and living conditions believed or alleged to be defective could constitute a clear hazard to the safety, health or security of seafarers or where the authorized officer has grounds to believe that any deficiencies constitute a serious breach of the requirements of this Convention (including seafarers' rights).

2 Where a more detailed inspection is carried out on a foreign ship in the port of a Member by authorized officers in the circumstances set out in subparagraph (a), (b) or (c) of paragraph 1 of this Standard, it shall in principle cover the matters listed in Appendix A5-Ⅲ.

3 在成员国港口的检查应由授权官员根据本守则和其他关于管理港口国监督检查的适用国际协议的规定来进行。任何此种检查应仅限于核实所检查的事项符合本公约条款和规则及本守则 A 部分所规定的相关要求。

4 根据本规则可能开展的检查应以有效的港口国检查和监督机制为基础,以帮助确保进入有关成员国港口的船舶上的海员工作和生活条件满足本公约的要求(包括海员权利)。

5 关于本规则第 4 款所述机制的信息,包括用于评价其有效性的方法,应包括在成员国根据《国际劳工组织章程》第二十二条提交的报告中。

标准 A5.2.1 在港口的检查

1 如果一授权官员登船进行检查并要求(如适用)出示海事劳工证书和海事劳工符合声明时发现:

（**a**） 未出示或未持有所要求的证书,或者持有虚假证书或所出示的证书未包含本公约所要求的信息或在其他方面无效;或

（**b**） 有明确理由相信该船舶上的工作和生活条件不符合本公约的要求;或

（**c**） 有合理的理由相信该船舶出于逃避符合本公约之目的而变更船旗;或

（**d**） 有投诉指控船舶上的具体工作和生活条件不符合本公约的要求;则可以进行更详细的检查以确定船上的工作和生活条件。如果相信或经指控工作和生活条件的缺陷会对海员的安全、健康和保安构成明显危害,或者授权官员有理由相信任何缺陷构成了对公约要求(包括海员权利)的严重违反,都要进行此种检查。

2 如果在成员国港口由授权官员在本标准第 1 款(a)、(b)或(c)项规定的情形中对外国船舶进行更详细的检查,该检查原则上应包括附录 A5-Ⅲ 中所列的事项。

3   In the case of a complaint under paragraph 1 (d) of this Standard, the inspection shall generally be limited to matters within the scope of the complaint, although a complaint, or its investigation, may provide clear grounds for a detailed inspection in accordance with paragraph 1 (b) of this Standard. For the purpose of paragraph 1 (d) of this Standard, "complaint" means information submitted by a seafarer, a professional body, an association, a trade union or, generally, any person with an interest in the safety of the ship, including an interest in safety or health hazards to seafarers on board.

4   Where, following a more detailed inspection, the working and living conditions on the ship are found not to conform to the requirements of this Convention, the authorized officer shall forthwith bring the deficiencies to the attention of the master of the ship, with required deadlines for their rectification. In the event that such deficiencies are considered by the authorized officer to be significant, or if they relate to a complaint made in accordance with paragraph 3 of this Standard, the authorized officer shall bring the deficiencies to the attention of the appropriate seafarers' and shipowners' organizations in the Member in which the inspection is carried out, and may:

(a)   notify a representative of the flag State;

(b)   provide the competent authorities of the next port of call with the relevant information.

5   The Member in which the inspection is carried out shall have the right to transmit a copy of the officer's report, which must be accompanied by any reply received from the competent authorities of the flag State within the prescribed deadline, to the Director-General of the International Labour Office with a view to such action as may be considered appropriate and expedient in order to ensure that a record is kept of such information and that it is brought to the attention of parties which might be interested in availing themselves of relevant recourse procedures.

6   Where, following a more detailed inspection by an authorized officer, the ship is found not to conform to the requirements of this Convention and:

(a)   the conditions on board are clearly hazardous to the safety, health or security of seafarers; or

(b)   the non-conformity constitutes a serious or repeated breach of the requirements of this Convention (including seafarers' rights);

the authorized officer shall take steps to ensure that the ship shall not proceed to sea until any non-conformities that fall within the scope of subparagraph (a) or (b) of this paragraph have been rectified, or until the authorized officer has accepted a plan of action to rectify such non-conformities and is satisfied that the plan will be implemented in an expeditious manner. If the ship is prevented from sailing, the authorized officer shall forthwith notify the flag State accordingly and invite a representative of the flag State to be present, if possible, requesting the flag State to reply within a prescribed deadline. The authorized officer shall also inform forthwith the appropriate shipowners' and seafarers' organizations in the port State in which the inspection was carried out.

3 在本标准第 1 款(d)项的投诉的情况下,检查一般应限于投诉范围内的事项,尽管一项投诉或其调查可能为根据本标准第 1 款(b)项进行更详细的检查提供明确理由。就本标准第 1 款(d)项而言,"投诉"系指由海员、专业机构、协会、工会或总体而言,由那些关心船舶安全,包括关心船上海员的安全或健康危害的任何人提交的信息。

4 如果在更详细检查后发现船上的工作和生活条件不符合本公约的要求,授权官员应立即请该船的船长注意这些缺陷并提出纠正这些缺陷的截止日期要求。如果授权官员认为这些缺陷为重大缺陷,或者这些缺陷涉及根据本标准第 3 款提出的投诉,授权官员应提请开展检查所在成员国的适当海员和船东组织注意这些缺陷,并且可以:

(a)   通知船旗国的代表;

(b)   向下一挂靠港口的主管当局提供有关信息。

5 开展检查所在的成员国应有权将检查员的报告的副本,其后必须附有所收到的船旗国的主管当局在规定的截止时间内作出的回应,转送国际劳工局局长,以便采取其可能认为适当和紧急的行动,确保关于此信息的记录得以保持,并确保提请可能会对利用相关追索程序感兴趣的各方注意。

6 如果授权官员进行更详细的检查后发现船舶不符合本公约的要求,并且:

(a)   船上条件明显危害海员的安全、健康或保安;或

(b)   不符合有关要求的情况构成对本公约要求(包括海员权利)的严重或屡次违反;

授权官员应采取措施确保只有在本款(a)或(b)项范围内的所有不符合情况得到纠正后,或者直到授权官员接受了纠正不符合情况的行动计划并认为该计划将会得到迅速实施后才允许船舶开航。如果船舶被禁止开航,授权官员应立即将有关情况通知船旗国并请船旗国的代表到场,若可能,要求船旗国在规定的期限内答复。授权官员还应立即通知开展检查的港口国的适当的船东组织和海员组织。

7 Each Member shall ensure that its authorized officers are given guidance, of the kind indicated in Part B of the Code, as to the kinds of circumstances justifying detention of a ship under paragraph 6 of this Standard.

8 When implementing their responsibilities under this Standard, each Member shall make all possible efforts to avoid a ship being unduly detained or delayed. If a ship is found to be unduly detained or delayed, compensation shall be paid for any loss or damage suffered. The burden of proof in each case shall be on the complainant.

Guideline B5. 2. 1 Inspections in port

1 The competent authority should develop an inspection policy for authorized officers carrying out inspections under Regulation 5. 2. 1. The objective of the policy should be to ensure consistency and to otherwise guide inspection and enforcement activities related to the requirements of this Convention (including seafarers' rights). Copies of this policy should be provided to all authorized officers and should be available to the public and shipowners and seafarers.

2 When developing a policy relating to the circumstances warranting a detention of the ship under Standard A5. 2. 1, paragraph 6, the competent authority should consider that, with respect to the breaches referred to in Standard A5. 2. 1, paragraph 6(b), the seriousness could be due to the nature of the deficiency concerned. This would be particularly relevant in the case of the violation of fundamental rights and principles or seafarers' employment and social rights under Articles Ⅲ and Ⅳ. For example, the employment of a person who is under age should be considered as a serious breach even if there is only one such person on board. In other cases, the number of different defects found during a particular inspection should be taken into account: for example, several instances of defects relating to accommodation or food and catering which do not threaten safety or health might be needed before they should be considered as constituting a serious breach.

3 Members should cooperate with each other to the maximum extent possible in the adoption of internationally agreed guidelines on inspection policies, especially those relating to the circumstances warranting the detention of a ship.

Regulation 5. 2. 2   Onshore seafarer complaint-handling procedures

1 Each Member shall ensure that seafarers on ships calling at a port in the Member's territory who allege a breach of the requirements of this Convention (including seafarers' rights) have the right to report such a complaint in order to facilitate a prompt and practical means of redress.

Standard A5. 2. 2   Onshore seafarer complaint-handling procedures

1 A complaint by a seafarer alleging a breach of the requirements of this Convention (including seafarers' rights) may be reported to an authorized officer in the port at which the seafarer's ship has called. In such cases, the authorized officer shall undertake an initial investigation.

7 各成员国应确保对其授权官员就本标准第 6 款中构成滞留船舶理由的情况按本守则 B 部分所指出的情况给以指导。

8 各成员国在履行其在本标准下的责任时,应尽一切可能努力避免船舶被不当滞留或延误。如果发现船舶被不当滞留或延误,应对所遭受的任何损失或破坏予以赔偿。在各种情况下举证的责任均在申诉方。

导则 B5.2.1 在港口的检查

1 主管当局应为按规则 5.2.1 进行检查的授权官员制定检查政策。政策的目标应为确保一贯性并在其他方面指导与本公约的要求(包括海员权利)有关的检查和执行活动。该政策的副本应提供给所有授权官员,并应使公众及船东和海员能够得到。

2 在制定关于标准 A5.2.1 第 6 款中构成滞留船舶正当理由之情形的政策时,主管当局应考虑到,关于标准 A5.2.1 第 6(b)款中所提及的违反,其严重性可以是因为有关缺陷的性质。这一点尤其关系到违反本公约第三条和第四条中的基本权利和原则或海员的就业和社会权利的情况。例如,雇用一个未成年人应被视为严重违反,即使船上只有一个这样的人。在其他情况下,应考虑到在一次特定的检查中所发现的不同缺陷的数量:例如,在被视为构成严重违反之前,可能需要有多种并不威胁安全或健康的关于起居舱室或食品和膳食服务的缺陷情况。

3 成员国应最大限度地相互合作,通过国际一致的检查政策导则,特别是那些关于构成滞留船舶正当理由的情形的导则。

规则 5.2.2 海员投诉的岸上处理程序

1 各成员国应确保,在该成员国领土内的港口挂靠的船舶上的指控违反本公约要求(包括海员权利)情况的海员,有权提出申诉以促进采取迅速而实际的解决方式。

标准 A5.2.2 海员投诉的岸上处理程序

1 海员指控违反本公约要求(包括海员权利)的投诉可向海员所在船舶挂靠的港口的授权官员报告。在这种情况下,授权官员应开展初步调查。

2 Where appropriate, given the nature of the complaint, the initial investigation shall include consideration of whether the on-board complaint procedures provided under Regulation 5.1.5 have been explored. The authorized officer may also conduct a more detailed inspection in accordance with Standard A5.2.1.

3 The authorized officer shall, where appropriate, seek to promote a resolution of the complaint at the ship-board level.

4 In the event that the investigation or the inspection provided under this Standard reveals a non-conformity that falls within the scope of paragraph 6 of Standard A5.2.1, the provisions of that paragraph shall be applied.

5 Where the provisions of paragraph 4 of this Standard do not apply, and the complaint has not been resolved at the ship-board level, the authorized officer shall forthwith notify the flag State, seeking, within a prescribed deadline, advice and a corrective plan of action.

6 Where the complaint has not been resolved following action taken in accordance with paragraph 5 of this Standard, the port State shall transmit a copy of the authorized officer's report to the Director-General. The report must be accompanied by any reply received within the prescribed deadline from the competent authority of the flag State. The appropriate shipowners' and seafarers' organizations in the port State shall be similarly informed. In addition, statistics and information regarding complaints that have been resolved shall be regularly submitted by the port State to the Director-General. Both such submissions are provided in order that, on the basis of such action as may be considered appropriate and expedient, a record is kept of such information and is brought to the attention of parties, including shipowners' and seafarers' organizations, which might be interested in availing themselves of relevant recourse procedures.

7 Appropriate steps shall be taken to safeguard the confidentiality of complaints made by seafarers.

Guideline B5.2.2   Onshore seafarer complaint-handling procedures

1 Where a complaint referred to in Standard A5.2.2 is dealt with by an authorized officer, the officer should first check whether the complaint is of a general nature which concerns all seafarers on the ship, or a category of them, or whether it relates only to the individual case of the seafarer concerned.

2 If the complaint is of a general nature, consideration should be given to undertaking a more detailed inspection in accordance with Standard A5.2.1.

3 If the complaint relates to an individual case, an examination of the results of any on-board complaint procedures for the resolution of the complaint concerned should be undertaken. If such procedures have not been explored, the authorized officer should suggest that the complainant take advantage of any such procedures available. There should be good reasons for considering a complaint before any onboard complaint procedures have been explored. These would include the inadequacy of, or undue delay in, the internal procedures or the complainant's fear of reprisal for lodging a complaint.

2 基于投诉的性质,凡适宜时,初步调查应包括考虑是否已探讨过通过规则 5.1.5 所规定的船上投诉程序来解决。授权官员还可以根据标准 A5.2.1 开展更详细的检查。

3 凡适宜时,授权官员应努力促成在船舶的层次上解决投诉。

4 如果根据本标准所规定的调查或检查发现的不符合情况属于标准 A5.2.1 第 6 款的范畴,应适用该款的规定。

5 如果本标准第 4 款的规定不适用,且该投诉未能在船舶的层次上得到解决,授权官员应立即通知船旗国,在规定的期限内征询建议及关于纠正的行动计划。

6 如果按本标准第 5 款采取行动后投诉问题未能得到解决,港口国应将一份授权官员报告的副本送交局长。该报告必须附有在规定的限期内从船旗国主管当局那里收到的答复。应以类似的方式通知港口国内适当的船东和海员组织。此外,港口国应定期将关于已解决投诉的统计资料和信息提交给局长。提交上述两种信息是为了在可能认为这些行动恰当且迅速的基础上,保持一份关于这些信息的记录,并使包括船东和海员组织在内的可能会对适用有关追索程序感兴趣的各方注意到这些信息。

7 应采取适当措施为提出投诉的海员保密。

导则 B5.2.2 海员投诉的岸上处理程序

1 如果标准 A5.2.2 中所述的投诉由授权官员来处理,该官员应首先核查该投诉是涉及该船上的所有海员或某一类海员的普遍性问题,还是只与该当事海员的个案有关。

2 如果该投诉是普遍性问题,应考虑根据标准 A5.2.1 进行一次更详细的检查。

3 如果投诉属于个案问题,应对解决有关投诉的任何船上投诉程序的结果予以考查。如果还没有诉诸该程序,授权官员应建议投诉人充分利用现有的此类程序。若在诉诸任何船上投诉程序之前就对投诉予以考虑,需要有充分的理由。这些理由包括内部程序不足或过分拖沓,或者投诉人害怕因提出投诉而遭到报复。

4   In any investigation of a complaint, the authorized officer should give the master, the shipowner and any other person involved in the complaint a proper opportunity to make known their views.

5   In the event that the flag State demonstrates, in response to the notification by the port State in accordance with paragraph 5 of Standard A5. 2. 2, that it will handle the matter, and that it has in place effective procedures for this purpose and has submitted an acceptable plan of action, the authorized officer may refrain from any further involvement with the complaint.

Regulation 5. 3

Labour-supplying responsibilities

Purpose: To ensure that each Member implements its responsibilities under this Convention as pertaining to seafarer recruitmentand placement and the social protection of its seafarers

1   Without prejudice to the principle of each Member's responsibility for the working and living conditions of seafarers on ships that fly its flag, the Member also has a responsibility to ensure the implementation of the requirements of this Convention regarding the recruitment and placement of seafarers as well as the social security protection of seafarers that are its nationals or are resident or are otherwise domiciled in its territory, to the extent that such responsibility is provided for in this Convention.

2   Detailed requirements for the implementation of paragraph 1 of this Regulation are found in the Code.

3   Each Member shall establish an effective inspection and monitoring system for enforcing its labour-supplying responsibilities under this Convention.

4   Information about the system referred to in paragraph 3 of this Regulation, including the method used for assessing its effectiveness, shall be included in the Member's reports pursuant to article 22 of the Constitution.

Standard A5. 3   Labour-supplying responsibilities

1   Each Member shall enforce the requirements of this Convention applicable to the operation and practice of seafarer recruitment and placement services established on its territory through a system of inspection and monitoring and legal proceedings for breaches of licensing and other operational requirements provided for in Standard A1. 4.

Guideline B5. 3   Labour-supplying responsibilities

1   Private seafarer recruitment and placement services established in the Member's territory and securing the services of a seafarer for a shipowner, wherever located, should be required to assume obligations to ensure the proper fulfilment by shipowners of the terms of their employment agreements concluded with seafarers.

4 在对投诉的任何调查中,授权官员应该给船长、船东和投诉所涉及的任何其他人员适当的机会来表明其观点。

5 如果船旗国在对港口国根据标准 A5.2.2 第 5 款所发通知的答复中已表明将处理该投诉,具备处理投诉的有效程序并提交了一份可接受的行动计划, 授权官员可不再进一步参与处理该投诉。

规则 5.3
劳工提供责任

目的:确保各成员国履行其在本公约下关于海员招募和安置以及对其海员提供社会保护的责任

1 在不妨碍各成员国对悬挂其旗帜船舶上的海员工作和生活条件的责任的原则的前提下,成员国还有责任确保实施本公约关于海员招募和安置的要求,以及对作为其国民或在其领土内定居或以其他方式居住于其领土的海员的社会保障保护的要求,只要本公约规定了此种责任。

2 实施本规则第 1 款的详细要求见守则。

3 各成员国应建立一个有效的检查和监督机制来执行其在本公约下的劳工提供责任。

4 关于本规则第 3 款所述机制的信息,包括用于评估其有效性的方法,应包括在成员国根据《国际劳工组织章程》第二十二条提交的报告中。

标准 A5.3　劳工提供责任

1 各成员国应通过一个检查和监督体制并通过对违反标准 A1.4 规定的许可证和其他操作性要求的情况采取法律程序,执行本公约中适用于在其领土上设立的海员招募和安置服务机构的运作与实践的要求。

导则 B5.3　劳工提供责任

1 在成员国领土内设立并为船东物色海员服务的私营海员招募和安置服务机构,无论其设在何处,均应要求其承担确保由船东妥善履行与海员订立的就业协议条款的义务。

Appendix A2- I
Evidence of financial security under
Regulation 2. 5, paragraph 2

The certificate or other documentary evidence referred to in Standard A2. 5. 2, paragraph 7, shall include the following information:

(**a**)   name of the ship;

(**b**)   port of registry of the ship;

(**c**)   call sign of the ship;

(**d**)   IMO number of the ship;

(**e**)   name and address of the provider or providers of the financial security;

(**f**)   contact details of the persons or entity responsible for handling seafarers' requests for relief;

(**g**)   name of the shipowner;

(**h**)   period of validity of the financial security; and

(**i**)   an attestation from the financial security provider that the financial security meets the requirements of Standard A2. 5. 2.

附录 A2-I
规则 2.5 第 2 款规定的财务担保证明

标准 A2.5.2 第 7 款提及的证书或其他证明文件应包括以下信息：

（**a**）　船舶名称；

（**b**）　船舶注册港口；

（**c**）　船舶呼号；

（**d**）　船舶的国际海事组织编号；

（**e**）　一个或多个财务担保机构的名称和地址；

（**f**）　负责处理海员救助要求的人员或机构的详细联系方式；

（**g**）　船东姓名；

（**h**）　财务担保的有效期；和

（**i**）　财务担保提供方出具的关于财务担保符合标准 A2.5.2 规定的证明。

Appendix A4- I
Evidence of financial security under Regulation 4. 2

The certificate or other documentary evidence of financial security required under Standard A4. 2. 1, paragraph 14, shall include the following information:

(**a**) name of the ship;

(**b**) port of registry of the ship;

(**c**) call sign of the ship;

(**d**) IMO number of the ship;

(**e**) name and address of the provider or providers of the financial security;

(**f**) contact details of the persons or entity responsible for handling seafarers' contractual claims;

(**g**) name of the shipowner;

(**h**) period of validity of the financial security; and

(**i**) an attestation from the financial security provider that the financial security meets the requirements of Standard A4. 2. 1.

附录 A4-Ⅰ
规则 4.2 规定的财务担保证明

标准 A4.2.1 第 14 款规定的财务担保证书或其他证明文件应包括以下信息：

（**a**） 船舶名称；

（**b**） 船舶注册港口；

（**c**） 船舶呼号；

（**d**） 船舶的国际海事组织编号；

（**e**） 一个或多个财务担保机构的名称和地址；

（**f**） 负责处理海员合同索赔的人员或机构的详细联系方式；

（**g**） 船东姓名；

（**h**） 财务担保的有效期；和

（**i**） 财务担保提供方出具的关于财务担保符合标准 A4.2.1 的规定的证明。

Appendix B4- I
Model Receipt and Release Form
referred to in Guideline B4. 2. 2

Ship (name, port of registry and IMO number) : _____

Incident (date and place) : _____

Seafarer/Legal heir and/or dependant : _____

Shipowner : _____

I, [Seafarer] [Seafarer's legal heir and/or dependant][1] hereby acknowledge receipt of the sum of [currency and amount] in satisfaction of the Shipowner's obligation to pay contractual compensation for personal injury and/or death under the terms and conditions of [my] [the Seafarer's] employment and I hereby release the Shipowner from their obligations under the said terms and conditions.

The payment is made without admission of liability of any claims and is accepted without prejudice to [my] [the Seafarer's legal heir and/or dependant's] right to pursue any claim at law in respect of negligence, tort, breach of statutory duty or any other legal redress available and arising out of the above incident.

Dated : _____

Seafarer/Legal heir and/or dependant : _____

Signed : _____

For acknowledgement : _____

Shipowner/Shipowner representative : _____

Signed : _____

Financial security provider : _____

Signed : _____

---

[1]   Delete as appropriate.

附录 B4-I
导则 B4.2.2 提及的收据和解除责任书范本

船舶(名称、注册港口和国际海事组织编号)：_____

事故(日期和地点)：_____

海员/法定继承人和/或被抚养人：_____

船东：_____

本人,[海员][海员的法定继承人和/或被抚养人]①兹声明收到船东为履行[本人][海员的]就业条款和条件所规定的义务而支付的对个人伤害和/或死亡的合同赔偿款项(货币和金额),本人兹免除船东根据所述条款和条件的规定承担的义务。

支付该款项并不意味承认对任何索赔负有责任,接受支付款项并不妨碍[本人][海员的法定继承人和/或被抚养人]*就任何疏忽、侵权、违反法定职责的情形提出任何法定赔偿要求或寻求任何其他可获得的、因本事故产生的法律补救。

日期：_____

海员/法定继承人和/或被抚养人：_____

签字：_____

确认方：_____

船东/船东代表：_____

签字：_____

财务担保提供方：_____

签字：_____

---

① 视情况删除。

Appendix A5- I

The working and living conditions of seafarers that must be inspected and approved by the flag State before certifying a ship in accordance with Standard A5. 1. 3, paragraph 1:

Minimum age

Medical certification

Qualifications of seafarers

Seafarers' employment agreements

Use of any licensed or certified or regulated private recruitment and placement service

Hours of work or rest

Manning levels for the ship

Accommodation

On-board recreational facilities

Food and catering

Health and safety and accident prevention

On-board medical care

On-board complaint procedures

Payment of wages

Financial security for repatriation

Financial security relating to shipowners' liability

附录 A5- I

在根据标准 A5.1.3 第 1 款向船舶发证以前必须经过检查并经船旗国批准的海员的工作和生活条件：

最低年龄

体检证书

海员资格

海员就业协议

使用任何有许可证的或者经发证或管理的私营招募和安置服务机构

工作和休息时间

船舶配员水平

起居舱室

船上娱乐设施

食品和膳食服务

健康和安全及防止事故

船上医疗

船上投诉程序

工资支付

对遣返的财务担保

与船东责任相关的财务担保

Appendix A5-II
Maritime Labour Certificate

(Note: This Certificate shall have a Declaration

of Maritime Labour Compliance attached)

Issued under the provisions of Article V and Title 5 of the

Maritime Labour Convention, 2006

(referred to below as "the Convention")

under the authority of the Government of:

_____

(full designation of the State whose flag the ship is entitled to fly)

by _____

(full designation and address of the competent authority or recognized organization

duly authorized under the provisions of the Convention)

Particulars of the ship

Name of ship: _____

Distinctive number or letters: _____

Port of registry: _____

Date of registry: _____

Gross tonnage: [1] _____

IMO number: _____

Type of ship: _____

_____

[1] For ships covered by the tonnage measurement interim scheme adopted by the IMO, the gross tonnage is that which is included in the REMARKS column of the International Tonnage Certificate (1969). See Article II (1)(c) of the Convention.

附录 A5-II
海事劳工证书

（注：本证书后应附有海事劳工符合声明）

本证书系根据《2006 年海事劳工公约》

（以下简称"公约"）第五条和标题五的规定，

经＿＿＿＿＿政府授权，

（船舶有权悬挂其旗帜国家的全称）

由＿＿＿＿＿签发

（根据公约规定正式授权的主管当局或认可组织的全称和地址）

船舶细节

船名：＿＿＿＿＿＿＿＿＿＿＿＿＿＿＿＿＿＿＿＿＿＿

船舶编号和呼号：＿＿＿＿＿＿＿＿＿＿＿＿＿＿＿＿

船籍港：＿＿＿＿＿＿＿＿＿＿＿＿＿＿＿＿＿＿＿＿

登记日期：＿＿＿＿＿＿＿＿＿＿＿＿＿＿＿＿＿＿

总吨位：①＿＿＿＿＿＿＿＿＿＿＿＿＿＿＿＿＿＿

国际海事组织编号：＿＿＿＿＿＿＿＿＿＿＿＿＿＿

船舶类型：＿＿＿＿＿＿＿＿＿＿＿＿＿＿＿＿＿＿

---

① 对于国际海事组织通过的吨位丈量临时表格所包括的船舶，总吨位为包括在《国际吨位证书（1969）》"备注"栏中的总吨位。见公约第二条第（1）（c）款。

Name and address of the shipowner: [1] _____

_____

_____

This is to certify:

1 That this ship has been inspected and verified to be in compliance with the requirements of the Convention, and the provisions of the attached Declaration of Maritime Labour Compliance.

2 That the seafarers' working and living conditions specified in Appendix A5- I of the Convention were found to correspond to the abovementioned country's national requirements implementing the Convention. These national requirements are summarized in the Declaration of Maritime Labour Compliance, Part I .

This Certificate is valid until _____ subject to inspections in accordance with Standards A5.1.3 and A5.1.4 of the Convention.

This Certificate is valid only when the Declaration of Maritime Labour Compliance issued

at _____ on _____ is attached.

Completion date of the inspection on which this Certificate is based was _____

Issued at _____ on _____

Signature of the duly authorized official issuing the Certificate

(Seal or stamp of issuing authority, as appropriate)

Endorsements for mandatory intermediate inspection and, if required, any additional inspection

This is to certify that the ship was inspected in accordance with Standards A5.1.3 and A5.1.4 of the Convention and that the seafarers' working and living conditions specified in Appendix A5- I of the Convention were found to correspond to the abovementioned country's national requirements implementing the Convention.

Intermediate inspection: _____   Signed: _____

(to be completed between the second   (Signature of authorized official)

and third anniversary dates)

Place: _____

---

[1] *Shipowner* means the owner of the ship or another organization or person, such as the manager, agent or bareboat charterer, who has assumed the responsibility for the operation of the ship from the owner and who, on assuming such responsibility, has agreed to take over the duties and responsibilities imposed on shipowners in accordance with this Convention, regardless of whether any other organizations or persons fulfil certain of the duties or responsibilities on behalf of the shipowner. See Article II (1) (j) of the Convention.

船东名称和地址①：＿＿＿＿＿＿＿＿＿＿＿＿＿＿＿＿＿＿＿＿＿＿＿＿＿＿＿＿＿＿＿＿＿

＿＿＿

兹证明：

1 本船舶已经过检验和核验,符合公约的要求和所附海事劳工符合声明的规定。

2 检查结果表明公约附录 A5-Ⅰ 中所规定的海员工作和生活条件符合上述国家实施公约的国家要求。这些国家要求被归纳在海事劳工符合声明的第 I 部分中。

本证书有效期至＿＿＿＿＿＿＿＿＿＿,但取决于根据公约的标准 A5.1.3 和 A5.1.4 的检查。

只有后面附有在＿＿＿＿＿＿＿＿＿于＿＿＿＿＿＿＿＿＿＿＿＿＿签发的海事劳工符合声明,本证书才有效。

本证书所依据的检查的完成日期为＿＿＿＿＿＿＿＿＿＿＿＿＿＿＿＿＿＿＿＿＿。

签发地点＿＿＿＿＿＿＿＿＿ 签发日期＿＿＿＿＿＿＿＿＿＿＿＿＿＿＿＿＿＿＿

经正式授权签发此证书的官员签字

(视情况,签发当局的钢印或盖章,如要求)

强制性中期检查以及任何附加检查(如要求)的签注

兹证明本船舶已按公约标准 A5.1.3 和 A5.1.4 经过检查,检查结果表明公约附录 A5-Ⅰ 所述的海员工作和生活条件符合前述国家实施公约的国家要求。

中期检查：＿＿＿＿＿＿＿＿＿＿＿＿ 签字：＿＿＿＿＿＿＿＿＿＿＿＿＿＿

(应在第 2 和第 3 个周年日之间完成) (经授权的官员签字)

地点：＿＿＿＿＿＿＿＿＿＿＿＿＿＿

---

① "船东"系指船舶所有人或从船舶所有人那里承担了船舶经营责任并在承担这种责任时已同意接受船东根据本公约所承担的职责和责任的另一组织或个人,如管理人、代理或光船承租人,无论是否有其他组织或个人代表船东履行了某些职责或责任。见公约第二条第(1)(j)款。

Date: _____

(Seal or stamp of the authority, as appropriate)

Additional endorsements (if required)

This is to certify that the ship was the subject of an additional inspection for the purpose of verifying that the ship continued to be in compliance with the national requirements implementing the Convention, as required by Standard A3.1, paragraph 3, of the Convention (re-registration or substantial alteration of accommodation) or for other reasons.

Additional inspection: Signed: _____

(if required)   (Signature of authorized official)

_____

Place: _____

Date: _____

(Seal or stamp of the authority, as appropriate)

Additional inspection: Signed: _____

(if required)   (Signature of authorized official)

Place: _____

Date: _____

(Seal or stamp of the authority, as appropriate)

Additional inspection: Signed: _____

(if required)   (Signature of authorized official)

Place: _____

Date: _____

(Seal or stamp of the authority, as appropriate)

日期：_____

（视情况，当局的钢印或盖章，如要求）

附加签注（如要求）

兹证明，按公约标准 A3.1 第 3 款的要求（重新登记或起居舱室的实质性改动）或出于其他原因，本船需受到一次附加检查以核验该船继续符合实施公约的国家要求。

附加检查： （如要求）	签字：_____ （经授权的官员签字） _____ 地点：_____ 日期：_____ （视情况，当局的钢印或盖章，如要求）
附加检查： （如要求）	签字：_____ （经授权的官员签字） 地点：_____ 日期：_____ （视情况，当局的钢印或盖章，如要求）
附加检查： （如要求）	签字：_____ （经授权的官员签字） 地点：_____ 日期：_____ （当局的钢印或盖章，如要求）

Extension after renewal inspection (if required)

This is to certify that, following a renewal inspection, the ship was found to continue to be in compliance with national laws and regulations or other measures implementing the requirements of the Convention, and that the present certificate is hereby extended, in accordance with paragraph 4 of Standard A5.1.3, until _____
(not more than five months after the expiry date of the existing certificate) to allow for the new certificate to be issued to and made available on board the ship.

Completion date of the renewal inspection on which this extension is based was:

_____

Signed: _____

(Signature of authorized official)

Place: _____

Date: _____

(Seal or stamp of the authority, as appropriate)

换证检查后延期(如要求)

兹证明,经换证检查,本船舶被认定仍符合国家法律、法规或实施本公约要求的其他措施,根据标准 A5.1.3 第 4 款,特此将本证书延期至＿＿＿＿＿＿＿＿＿＿＿＿＿＿＿＿＿＿

(不超过现有证书到期之日起五个月),以便能发给该船舶新证书并随船携带该证书。本延期所依据的换证检查的完成日期是:＿＿＿＿＿＿＿＿＿＿＿＿＿＿＿＿＿＿＿＿＿

签字:＿＿＿＿＿＿＿＿＿＿＿＿＿＿＿＿＿

(经授权的官员签字)

地点:＿＿＿＿＿＿＿＿＿＿＿＿＿＿＿＿

日期:＿＿＿＿＿＿＿＿＿＿＿＿＿＿＿＿

(视情况,当局的钢印或盖章,如要求)

Maritime Labour Convention, 2006

Part I
Declaration of Maritime Labour Compliance

(Note: This Declaration must be attached to the ship's Maritime Labour Certificate)

Issued under the authority of: _____ [insert name of competent authority as defined in Article II, paragraph 1(a), of the Convention]

With respect to the provisions of the Maritime Labour Convention, 2006, the following referenced ship:

Name of ship	IMO number	Gross tonnage

is maintained in accordance with Standard A5.1.3 of the Convention.

The undersigned declares, on behalf of the abovementioned competent authority, that:

(a) the provisions of the Maritime Labour Convention are fully embodied in the national requirements referred to below;

(b) these national requirements are contained in the national provisions referenced below; explanations concerning the content of those provisions are provided where necessary;

(c) the details of any substantial equivalencies under Article VI, paragraphs 3 and 4, are provided <under the corresponding national requirement listed below> <in the section provided for this purpose below> (strike out the statement which is not applicable);

(d) any exemptions granted by the competent authority in accordance with Title 3 are clearly indicated in the section provided for this purpose below; and

(e) any ship-type specific requirements under national legislation are also referenced under the requirements concerned.

2006 年海事劳工公约

第 I 部分
海事劳工符合声明

(注:本声明必须附于船舶的海事劳工证书之后)

在_____(填入公约第二条第 1(a)款定义的主管当局的名称)的授权下签发

就《2005 年海事劳工公约》的规定而言,下述船舶:

船名	国际海事组织编号	总吨位

与公约标准 A5.1.3 保持一致。

下面的签字者代表上述主管当局声明:

(a) 《海事劳工公约》的规定已充分体现在下述国家要求之中;

(b) 这些国家要求收录在下文所述的国家规定中;凡必要时提供了关于这些规定内容的解释;

(c) 根据第六条第 3 款和第 4 款的任何实质上等效的细节在<下文所列的相应国内要求下><下文为此目的而设的一节中>(删去不适用的陈述)提供;

(d) 主管机关根据标题三所准予的任何免除在下文专门部分明确指出;以及

(e) 在有关要求中还提及了国家立法中对任何船舶类型的具体要求。

1   Minimum age (Regulation 1. 1) _____

2   Medical certification (Regulation 1. 2) _____

3   Qualifications of seafarers (Regulation 1. 3) _____

4   Seafarers' employment agreements (Regulation 2. 1) _____

5   Use of any licensed or certified or regulated private recruitment and placement service (Regulation 1. 4) _____

6   Hours of work or rest (Regulation 2. 3) _____

7   Manning levels for the ship (Regulation 2. 7) _____

8   Accommodation (Regulation 3. 1) _____

9   On-board recreational facilities (Regulation 3. 1) _____

10   Food and catering (Regulation 3. 2) _____

11   Health and safety and accident prevention (Regulation 4. 3) _____

12   On-board medical care (Regulation 4. 1) _____

13   On-board complaint procedures (Regulation 5. 1. 5) _____

14   Payment of wages (Regulation 2. 2) _____

15   Financial security for repatriation (Regulation 2. 5) _____

16   Financial security relating to shipowners' liability (Regulation 4. 2) _____

Name: _____

Title: _____

Signature: _____

Place: _____

Date: _____

(Seal or stamp of the authority, as appropriate)

Substantial equivalencies

(Note: Strike out the statement which is not applicable)

The following substantial equivalencies, as provided under Article VI, paragraphs 3 and 4, of the Convention, except where stated above, are noted (insert description if applicable):

_____

_____

1 最低年龄（规则 1.1）_____

2 体检证书（规则 1.2）_____

3 海员的资格（规则 1.3）_____

4 海员就业协议（规则 2.1）_____

5 使用任何经许可或发证或管理的私营招募和安置服务机构（规则 1.4）_____

6 工作和休息时间（规则 2.3）_____

7 船舶配员水平（规则 2.7）_____

8 起居舱室（规则 3.1）_____

9 船上娱乐设施（规则 3.1）_____

10 食品和膳食服务（规则 3.2）_____

11 健康和安全及防止事故（规则 4.3）_____

12 船上医疗（规则 4.1）_____

13 船上投诉程序（规则 5.1.5）_____

14 工资支付（规则 2.2）_____

15 对遣返的财务担保（规则 2.5）_____

16 与船东责任相关的财务担保（规则 4.2）_____

姓名：_____

职务：_____

签字：_____

地点：_____

日期：_____

（视情况，当局的钢印或盖章）

实质上等效

（注：划掉不适用的陈述）

除上述内容外，按本公约第六条第 3 和 4 款规定的实质上等效记录如下（如适用，填入描述）：

_____

_____

No equivalency has been granted.

Name: _____

Title: _____

Signature: _____

Place: _____

Date: _____

(Seal or stamp of the authority, as appropriate)

Exemptions

(Note: Strike out the statement which is not applicable)

The following exemptions granted by the competent authority as provided in Title 3 of the Convention are noted:

_____

_____

No exemption has been granted.

Name: _____

Title: _____

Signature: _____

Place: _____

Date: _____

(Seal or stamp of the authority, as appropriate)

未准许等效。

姓名：_____

职务：_____

签字：_____

地点：_____

日期：_____

(视情况,当局的钢印或盖章)

免除

(注:划掉不适用的陈述)

主管机关根据本公约标题三的规定准许的免除如下:

_____

未准许免除。

姓名：_____

职务：_____

签字：_____

地点：_____

日期：_____

(视情况,当局的钢印或盖章,如要求)

Part Ⅱ
Declaration of Maritime Labour Compliance

Measures adopted to ensure ongoing compliance between inspections

The following measures have been drawn up by the shipowner, named in the Maritime Labour Certificate to which this Declaration is attached, to ensure ongoing compliance between inspections:

(State below the measures drawn up to ensure compliance with each of the items in Part Ⅰ)

1   Minimum age (Regulation 1.1)   ☐

2   Medical certification (Regulation 1.2)   ☐

3   Qualifications of seafarers (Regulation 1.3)   ☐

4   Seafarers' employment agreements (Regulation 2.1)   ☐

5   Use of any licensed or certified or regulated private recruitment

    and placement service (Regulation 1.4)   ☐

6   Hours of work or rest (Regulation 2.3)   ☐

7   Manning levels for the ship (Regulation 2.7)   ☐

8   Accommodation (Regulation 3.1)   ☐

9   On-board recreational facilities (Regulation 3.1)   ☐

10   Food and catering (Regulation 3.2)   ☐

11   Health and safety and accident prevention (Regulation 4.3)   ☐

12   On-board medical care (Regulation 4.1)   ☐

13   On-board complaint procedures (Regulation 5.1.5)   ☐

14   Payment of wages (Regulation 2.2)   ☐

15   Financial security for repatriation (Regulation 2.5)   ☐

16   Financial security relating to shipowners' liability (Regulation 4.2)   ☐

I hereby certify that the above measures have been drawn up to ensure ongoing compliance, between inspections, with the requirements listed in Part Ⅰ.·

第 II 部分
海事劳工符合声明

为确保检查之间持续符合所采取的措施

后附本声明的海事劳工证书中具名的船东制定了以下措施来确保检查之间的持续符合：

（为确保符合第 I 部分中的各项要求而制定的措施陈述如下）

1 最低年龄（规则 1.1） .... ☐

2 体检证书（规则 1.2） .... ☐

3 海员的资格（规则 1.3） .... ☐

4 海员就业协议（规则 2.1） .... ☐

5 使用任何经许可或发证或管理的私营招募和安置服务机构（规则 1.4） .... ☐

6 工作和休息时间（规则 2.3） .... ☐

7 船舶配员水平（规则 2.7） .... ☐

8 起居舱室（规则 3.1） .... ☐

9 船上娱乐设施（规则 3.1） .... ☐

10 食品和膳食服务（规则 3.2） .... ☐

11 健康和安全及防止事故（规则 4.3） .... ☐

12 船上医疗（规则 4.1） .... ☐

13 船上投诉程序（规则 5.1.5） .... ☐

14 工资支付（规则 2.2） .... ☐

15 对遣返的财务担保（规则 2.5） .... ☐

16 与船东责任相关的财务担保（规则 4.2） .... ☐

我特此证明为确保检查之间持续符合第 I 部分所列的要求而制定了上述措施。

Name of shipowner[1]: _____

Company address: _____

Name of the authorized signatory: _____

_____

Title: _____

Signature of the authorized signatory: _____

_____

Date: _____

(Stamp or seal of the shipowner)

The above measures have been reviewed by (insert name of competent authority or duly recognized organization) and, following inspection of the ship, have been determined as meeting the purposes set out under Standard A5.1.3, paragraph 10(b), regarding measures to ensure initial and ongoing compliance with the requirements set out in Part I of this Declaration.

Name: _____

Title: _____

Address: _____

_____

_____

Signature: _____

Place: _____

Date: _____

(Seal or stamp of the authority, as appropriate)

---

[1] *Shipowner* means the owner of the ship or another organization or person, such as the manager, agent or bareboat charterer, who has assumed the responsibility for the operation of the ship from the owner and who, on assuming such responsibility, has agreed to take over the duties and responsibilities imposed on shipowners in accordance with this Convention, regardless of whether any other organizations or persons fulfil certain of the duties or responsibilities on behalf of the shipowner. See Article II(1)(j) of the Convention.

船东^①姓名_____

公司地址：_____

授权签字人姓名：_____

职务：_____

授权签字人签字：_____

日期：_____

（船东的钢印或盖章）

上述措施已经过（填入主管当局或正式认可组织的名称）审查，并且在对船舶进行检查后，确定已满足了标准 A5.1.3 第 10 款（b）关于确保最初和持续符合本声明第 I 部分所列要求的目标。

姓名：_____

职务：_____

地址：_____

_____

_____

签字：_____

地点：_____

日期：_____

（视情况，当局的钢印或盖章）

---

① "船东"系指船舶所有人或从船舶所有人那里承担了船舶经营责任并在承担这种责任时已同意接受船东根据本公约所承担的职责和责任的另一组织或个人，如管理人、代理或光船承租人，无论是否有其他组织或个人代表船东履行了某些职责或责任。见公约第二条第（1）（j）款。

Interim Maritime Labour Certificate

Issued under the provisions of Article V and Title 5 of the

Maritime Labour Convention, 2006

(referred to below as "the Convention")

under the authority of the Government of:

_____

(full designation of the State whose flag the ship is entitled to fly)

by _____

(full designation and address of the competent authority or recognized organization

duly authorized under the provisions of the Convention)

Particulars of the ship

Name of ship:_____

Distinctive number or letters:_____

Port of registry:_____

Date of registry:_____

Gross tonnage^{①}:_____

IMO number:_____

Type of ship:_____

Name and address of the shipowner:^{②}_____

_____

This is to certify, for the purposes of Standard A5.1.3, paragraph 7, of the Convention, that:

(**a**) this ship has been inspected, as far as reasonable and practicable, for the matters listed in Appendix A5-I to the Convention, taking into account verification of items under (b), (c) and (d) below;

(**b**) the shipowner has demonstrated to the competent authority or recognized organization that the ship has adequate procedures to comply with the Convention;

---

① For ships covered by the tonnage measurement interim scheme adopted by the IMO, the gross tonnage is that which is included in the REMARKS column of the International Tonnage Certificate (1969). See Article II(1)(c) of the Convention.
② _Shipowner_ means the owner of the ship or another organization or person, such as the manager, agent or bareboat charterer, who has assumed the responsibility for the operation of the ship from the owner and who, on assuming such responsibility, has agreed to take over the duties and responsibilities imposed on shipowners in accordance with this Convention, regardless of whether any other organizations or persons fulfil certain of the duties or responsibilities on behalf of the shipowner. See Article II (1)(j) of the Convention.

临时海事劳工证书

本证书系根据《2006 年海事劳工公约》

（以下简称"公约"）第五条和标题五的规定

经＿＿＿＿＿＿＿＿＿＿＿＿政府授权

（船舶有权悬挂其旗帜的国家的全称）

由＿＿＿＿＿＿＿＿＿＿＿＿＿＿签发

（根据公约的规定正式授权的主管当局或认可组织的全称和地址）

船舶细节

船名：＿＿＿＿＿＿＿＿＿＿＿＿＿＿＿＿＿＿＿＿＿＿＿＿＿＿

船舶编号或呼号：＿＿＿＿＿＿＿＿＿＿＿＿＿＿＿＿＿＿＿＿

船籍港：＿＿＿＿＿＿＿＿＿＿＿＿＿＿＿＿＿＿＿＿＿＿＿＿＿

登记日期：＿＿＿＿＿＿＿＿＿＿＿＿＿＿＿＿＿＿＿＿＿＿＿＿

总吨位①：＿＿＿＿＿＿＿＿＿＿＿＿＿＿＿＿＿＿＿＿＿＿＿＿

国际海事组织编号＿＿＿＿＿＿＿＿＿＿＿＿＿＿＿＿＿＿＿＿＿

船舶类型＿＿＿＿＿＿＿＿＿＿＿＿＿＿＿＿＿＿＿＿＿＿＿＿＿＿

船东②名称和地址：＿＿＿＿＿＿＿＿＿＿＿＿＿＿＿＿＿＿＿＿

兹证明，就公约标准 A5.1.3 第 7 款而言：

（a）　本船舶已对本公约附录 A5-Ⅰ 所列事项进行过合理和实际可行的检查，并考虑到了下文（b）、（c）和（d）项的核查；

（b）　船东已向主管当局或认可组织表明本船有遵守公约的适当程序；

---

① 对于国际海事组织通过的吨位丈量临时表格所包括的船舶，总吨位为包括在《国际吨位证书（1969）》"备注"栏中的总吨位，见公约第二条第（1）（c）款。
② "船东"系指船舶所有人或从船舶所有人那里承担了船舶经营责任并在承担这种责任时已同意接受船东根据本公约所承担的职责和责任的另一组织或个人，如管理人、代理或光船承租人，无论是否有其他组织或个人代表船东履行了某些职责或责任。见公约第二条第（1）（j）款。

(**c**) the master is familiar with the requirements of the Convention and the responsibilities for implementation; and

(**d**) relevant information has been submitted to the competent authority or recognized organization to produce a Declaration of Maritime Labour Compliance.

This Certificate is valid until _____ subject to inspections in accordance with Standards A5. 1. 3 and A5. 1. 4.

Completion date of the inspection referred to under (a) above was _____

Issued at _____ on _____

Signature of the duly authorized official

issuing the interim certificate: _____

(Seal or stamp of issuing authority, as appropriate)

（c）　船长熟悉公约的要求以及实施公约的责任；且

（d）　制作海事劳工符合声明的相关信息已提交给主管当局或认可组织。

本证书有效期至＿＿＿＿＿＿＿＿＿＿，但取决于根据标准 5.1.3 和 5.1.4 的检查。

上面(a)中所述之检查的完成日期为 ＿＿＿＿＿＿＿＿＿＿＿＿＿＿＿＿＿＿＿

签发地点＿＿＿＿＿＿＿＿＿＿＿＿＿签发日期＿＿＿＿＿＿＿＿＿＿＿＿＿＿＿

经正式授权签发临时证书的官员签字 ＿＿＿＿＿＿＿＿＿＿＿＿＿＿＿＿＿＿＿

（视情况，发证当局的钢印或盖章）

Appendix A5-III

General areas that are subject to a detailed inspection by an authorized officer in a port of a Member carrying out a port State inspection pursuant to Standard A5.2.1:

Minimum age

Medical certification

Qualifications of seafarers

Seafarers' employment agreements

Use of any licensed or certified or regulated private recruitment

and placement service

Hours of work or rest

Manning levels for the ship

Accommodation

On-board recreational facilities

Food and catering

Health and safety and accident prevention

On-board medical care

On-board complaint procedures

Payment of wages

Financial security for repatriation

Financial security relating to shipowners' liability

附录 A5-Ⅲ

成员国港口的授权官员在根据标准 A5.2.1 开展港口国检查时将进行详细检查的一般领域：

最低年龄

体检证书

海员资格

海员就业协议

使用任何有许可证的或经发证或者管理的私营招募和安置服务机构

工作和休息时间

船舶配员水平

起居舱室

船上娱乐设施

食品和膳食服务

健康和安全及防止事故

船上医疗

船上投诉程序

工资支付

对遣返的财务担保

与船东责任相关的财务担保

Appendix B5- I   Example of a National Declaration

See Guideline B5. 1. 3, paragraph 5

Maritime Labour Convention, 2006

Part I
Declaration of Maritime Labour Compliance

(Note: This Declaration must be attached to the ship's Maritime Labour Certificate)

Issued under the authority of: The Ministry of Maritime Transport of Xxxxxx

With respect to the provisions of the Maritime Labour Convention, 2006, the following referenced ship:

Name of ship	IMO number	Gross tonnage
M. S. EXAMPLE	12345	1,000

is maintained in accordance with Standard A5. 1. 3 of the Convention.

The undersigned declares, on behalf of the abovementioned competent authority, that:

(a)   the provisions of the Maritime Labour Convention are fully embodied in the national requirements referred to below;

(b)   these national requirements are contained in the national provisions referenced below; explanations concerning the content of those provisions are provided where necessary;

(c)   the details of any substantial equivalencies under Article VI, paragraphs 3 and 4, are provided <under the corresponding national requirement listed below> <in the section provided for this purpose below> (strike out the statement which is not applicable);

(d)   any exemptions granted by the competent authority in accordance with Title 3 are clearly indicated in the section provided for this purpose below; and

(e)   any ship-type specific requirements under national legislation are also referenced under the requirements concerned.

附录 B5-Ⅰ 国家声明样本

见导则 B5.1.3 第 5 款

2006 年海事劳工公约

第Ⅰ部分
海事劳工符合声明

（注：本声明必须附在船舶的海事劳工证书之后）

在 Xxxxxx 国海运部的授权下签发

就《2006 年海事劳工公约》的规定而言，下述船舶：

船名	国际海事组织编号	总吨位
M. S. EXAMPLE	12345	1 000

与公约标准 A5.1.3 保持一致。

下面的签字者代表上述主管当局声明：

（**a**） 《海事劳工公约》的规定已充分体现在下述国家要求之中；

（**b**） 这些国家要求收录在下文所述的国家规定中；凡必要时提供了关于这些规定内容的解释；

（**c**） 根据第六条第 3 款和第 4 款的任何实质上等效的细节在<下文所列的相应国家要求下> <下文为此目的而设的一节中>（删去不适用的陈述）提供；

（**d**） 主管机关根据标题三所准予的任何免除在下文专门部分明确指出；以及

（**e**） 在有关要求中还提及了国家立法对任何船舶类型的具体要求。

1 Minimum age (Regulation 1. 1)

Shipping Law, No. 123 of 1905, as amended ("Law"), Chapter X; Shipping Regulations ("Regulations"), 2006, Rules 1111−1222.

Minimum ages are those referred to in the Convention.

"Night" means 9 p. m. to 6 a. m. unless the Ministry of Maritime Transport.

("Ministry") approves a different period.

Examples of hazardous work restricted to 18-year-olds or over are listed in Schedule A hereto. In the case of cargo ships, no one under 18 may work in the areas marked on the ship's plan (to be attached to this Declaration) as "hazardous area".

2 Medical certification (Regulation 1. 2)

Law, Chapter XI; Regulations, Rules 1223−1233.

Medical certificates shall conform to the STCW requirements, where applicable; in other cases, the STCW requirements are applied with any necessary adjustments.

Qualified opticians on list approved by Ministry may issue certificates concerning eyesight.

Medical examinations follow the ILO/WHO Guidelines referred to in Guideline B1. 2. 1.

----

1   最低年龄(规则 1.1)

经修正的《航运法》1905 年第 123 号("法律"),第十章;2006 年航运法规("法规"),第 1111–1222 条。

最低年龄为公约中所述的最低年龄。

除非海运部("部")批准了一个不同的时段,"夜间"系指晚 9 点至早 6 点。

关于仅限于 18 岁或以上的人员从事危害性工作的例子列于下表 A。对于货船来说,任何 18 岁以下的人都不得在船舶平面图(将附在本声明之后)中被标为"危险区域"的区域内工作。

2   体检证书(规则 1.2)

法律第十一章;法规第 1223–1233 条。

凡适宜,体检证书应符合 STCW 公约的要求,在其他情况下,经过相应必要调整后适用 STCW 公约的要求。

经部批准的清单上的合格眼镜商可以签发关于视力的证书。

按导则 B1.2.1 中所述的 ILO/WHO 导则进行体检。

Part II
Declaration of Maritime Labour Compliance

Measures adopted to ensure ongoing compliance between inspections

The following measures have been drawn up by the shipowner, named in the Maritime Labour Certificate to which this Declaration is attached, to ensure ongoing compliance between inspections:

(State below the measures drawn up to ensure compliance with each of the items in Part I)

1 Minimum age (Regulation 1. 1) ☒

Date of birth of each seafarer is noted against his/her name on the crew list.

The list is checked at the beginning of each voyage by the master or officer acting on his or her behalf ("competent officer"), who records the date of such verification.

Each seafarer under 18 receives, at the time of engagement, a note prohibiting him/her from performing night work or the work specifically listed as hazardous (see Part I , section 1, above) and any other hazardous work, and requiring him/her to consult the competent officer in case of doubt. A copy of the note, with the seafarer's signature under "received and read", and the date of signature, is kept by the competent officer.

2 Medical certification (Regulation 1. 2) ☒

The medical certificates are kept in strict confidence by the competent officer, together with a list, prepared under the competent officer's responsibility and stating for each seafarer on board: the functions of the seafarer, the date of the current medical certificate(s) and the health status noted on the certificate concerned.

In any case of possible doubt as to whether the seafarer is medically fit for a particular function or functions, the competent officer consults the seafarer's doctor or another qualified practitioner and records a summary of the practitioner's conclusions, as well as the practitioner's name and telephone number and the date of the consultation.

第 II 部分
海事劳工符合声明

为确保在检查之间持续符合所采取的措施

在后附本声明的海事劳工证书中具名的船东制定了以下措施以确保检查之间的持续符合：

（为确保符合第 I 部分中的各项要求而制定的措施陈述如下）

1 最低年龄（规则 1.1） $\boxed{X}$

每一海员的出生日期应在船员清单中的姓名旁注明。

在每次航程开始时由船长或代表船长的高级船员（"主管高级船员"）核查清单，并记录核查的日期。

在受聘时，每个 18 岁以下的海员收到一份禁止其从事夜间工作或从事被特别列为有害的工作（见上文第 I 部分第 1 节）或任何其他有害工作的通知，并要求该海员在有疑问时与主管高级船员协商。经海员签署"收到并已阅"字样的该通知副本，连同签字日期，由主管高级船员保存。

2 体检证书（规则 1.2） $\boxed{X}$

体检证书应与主管高级船员负责准备的记述船上每一船员职务、当前体检证书的日期和有关证书上记录的海员健康状况的清单一起，由主管高级船员在严格保密的条件下保管。

在对海员的身体是否适合某一特定职责或某些职责可能存在疑问的情况下，主管高级船员将咨询海员的医生或另一名合格的开业医生，并记录该开业医生的结论概要以及开业医生的姓名、电话号码和咨询日期。